The Blue Moment

by the same author

Enzo Ferrari: A Life
The Death of Ayrton Senna
Long Distance Call
The View from the High Board
Racers
The Perfect 10
The Last Road Race

Richard Williams

The Blue Moment

Miles Davis's *Kind of Blue*
and the Remaking of Modern Music

W. W. Norton & Company
New York London

First published in Great Britain in 2009 by Faber and Faber Ltd.

"The Man with the Blue Guitar" from *The Collected Poems of Wallace Stevens* by Wallace Stevens, copyright 1954 by Wallace Stevens and renewed 1982 by Holly Stevens. Used by permission of Alfred A. Knopf, a division of Random House, Inc.

For information about permission to reproduce selections from this book, write to Permissions, W. W. Norton & Company, Inc., 500 Fifth Avenue, New York, NY 10110

For information about special discounts for bulk purchases, please contact W. W. Norton Special Sales at specialsales@wwnorton.com or 800-233-4830

Manufacturing by Courier Westford

Library of Congress Cataloging-in-Publication Data

Williams, Richard, 1947–
    The Blue Moment : Miles Davis's Kind of blue and the remaking of modern music / Richard Williams. — 1st American ed.
        p. cm.
    "First published in Great Britain in 2009 by Faber and Faber Ltd."
    Includes bibliographical references and index.
    ISBN 978-0-393-07663-9 (hardcover)
1. Davis, Miles. Kind of blue. 2. Davis, Miles—Influence. 3. Music—20th century—History and criticism. 4. Jazz—1961–1970—History and criticism. I. Title.
ML419.D39W52 2010
785'.32196165—dc22   2009053270

W. W. Norton & Company, Inc.
500 Fifth Avenue, New York, N.Y. 10110
www.wwnorton.com

W. W. Norton & Company Ltd.
Castle House, 75/76 Wells Street, London W1T 3QT

1 2 3 4 5 6 7 8 9 0

In memory of Robert John Partridge (1948–2008)

The man bent over his guitar,
A shearsman of sorts. The day was green.

They said, 'You have a blue guitar,
You do not play things as they are.'

The man replied, 'Things as they are
Are changed upon the blue guitar.'

And they said then, 'But play, you must,
A tune beyond us, yet ourselves,

A tune upon the blue guitar
Of things exactly as they are.'

Wallace Stevens, 'The Man with the Blue Guitar' (1937)

. . . a winter twlight called, in Finnish, *sininen hetki* or
the 'blue moment'. It is as if blue light rises out of the
snow and, because everything is covered in snow, everything turns blue, so the world is full of its own space
and silence and not empty at all.

Lavinia Greenlaw, 'The Arctic' (*Granta* 101, 2008)

Contents

1 Introduction

It is the most singular of sounds, yet among the most ubiquitous. It is the sound of isolation that has sold itself to millions.

Lovers give each other Miles Davis's *Kind of Blue*, even though its mood offers no consolation, let alone ecstasy. But those who give it want to share its richness of spirit, its awareness of the infinite, and its extraordinary quality of constantly revealing more to those who know it best. Sometimes perhaps they are saying, if you like this, too, then we have a basis for something.

For many people it is the only jazz album they own. They may have bought it after hearing it at a friend's house, or in a record shop, or in the background at a restaurant: something that imprinted itself during a casual encounter, the most exquisitely refined of ambient music. Yet there are life-long students of jazz with vast collections covering the entire history of the idiom who would unhesitatingly nominate it as the item which, if they had to choose just one, they would save from a burning house.

So there it is, in the rack at a small airport, the only representative of jazz, sitting among the Ibiza dance compilations and power-ballad divas. But *Kind of Blue* is not the equivalent of a temporary and aberrant fad for the sound of Irish pipes or Bulgarian female choirs. It is not, in that sense, a phenomenon. Its increasing success over forty years is a wholly organic process, the consequence of its intrinsic virtues and of its unique appeal to a particular layer of the human spirit.

It began its life, in 1959, with a series of warm reviews and the unqualified admiration of other musicians – at least those of a similar age and tendency, which meant virtually an entire generation. They were swift to absorb *Kind of Blue*, to replicate its methods and its mannerisms, but its essence could never be recaptured. Not even, as it turned out, by the man who made it. Miles Davis spent the remaining thirty years of his life as the leading figure in jazz, initiating trends great and small, often putting himself at the centre of the music's frequent crises of identity. But he never tried to do again the thing that he and six other musicians had done during the course of two days in the spring of 1959. He moved on, as he usually did.

If it could not be counterfeited, what happened to it was something much more interesting, an effect that could only be seen in hindsight. *Kind of Blue*'s atmosphere – slow, rapt, dark, meditative, luminous – began to become all-pervasive. It was as if Miles Davis had tapped into something more profound than a taste for a particular set of musical sounds: he had uncovered a desire to change the scenery of life.

Before *Kind of Blue* there had been slow jazz, mournful jazz, romantic jazz, astringent jazz. But there had never been anything that so carefully and single-mindedly cultivated an atmosphere of reflection and introspection, to such a degree that the mood itself became an art object. *Kind of Blue* seemed to have taken place in a sealed environment,

2

with all its individual sensibilities pointing inwards. This is what gives it that extraordinary sense of focus, of concentration, of distillation. The musicians seem to have been spellbound. No wonder its forty-odd minutes of music were made in barely nine hours, and that it was never repeated.

But in its ability to combine complexity of content with a powerful sense of ambiance, it has become one of the most influential albums of our time. You can't put on an ECM album, for instance, without participating in the legacy of *Kind of Blue*: in particular the concern for a sense of space within the music, for a unity of atmosphere, and for the desire to create a mood of calm contemplation in which the troubled Western soul can take its rest.

A late summer warmth is filling the streets of central Barcelona. Just off the Plaça Catalunya, near the top of the Rambla, two young musicians are busking. One plays a metre-long didgeridoo, the ancient wooden instrument associated with Australia's aboriginal people, a sort of rustic contra-bass pipe suitable mainly for the production of low drones. The other is playing a hang, a newly fashionable steel hand-drum that looks like two woks welded together, the smooth surface of its upper hemisphere interrupted by half a dozen large dimples. A phenomenon called the Helmholtz resonance, which exploits the sounds produced by air in a cavity, allows the hang to produce a gentle melodic *bong*, like a Zen monk's version of a Trinidadian steel pan. The duo's minimalist music is static, almost heat-struck; it lacks obvious thematic material and seems to have no beginning or ending, no specific geographical origin or cultural inflections. A dozen listeners seem drawn more to the curious nature of the instruments than to the music itself.

A few streets away, around the corner from the Plaça de Saint-Jaume in the old quarter, a bigger group is performing in the mouth of an alleyway. This one has two hang players, plus a saxophonist whose soprano instrument has an elegantly curved neck, and a man manipulating an Indian tambura with one hand to produce a quiet background drone while playing a softly skipping rhythm on the skin of an Irish bodhrán, a single-headed drum, with the other. Their music, which has drawn a crowd of tourists of all types and ages, is similarly unaggressive. Again this is a music of resources rather than themes. Yet it has a sense of space, of balance, of containment, of refined simplicity. The absence of harmonic movement and the sound of the hang drums – their notes like heavy raindrops, splashing against the drone – invites the saxophonist to shape his improvised phrases with contemplative grace.

And I'm thinking as I walk away, the sound of the instruments fading into the early-evening hubbub, that this music could never have happened without *Kind of Blue*.

It is half a century since Miles Davis walked into a studio in a converted church in midtown Manhattan and directed his sextet through five pieces of music that have come to stand not just for a certain kind of jazz – almost, indeed, for jazz itself – but for an entire scope of feeling. With this record Davis introduced the listeners of the Western world to a music suffused with a kind of mild exoticism that had its roots in Eastern philosophies.

Bill Evans, his pianist, supplied the album with a set of explanatory notes in which the act of the music's creation is compared to those Japanese artists who spend a day preparing their brushes and paints before executing their delicate ideograms with a single indelible stroke. Earlier forms of jazz had found room for delicacy – in the cornet playing of Bix Beiderbecke, the piano solos of Teddy Wilson or the neoclassical inventions of the Modern Jazz Quartet – but it had never been so single-mindedly focused into an entire methodology as it was in *Kind of Blue*.

At first the album attracted puzzlement as well as admiration. When the English critic Benny Green called it 'a straw in the wind as far as conventional jazz-making techniques were concerned' and added that it 'questioned the tenets of jazz-making more thoroughly than anything since Charlie Parker', he was not extending the warmest of welcomes. Green contributed a measured sleeve note to the British release of the album, but when Davis and his group arrived in Britain a few months later, while the album's initial reverberations were still spreading, his reservations were apparent. 'The myth that jazz is essentially a good-time music was finally laid to rest last week when the American trumpeter Miles Davis opened his long-awaited British tour,' Green wrote in the *Observer*. 'At the Gaumont, Hammersmith, Davis somehow managed to recreate, and even intensify, the hypnotic effect of recordings which have obliged us all to stop in our tracks and ask once again, "What *is* jazz, anyway?" . . . To put it briefly, Davis has succeeded in introducing into the jazz context a new aesthetic. Every note he plays is tinged with the disturbing melancholia of a highly sophisticated and super-sensitive artist. Nowhere is there any trace of the unselfconscious joy at being alive of Louis Armstrong, or the irrepressible good spirits of Davis's great contemporary, Dizzy Gillespie. Suddenly, through the prism of Davis's conception, all other jazz appears a Panglossian affair concerned with the release of tension rather than the expression of it. With Miles Davis, introspection enters the jazz world . . .' That world – and a far wider one, too – was ready for it. Introspection was becoming so much a part of the psychological apparatus of mid-century Western man and woman that Davis turned out to have manufactured the soundtrack to their inner lives.

Green was not alone in his lament for the hedonistic expressionism of Armstrong and Gillespie. In the *New Yorker*, Whitney Balliett fretted over Davis's espousal of an approach 'that is brooding, melancholy, perhaps self-pitying, and extremely close to the sentimental'. Balliett called him the Young Werther of jazz, referring to Goethe's doomed romantic hero. The novelist Kingsley Amis heard Davis in New York the year before *Kind of Blue* was recorded, and wrote: 'The sound of Miles Davis's trumpet, introverted, gloomy, sour in both senses, refuses to go away. I heard the future, and it sounded horrible.' But these were vain cries. Far from distorting the mood of the time, Davis had caught it. By isolating a single strand of jazz, and expanding it into a vehicle for the expression of his own temperament, he not only changed jazz but gave it a new lease of life, a compass bearing by which it could navigate through the difficult times to come. He ensured that, as rhythm and blues and rock 'n' roll – the music of the post-

war 'youthquake', as *Time* magazine termed it – relegated
jazz to the fringes of popular culture, it had something to
say that was relevant to its time and would not expire from
obsolescence. Under sustained assault from all sides, cultural and commercial, it would somehow retain its quality of
coolness. And even more than that, *Kind of Blue* helped
open the way to developments in music undreamed of on
those two days in New York in the spring of 1959 when the
tapes started running.

The album's story has been told before. Those seeking the
details of its origins are directed to Ashley Kahn's *Kind of
Blue: The Making of Miles Davis's Masterpiece* (Da Capo)
and Eric Nisenson's *The Making of Kind of Blue: Miles
Davis and His Masterpiece* (St Martin's Press), both published in 2000. Kahn's volume is an exemplary piece of
investigative reporting: he listened to the original master
tapes, talked to the surviving witnesses and unearthed the
record company's memoranda and payment schedules.
Nisenson delves more deeply into the personalities involved
in the genesis of the album, and into the musicology. In
terms of narrative history, at any rate, little scope remains.

This book's intentions are quite different. The task here is
not just to describe the album's origins and the context in
which it made its appearance but to look at what happened
next: to follow trails in order to find connections, identify
direct influences, tease out correspondences and locate
interesting pre-echoes and intriguing coincidences. If some
of the links seem tenuous, it is worth considering that
movements in music are sometimes given their definition as
much by barely detectable undercurrents as by tidal waves.

And there is no ambition to present a definitive survey; that way madness lies. After fifty years, these connections and correspondences stretch into infinity.

Like the ripples from a pebble dropped into an ever-expanding lagoon, the effect created by *Kind of Blue* spread far beyond its immediate environment. Quickly recognised as a major achievement, it gradually acquired the standing of a classic. But then, some time in the 1990s, its status changed more radically. First, as jazz acquired a new public, it became pre-eminent, outranking any collection by such pre-LP artists as Louis Armstrong and Charlie Parker or even such later bestsellers as Dave Brubeck's *Time Out*, John Coltrane's *A Love Supreme* and Keith Jarrett's *Köln Concert*. And in becoming the one jazz album that even non-jazz fans found themselves owning, it permeated layers of taste and consciousness that no jazz record had previously reached.

How thoroughly it has penetrated the universal consciousness could be seen in two remarks made within 24 hours of each other, only a few months before the album celebrated its fiftieth birthday. In a newspaper column devoted to his detestation of jazz, the English humorist Dom Joly reserved a grudging respect for one exception. 'I do have to admit to owning Miles Davis's *Kind of Blue*,' he wrote. 'It's good for wafting over the pool on a sunny day or as a gentle soundtrack to a dull dinner party. If I had a lift then I'd pipe it through my lift speakers.' From the actress Kristin Scott-Thomas, by contrast, it drew a fond memory illustrating its ability to enhance an emotional landscape. 'I'd just met my future husband,' she told a radio interviewer. 'He's French, and we were driving to his grandmother's country house in Normandy in a Peugeot *quatre-cent-quatre* with a leaking roof and this music on the tape deck. So when I hear it, it reminds me of the smell of old leather and being tremendously in love and going to the seaside.'

Within the jazz world, however, some observers have always found it difficult to accept that a single recording, and such a seemingly self-conscious one at that, should have become the focus of such attention. In a book on Davis's recordings published in 2005, a couple of years before his early death, the critic Richard Cook described *Kind of Blue* as 'the hippest easy-listening album of them all'. He would have given a wry nod of recognition to Dom Joly's comments. To Cook and those who share his opinion, *Kind of Blue* is undeserving of such exceptional treatment. It was, he wrote, harder to say what it was not than what it was: 'It is not troubling, not abrasive, not much like the other jazz of its period, and not difficult to assimilate.' In Cook's view, *Milestones* – the album which preceded *Kind of Blue* by a year – was a better jazz record: 'more swinging, more powerful, a superior showcase for the sextet as a working ensemble'.

For others, however, *Kind of Blue* provided a window on the future. In Japan, Toru Takemitsu listened and absorbed its lessons. The young American composers who became known as the minimalists – La Monte Young, Terry Riley, Steve Reich and Philip Glass – grew up pondering its implications before striking out on their own paths. Their influence would be absorbed by the Welsh viola player and composer John Cale, a member of the Velvet Underground, the Andy Warhol-sponsored ensemble who laboured in obscurity throughout their short lifetime but would ultimately become, through their influence on art rock and punk rock, the most widely emulated rock group since the Beatles, and by the English experimentalist Brian Eno, whose art-school explorations led to his groundbreaking work with the group Roxy Music and thence, via his associations with Robert Fripp, David Bowie, Talking Heads, Jon Hassell and U2, to his invention of ambient and generative music, with which he added another extension to the house that Davis built.

Sometimes the impact was tangential. During his freshman year at Harvard, the music student John Adams carried the scores of Pierre Boulez around with him 'hoping that somehow, perhaps by osmosis, they would reveal themselves to me and make me love them as I loved Mozart and Miles Davis's *Kind of Blue*.' Adams would go on to become a prolific composer of works including the opera *Nixon in China*, a wonderful violin concerto and a striking threnody for the victims of 9/11, *On the Transmigration of Souls*, none of which bore the explicit imprint of *Kind of Blue*. At other times the effect was integral. For Manfred Eicher, a young German double-bassist seemingly heading for a career in the classical world, Davis's album opened up a new universe of music and thought. Eicher went on to found ECM Records, a label whose recordings of the American pianist Keith Jarrett, the Norwegian saxophonist Jan Garbarek, the Polish trumpeter Tomasz Stanko and many others could be said to extend the values of *Kind of Blue*, starting with its air of contemplative minimalism. 'The fewer words you use,' Eicher once observed, in what could stand as a mission statement, 'the more intense the dialogue.' By the time he said that, his albums had sold in millions around the world and he understood perhaps as well as anyone in the world the ability of music with such qualities to attract listeners in large numbers.

Over on another part of the spectrum of contemporary music, the guitarists Andy Summers, Duane Allman and Chris Rea were profoundly affected by exposure to *Kind of Blue*: the first in the 1960s, the last in the early 1990s. For the inquisitive Summers, growing up in the early 60s and heading for a berth in Zoot Money's Big Roll Band before finding worldwide fame alongside Sting and Stewart Copeland in the Police, it formed the centrepiece of a vast tapestry of cultural influences that ranged from Jack Kerouac to Hamza Al-Din. For Rea, it provided a beacon of inspiration as he struggled, after surviving a life-threatening illness, to free himself from the limitations imposed by the world of commercial popular music.

Then there is Robert Wyatt, who began his professional career in the middle 1960s as a drummer with the Soft Machine before an accident forced him to concentrate on singing and composing, and who writes music by 'finding a harmonic layer, maybe just a chord, and populating it with notes'. This is his response to the blueprint laid down by Davis and his friend and associate Gil Evans in the months leading up to *Kind of Blue*, when they explored the possibility of abandoning the conventional cycles of chords on which popular songs – the customary vehicles for jazz improvising – are built, putting in their place a set of slowly moving or even static harmonic guidelines that eradicated the old parameters in favour of creating space for thought and action: the 'harmonic layer' which Wyatt, like many others in their different ways, uses as the foundation of his pieces.

So this is, for many listeners, an addictive substance. When you fall in love with *Kind of Blue* you just want to keep on buying it, a fact that its commercial copyright owners recognised years ago. How many people around the world bought the vinyl album, replaced it when its grooves wore out, bought the pre-recorded cassette for their car stereo, bought the CD when the technology changed, then a remastered disc, then the MasterSound CD with the extra track and the pitch correction and the previously unseen session photographs, then the Millennium Edition in its numbered miniature replica cardboard jacket, then the Japanese mini-disc, then the steel-slipcased boxed set with even more previously unseen session photographs, then the two-disc release with the original album accompanied by an hour-long DVD documentary, and finally – for now – the $100 fiftieth anniversary 'collectors' edition', a twelve-by-twelve slip-cased set including a blue vinyl LP disc, two CDs including unreleased false starts and studio chatter, the aforementioned film documentary, prints of half a dozen original session photographs, a facsimile of Bill Evans's original handwritten sleeve notes, a reprint of a Columbia Records publicity pamphlet and a large poster, all intended

to help the record industry survive the crisis of download-
ing? One, at least, and probably many more.

Time and again, however, *Kind of Blue* rises above such
attempts to fetishise it. Whenever it is played, in whatever
circumstances, it provides further evidence that its essence
remains undisturbed, a rare example of human perfection,
never needing to raise its voice to make itself heard but
speaking more clearly as the years go by.

2 Into the Blue

Welcome to the modern world

A teenage party on a Saturday night in the summer holidays of 1963. One year earlier, we'd learnt to do the Twist – the first dance that hadn't been endorsed by the example of the adult world. The Twist was a non-contact dance, which made it somehow more attractive than the sort of stuff our parents did, or even our older brothers and sisters, whose jiving to early rock 'n' roll was altogether too unreflective, too unconsidered, too wholehearted for our developing taste. We were growing up into a world of extreme self-consciousness, in which personal style was taking precedence over almost every other consideration, and for a while the Twist was one way of showing it.

Not, that is, the version of the Twist that you saw in news clips of Manhattan socialites dancing in a self-consciously déclassé style at the Peppermint Lounge. That kind of frantic gyrating – a thuddingly literal interpretation of the Arthur Murray School instruction leaflet, which told you to pretend that you were drying your back with a towel held lengthways in both hands at waist height while pretending to extinguish cigarette butts with both feet – represented an impulse towards public display which had nothing to do with the real-life version. When you were dancing the Twist properly, you had the sensation of both being with your partner and being by yourself. To borrow the title and modify the sentiment of a great torch song from an earlier era, you were alone together. If you were dancing in a state of some sort of mutual physical understanding, that was good. Essential, even, if you had designs on your partner. But to imitate or duplicate each other's moves was considered crass.

In any case, by the summer of 1963 the Twist was on its way out in our micro-segment of society, slowly being replaced by less emphatic and more personal variations which generally involved a reduction of physical effort. The apogee of this development came when boys and girls returned from family holidays in France proclaiming the existence of a dance called *le Slow*, which, whether they had it right or not, allegedly involved nothing more than the almost imperceptible flexing of the right knee. Done with the appropriate rigour, it was the most perfect dance next to complete immobility, a homage to the kind of cool embodied by Alain Delon and Marcello Mastroianni. Infinitely adaptable, and rechristened the Shake, it became the signature dance-floor movement of the mid-60s modernist.

This was also the first Beatles summer, the success of 'Please Please Me' and 'From Me to You' presaging a flood of number one hits for other Liverpool groups. Gerry and the Pacemakers ('How Do You Do It?' and 'I Like It'), Billy J Kramer and the Dakotas ('Do You Want to Know a Secret?'), and the Searchers ('Sweets for My Sweet') enjoyed their moment in the limelight while the Fab Four bided their time before, in September, unleashing 'She Loves You', the song that secured their universality. Naturally, there was a price to pay for such acclaim. The Beatles were, in fact, already uncool. Our parents were beginning to fall under their spell, which was not good news.

But for us, that summer was beginning to reveal other songs which engaged the ear on a different level: the proto-type soul music of 'Hello Stranger' by Barbara Lewis, 'Two Lovers' by Mary Wells, 'Heat Wave' by Martha and the Vandellas, 'Mickey's Monkey' by the Miracles, 'You're No Good' by Betty Everett, 'Don't Make Me Over' by Dionne Warwick, and 'Cry Baby' by Garnett Mimms and the Enchanters. These songs and the way they were performed seemed not just more exotic but much, much more real.

Between them, the rise of the beat groups and the soul singers dealt a death blow to the Trad boom, Britain's well-intentioned but awkward revival of New Orleans jazz, in which the rugged virtues of the original were conscientiously ironed out, thereby creating some of the most innocuous and deracinated music ever presented for public consumption. The phenomenon burnt out after the commercial success of the *Ball, Barber and Bilk* albums on the cut-price Golden Guinea label and of Kenny Ball's 'Midnight in Moscow' and Acker Bilk's 'Stranger on the Shore' in the singles charts, when the men in silly hats and matching fancy waistcoats with clarinets and banjos were finally obliterated by the Mersey Sound and the emergence of young white groups with guitars playing a more immediately relevant form of black American popular music.

The party began in the daylight of a long summer evening and was eventually illuminated by candles in Chianti flasks, a gesture of misguided yearning for an older, more sophisticated world. Into this atmosphere, during a moment's pause in the activity, came the sound of *Kind of Blue*. And at that point, for all the impact it made, it might as well have been some piece of strict-tempo porridge by Victor Sylvester or Lawrence Welk. After a few minutes of total indifference it was replaced by something more in tune with the prevailing mood of adolescent hedonism. Modern jazz was not really a part of this world.

But *Kind of Blue* would not be so easily brushed aside. Back at home it resumed its place of honour on the Dansette turntable, a text to be studied and memorised. At that age all you want to do is absorb new information, and the memory offers plenty of spare capacity. Already it was apparent that *Kind of Blue* would be occupying a special place in the expanding mental library.

I had first heard it only a few weeks earlier on the Voice of America's nightly *Jazz Hour* programme, presented by Willis Conover, a man who introduced jazz records in a tone of impeccable sobriety but probably did more for the image of the United States around the world than any president you could mention. Conover's work amounted, in the view of the State Department, which ran the network, to a tacit endorsement of international capitalism and the free-market system. It made him a particular hero among listeners behind the Iron Curtain, to whom the sound of jazz symbolised the free world and all its social and material benefits. His precise enunciation of song titles and musicians' names helped him communicate with those whose command of English was limited or non-existent.

My own initial exposure to Miles Davis had come the previous year, when an older boy brought a copy of a seven-inch EP to a meeting of the school jazz society. It contained just two tracks, 'Milestones' and 'Two Bass Hit', and lots of things about it impressed me. The sleeve design juxtaposed tightly cropped vertical photographs of the three horn players: Davis, John Coltrane and Cannonball Adderley, all in the act of playing. They certainly looked glamorous, in the way that black American jazz musicians, young or old, were always likely to do to a fourteen-year-old schoolboy in England, but the set of their faces and their bodies also delivered a powerful message that what they were doing was serious and important. The music reinforced the suggestion. The sextet's version of 'Two Bass Hit', a bebop tune written in the late forties by Dizzy Gillespie and his pianist of the time, John Lewis, was perfectly fine, a solid performance in the hard-swinging post-bop idiom. But 'Milestones' was something else altogether. Here was a piece of jazz that redefined the 'modern' in modern jazz. It had a special atmosphere, one which appeared to break the link with conventional popular song formats – the 32-bar Broadway ballad and the 12-bar blues – without needing to venture into the intimidating abstraction of contemporary classical music.

Only later did it become clear what Davis had done, when 'Milestones' revealed itself to have been his first significant attempt at constructing a piece of jazz based on what became known as the modal principle, in which the repeating cycles of chords that underpinned the familiar ballads and blues were abandoned in favour of improvisations based on scales or modes, changing – if they changed at all – much more slowly than the old chord sequences.

Although in a sense this merely substituted one set of sign-posts for another, in fact the open-ended nature of the new structures coincided with much larger shifts in consciousness, and in the way we listened to music.

Formerly determined by the capacity of one side of a ten-inch 78rpm disc, the length of a tune no longer needed to be restricted to an otherwise arbitrary maximum of three minutes. Classical music had navigated the original limitations by using larger twelve-inch discs and multiple volumes in slip cases, but jazz had found its way into the world as a branch of popular music and only now, having made the decisive move away from the ballroom and the cabaret, was it in a position to establish a more independent existence.

Improvements in recording technology had enabled engineers and producers to elevate the work of the rhythm section almost to the level of that of the soloist, while enhancing the identity of the individual instruments and investing each part of the music with a greater significance. The piano, bass and drums were no longer creating a platform but participating in the dialogue, and one way in which the increased strength of their contribution affected the music was to allow the soloist to play less without reducing the music's density or diminishing its impact.

Through these changes the music's structures were being expanded, which meant, in general, both a chronological lengthening and a reduction of incident within those structures. Improvisers were being given less material to work with and more time in which to explore it. The result of this was to make the music more reflective, more relaxed, sometimes more introverted, sometimes more poised – more of just about everything that suited Miles Davis, in fact.

The fact that it took place at a time of increasing interest in art forms which also had a different understanding of time – from the compressed but weightless seventeen-syllable haiku poems of Japan to the extended ragas of Indian classical music – could hardly have been an accident. One read a haiku and let its echoes resonate, or allowed a raga to distend Western clock-time. Nor was it by chance that Andy Warhol was discovering the appeal of repetition in his artworks: the triple Elvis, the multiplied car crash, the endless Marilyns. In one sense it would be ludicrous to make a comparison between serial printings of a silkscreened image of Elvis Presley and an improvised solo by Miles Davis, even one reproduced for mass consumption on a vinyl disc, but there was a deeper relationship between Warhol's conception of time and the changing forms of Davis's music. We were all ready to look at or listen to less, and to take more time over it.

It was while wandering round Osborne House, a mansion built for Queen Victoria on the Isle of Wight, that a possible explanation of this phenomenon came to me. The monarch's living quarters, preserved with their original decoration, fittings and furniture intact almost a hundred years after her death, looked appallingly cluttered. Surely she and Prince Albert and their children could hardly move for stools and occasional tables and framed photographs and imperial mementos. Nor was there anywhere for their eyes to rest, thanks to the endless variety of stripes and other patterns covering every available surface, as well as the astonishing profusion of objects. How on earth could they live amid such spatial and visual chaos? Why, with unlimited resources in terms of space and time, would they choose practically to bury themselves under such an avalanche? The answer must be that Victoria and Albert and their contemporaries were not subject to the barrage of sensory stimuli that became commonplace during the second half of the twentieth century. Unlike us, they were not besieged by 24-hour television programming, by music in lifts and supermarkets, by posters covering every urban surface, by brightly coloured junk mail, by newsagents' racks bursting with a thousand periodicals, by T-shirt messages and commercial logos everywhere, by text messages and emails and cold-calling. In our normal lives, we can hardly escape the permanent storm of visual and aural signals. One way of achieving peace within it has been to adapt the nature of art in order to give us less information and more feeling: hence, in painting, the arrival of the minimalism of Barnett Newman, the contemplative abstract expressionism of Mark Rothko, the quiet grid patterns of Agnes Martin, and the apparently content-free white on white canvases of Robert Ryman, a sometime jazz musician.

Had Ryman stuck with his career in jazz he might have found a way to make the musical equivalent of his canvases. But it was Miles Davis who, with the support and encouragement of several trusting and visionary colleagues, took the decisive step away from the belief that what you did was load music up with all the freight it could carry. 'Less is more' is said to be a nineteenth-century proverb, but it has become identified with another definitively twentieth-century figure: Ludwig Mies van der Rohe, who ran the Bauhaus school in Germany in the early 1930s and, after moving to the United States to escape Hitler, became the leader of the modernist movement in design and architecture. What had happened to chairs and buildings – a simplification of outline and surface concealing a complex response to the modern world – was about to happen to music, and Davis was to be its principal agent. Miles was becoming its Mies.

It was no surprise to find Davis in the vanguard of these developments. In the descriptions of his work published in music papers and magazines, writers and critics always made him sound interesting and appealing, as if he possessed some sort of presence or depth that held him apart from his contemporaries and colleagues. Some of that quality, whatever it may have been, was audible in the five and three-quarter minutes of 'Milestones', in which the three solos – alto saxophone, flügelhorn, tenor saxophone – flowed into each other like three planes of the same object, supported by a rhythm section clearly aware of its duty to produce something more focused and carefully integrated with the material than the usual combo blowing session would demand. But when Willis Conover's engineer cued up side two, track one of *Kind of Blue* and sent it over the airwaves from the VOA's transmitters in northern Europe, what had been merely a promise was instantly fulfilled.

The subdued mid-range piano tremolo, the lulling triple-metre bass vamp and the wire brushes rustling on a snare drum that formed the introduction to 'All Blues' also ushered a new scope of feeling into the world. As the two saxophones entered, riding the bass line with a simple har-monised figure that see-sawed between two chords, they seemed to be playing something that reflected distant roots in black church music, filtered through a very modern sensibility. The arrival of the solo muted trumpet completed the combination, a silvery contrast to the warm grain of the reeds, squeezing out a line of melody so pure and simple that it gave the impression of having been distilled from some far more complex subject. The most obvious hallmark of all this was restraint, but behind the economy of gesture and effort appeared to lie enormous reserves of intensity.

Every second of its eleven and a half minutes seemed to reveal some new element of truth or beauty. It was a blues, at least in its twelve-bar form, but it was not like any blues previously encountered. In the moment that the theme ended, for example, during a four-bar interlude while Miles removed the mute from his trumpet, the drummer, Jimmy Cobb, was adroitly switching from his brushes to his sticks – one hand at a time – with an effect that re-shaded the whole ambiance of the track, inviting the soloist to embark on an exploration of a mood that did not rely on the conventional blues triggers of lamentation or exhilaration but traced with great precision an emotional contour somehow closer to painting or literature than to anything else going on in music at the time.

Its glow was quiet, even subdued. The individual sounds were delicate and nuanced. There was no showing off. No one was muscling in to have their say. Yet the impression was of great firmness and resilience and resolution, and a sense of perfection within the moment – despite the fact that since this was jazz, and modern jazz at that, therefore it must have been predominantly improvised. And although it sounded completely new, it also sounded somehow definitive. But in 1963, at least, it was not something to play in the background at parties, while people ate and drank and danced and looked each other over. That was still some way in its future.

3 The Sound of Blue

Blue valentines. Blue kisses. Blue velvet. Way to blue

When Miles Davis called his album *Kind of Blue* he caught many strands of meaning in a single casual phrase. As a jazz musician he could automatically be assumed to be making a reference to the blues, the African American form that invaded and eventually dominated the popular music of the twentieth century and beyond. But by the time Davis made the album in 1959, he and the blues were already far beyond the standard definition of a twelve-bar form with certain tonal characteristics (including the intervals of the flattened third and seventh) which had been brought up the Mississippi river by people leaving the poverty of the Delta plantations in order to make new lives in the industrial centres of Illinois and Michigan. The blues had become an emotion, or a span of emotions, generally reckoned to range from mild ennui to suicidal despair. Davis's blues were located at the more sophisticated end of the musical and emotional spectrum, where ennui wore a nice raincoat and suicide demanded an elegant setting. The child of a comfortable middle-class family, arriving in New York at the age of eighteen to study at the Juilliard Conservatory, Davis moved with relative ease through worlds outside the strict confines of his chosen profession, broadening his experience and sharpening his sophistication at the same time as establishing and reaffirming his credentials in jazz. Open to new feelings and new influences, he was able to redefine not only the particular internal characteristics of his music but also its place in the world.

Although 'blue' is the word on which the title's primary meaning depends, 'kind of' is just as significant. Apparently offhand, almost disdainful of itself, it is the shrug that half-conceals real depth of thought and feeling. It mirrored not just the tide of informality and intimacy that was beginning to sweep across the Western world but also the existential-ist mode of the time, the reluctance of a certain kind of mid-century man to make a commitment to the agenda of the straight universe. As with the music, so with the title: the more you examine *Kind of Blue*, the more there is to think about.

Blue is, in any case, something of a charged subject. Throughout history, our relationship with it has never been quite straightforward. It is, in that sense, the colour of equivocation, of uncertainty. *L'heure bleue* is a time between work and play, between day and night, between zones of existence, between one kind of life and another, a time defined by transience and evanescence. To Wallace Stevens, inspired in 1937 by the memory of a masterpiece from Picasso's blue period (*The Old Guitarist*, 1903) and by the artist's subsequent adventures in surrealism to create his great poem 'The Man with the Blue Guitar', it symbol-ised the freedom of the imagination, while in the minds of those mostly anonymous songsters who laid the founda-tions for what the twentieth century came to call the blues, it represented the means by which to express the most basic realities of daily life.

Successive ages have exalted and derided it. In the Neolithic era the peoples of Asia were already using dyes from the indigo plant; when it was exported, in the form of compressed blocks, the Romans jumped to the wrong conclusion about its origin and gave it a name, *lapis indicus*, stone of India, from which its modern name is derived. Woad, extracted from the leaves of a herb of the mustard family, was used for body decoration by the Celtic and German tribes of antiquity. A kind of blue was the first synthetic colour, created to the order of a king of ancient Egypt who wished to reproduce the hue of lapis lazuli, the semi-precious stone, veined with iron pyrite (or 'fool's gold'), that came from China, Siberia, Afghanistan, Tibet and Iran to adorn the jewellery of the pharaohs. Medieval lapidarists believed sapphire to have the power to cure disease by cooling the inner organs. When cobalt from Bohemia or Persia was needed for stained glass, rich patrons provided cathedral architects with the materials. And Prussian blue, developed in Germany in the early eighteenth century, was the first synthetic colour produced by modern industrial methods.

Not everyone was attracted by it. The ancient Greeks and Romans had little time – and no single defining word – for it, omitting it from their analyses of the colours of the rainbow and leading to evolutionary theories proposing that they could not actually 'see' it as we do. They preferred white, black and red. The creators of the Parthenon used it sparingly, and only as a background. The Romans, influenced by the sight of woad-wearing barbarians, looked down on it. It was good for little except mourning dress, and blue eyes were considered a deformity.

It remained a neglected hue as Europe's middle ages began, ignored by kings and courtiers until the eleventh and twelfth centuries, when it began to acquire a significance in Christianity as the colour of the Virgin Mary's cloak. Stained-glass makers in the cathedrals of northern France – Chartres, Le Mans and notably Saint-Denis, the burial place of kings – used cobalt in the manufacture of a glass through which light filtered to create a holy luminosity. Eventually Louis IX, who reigned in the early thirteenth century, would be depicted in blue robes. Across the English channel, it became the colour of King Arthur. In parallel with these developments, its use in heraldry multiplied vastly between the twelfth and fifteenth centuries, underlining its newly exalted standing. When knights dressed in blue, the colour became a symbol of their courage and virtue.

The spread was encouraged by improvements in dyeing techniques, enabling the creation of brighter and more stable shades; eventually the fashions spread from France to Germany and Italy. Merchants of madder, a common herb that was the principal source of red dye, attempted to preserve their market share by persuading the creators of the stained-glass windows and the painters of frescoes to limit their use of blue to the depiction of hell and the devils who presided over it, but they could not hold back the tide. By the end of the sixteenth century, blue had become ubiquitous throughout Western Europe and was accepted, the historian Michel Pastoureau records, as a colour 'of joy, love, loyalty, peace and comfort'. Further advances in dyeing methods, however, had allowed black to take over as a colour denoting nobility in the fourteenth and fifteenth centuries. This suited the Protestants of the Reformation, who were naturally suspicious of bright colours and decoration; while developing a moral hierarchy of colours, eventually they permitted the restrained use of dark blue alongside their preferred black and white.

As the use of red declined, blue gradually advanced towards a popularity that it has never relinquished, greatly enriching producers of the pastel made from woad in such places as Thuringia and parts of the Languedoc. Isaac Newton's experiments in the late seventeenth century, establishing its place in the centre of the newly discovered spectrum, seemed to confirm its pre-eminence, and the discovery (through a chemical accident) of Prussian blue in Berlin at the beginning of the eighteenth century gave painters a rich new hue for their palettes.

To satisfy the growing demand for blue, particularly in the clothing market, the importers of indigo, which was many times more expensive than woad but of vastly higher quality, began to overcome old protectionist laws. The discovery of an even more effective type of indigo by explorers in the Caribbean, Mexico and the Andes, coupled with the cheapness of slave labour, brought down its price at the expense of the original sources in Asia. When indigo dyeing was finally permitted throughout France in 1737, it heralded the end of the woad industry. A century and a half later, German scientists perfected a method of synthesising an artificial indigo that could be produced in industrial quantities, and in turn its success led inexorably to the decline and fall of the plantations, east and west.

So common was the use of blue that to Camille Pissarro

it was merely the colour of underpants. 'Seeing blue' was a disease, the painter wrote to his son in 1883, adding that it needed the accompaniment of orange to bring it to useful life. For Goethe, however, the question had been a great deal more complicated. When he rigged out the hero of *The Sorrows of Young Werther* (1774) in a blue dress coat, the book's phenomenal success generated a fashion craze among those drawn to the new cult of Romanticism. Thirty-six years later, in his highly unscientific but widely noticed *Theory of Colours*, he divided the spectrum into positive and negative hues. 'The colours on the plus side are yellow, red-yellow (orange), yellow-red (minium, cinnabar). The feelings they excite are quick, lively, aspiring . . . The colours on the minus side are blue, red-blue and blue-red. They produce a restless, susceptible, anxious impression. As yellow is always accompanied with the light, so it may be said that blue brings a principle of darkness with it.'

Goethe dismissed Newton's findings and either knew nothing of the discovery of wave theory by his contemporary, Thomas Young, or chose to ignore it. His view of colour was entirely subjective – the poet's response rather than the scientist's. On blue he wrote: 'This colour has a peculiar and almost indescribable effect on the eye. As a hue it is powerful, but it is on the negative side, and in its highest purity is, as it were, a stimulating negation. Its appearance, then, is a kind of contradiction between excitement and repose.'

In its contradictions resided its allure. 'As the upper sky and distant mountains appear blue, so a blue surface seems to retire from us,' he continued. 'But as we readily follow an agreeable object that flies from us, so we love to contemplate blue, not because it advances towards us, but because it draws us after it. Blue gives us an impression of cold and thus, again, reminds of shade.' He concluded with two rather comfortless assertions: 'Rooms which are hung with pure blue appear in some degree larger, but at the same time empty and cold'; and 'The appearance of objects seen through a blue glass is gloomy and melancholy.' Perhaps that was the atmosphere Rainer Maria Rilke, the great German lyric poet of the early twentieth century, was after when he wrote such works as the *Duino Elegies* and the *Sonnets to Orpheus*, poems of solitude and anxiety, only on blue paper.

To many, however, it is the colour of the sea and the sky, and of the summer. But even Matisse, who borrowed the ecstatic blues of the Côte d'Azur and spoke of being 'pierced in the heart' by the particular blue of a butterfly's wings, cherished its natural ambiguities. 'What a difference there is between a black tinted with Prussian blue and a black tinted with ultramarine,' he wrote. 'The black with ultramarine has the warmth of tropical nights, but tinted with Prussian blue it has the chill of a glacier . . .'

Blue is the colour of distance, of the sky and of the far-off hills. Cézanne believed that only by adding an element of blue to every colour on his palette could he create the sensation of natural light, of objects viewed through air. It is the colour of partings, of tears, of absences, of longing, of stoicism, of emotions controlled or examined in solitary contemplation. And yet of all the colours of the spectrum, only violet has a shorter wavelength than blue, which therefore generates a high degree of energy. The blue flame is the fiercest. Red, at the other end of the waveband, is a low-energy colour. The excitement red creates is, in that sense, as much an illusion as the aloofness and passivity of blue. But it is a popular illusion: an experiment once showed that people in a room painted in blues and greens complained of the cold when the temperature fell to 59 degrees Fahrenheit; when the room was repainted in reds and yellows, they were still feeling warm at 54 degrees.

Although blue is hard to find in nature, outside the tones of the sky and the sea, it has long secured its place in the demotic life of the world: in the French workman's *bleu de travail*, the indigo wraps of the nomadic Tuaregs, the blue denim trousers of workers in the nineteenth-century gold mines of California's Sierra Nevada, where Levi Strauss turned surplus tent fabric into hard-wearing apparel before sending to southern France for supplies of denim, an indigo-dyed twill fabric manufactured in what had once been an output of the Roman empire: *serge de Nîmes*. In the twentieth century it became first the colour of efficiency – J. Edgar Hoover's FBI men wore dark blue suits, as did most post-war business executives, often adding pale blue shirts, navy blue polka dot ties, and dark blue socks. By the 1960s, a survey showed that 80 per cent of West German companies used the colour blue in their corporate identities. Simultaneously, however, blue began to be accepted as the colour of laid-back leisure in denim's leap from working gear to fashion apparel. Bob Dylan wears denim in the cover photographs of both *Freewheelin'* and *The Times They Are a-Changin'*, his second and third albums, with

which he proposed not only a new sound but a new style –
pre-owned, weathered, authentic – for a generation seeking
escape routes from the culture into which it had been born.

A tune beyond us, yet ourselves. The blue sign on the door
of Picasso's studio in the Montmartre apartment building
known as the Bâteau Lavoir during his first years in Paris
read: RENDEZ-VOUS DES POÈTES. These were the years of
his friendship with Guillaume Apollinaire, his life and his
art fuelled by opium, hashish, laudanum and alcohol: the
years of the blue period. The colour had become an obsession with symbolist Paris two decades earlier. John
Richardson, Picasso's biographer, describes a glass bowl by
Emile Galle, exhibited at the 1892 Salon, inscribed with a
verse by the symbolist poet Maurice Rollinat: 'How many
times a languid / Memory shows the heart / Its blue and
melancholy flower.' Richardson also quotes the claim by the
poet Jaime Sabartes that his friend and fellow Catalan
believed at the time that 'art emanates from Sadness and
Pain . . . Sadness lends itself to meditation . . . grief is at the
basis of life. We are passing through . . . a period of uncertainty that everyone regards from the viewpoint of his own
misery . . . a period of grief, of sadness . . . Life with all its
torments is at the core of [Picasso's] theory of art. If we
demand sincerity of the artist, we must remember that sincerity cannot be found outside the realm of grief.'

Richardson, however, is scornful of the 'twisted senti-
mentality' of the blue period: Examining Picasso's parade of
drudges and harlots and beggars, inspired by encounters in
bars and prisons and hospitals, he reaches a series of dis-

dainful conclusions. 'There is more romantic agony than social criticism to Blue period imagery,' he writes. 'Over the years (these paintings) have become popular favourites. Very rich people consistently pay higher prices for them than for any other examples of twentieth-century art. These distillations of suffering and want either exorcise the guilt of mammon or else make it the more enjoyable.'

Once Picasso had abandoned his preoccupation with blue, the Blaue Reiter (blue rider) movement took over. Founded in Germany in 1911 by a group including Wassily Kandinsky and Auguste Macke, the movement tried to identify and promote a set of specific colour identities, described by Franz Marc, co-author of the *Blaue Reiter Almanac*, who wrote: 'Blue is the male principle, sharp and spiritual, yellow the female principle . . . soft, cheerful and sensual, red the material, brutal and heavy and ever the colour which must be resisted and overcome by the other two . . .'

But no artist would be more closely identified with the colour than the prankster, visionary, pioneer performance artist and confirmed monochromaticist Yves Klein, who was born in 1928 under the blue sky of Nice and devoted most of his brief career to creating works solely composed of a deep and vibrant colour he formulated and christened International Klein Blue (IKB). 'Blue evokes the sea and the sky; after all, these are the most abstract things in the tangible and visible world,' he wrote, describing its 'enchanting emptiness' and concluding that it exerts its attraction 'not because it enters inside us but because it draws us in its wake'.

In 1957 Klein exhibited seven all-blue canvases at the

Gallery Apollinaire in Milan, as part of the launch of a movement called New Realism. The following year he presented for inspection by the Parisian public a totally empty gallery at number 3, rue des Beaux Arts in Saint-Germain des Prés, the room painted a uniform white save for a canopy and windows in IKB. Later he created an amusing scandal at his own International Gallery for Contemporary Art when several young women were covered in IKB and invited to lie on rolls of paper, leaving impressions (which he called *anthropometries*) strikingly similar to Matisse's famous *Nu bleu debout* of 1952. In 1958 he wrote to the secretary-general of the United Nations' International Geophysical Year proposing the creation of a Blue Sea to go with the Red and Black Seas. Later that year, as the Cold War approached its climax, he corresponded with the chairman of the International Conference on the Detection of Atomic Explosions, noting the proposed creation of the so-called 'cobalt bomb' – in which the destructive power of hydrogen bombs would be increased by addition of cobalt-60, an isotope used in radiotherapy – and suggesting instead that the bombs should be coated with IKB, as a way of creating visible fallout and adding a bit of cheerfulness to an essentially glum event. He sent copies of his letter to the Dalai Lama, the Pope, Bertrand Russell, Albert Schweitzer and the editor of the *Christian Science Monitor*. (And in November 2008, while the world was experiencing a financial meltdown, one of his all-blue panels, with sponges and pebbles glued on, went for $21.6 million in a sale at Sotheby's in New York; that day the Dow Jones index plunged 413 points.)

Yet blue had already irradiated the world in another form. In the early years of the twentieth century a variety of musical traditions coalesced among the African American population of the United States to form the music we know as the blues: songs of lamentation or complaint, usually to do with poor social conditions or, more regularly, lost love. The use of the term 'blue' among black people to denote an unhappy state of mind was first recorded in 1860, although in Europe the phrase 'the blue devils' had gained currency 200 years earlier as a synonym for depression, itself replaced in more recent times by the image of the black dog (while the Blue Devils became the name of a particularly potent Kansas City band of the 1930s).

As the blues colonised and refashioned the forms of music that surrounded it, from ragtime piano music and the Broadway torch song to the Kentucky mountain ballad, so the colour and the sound became synonymous. This itself was nothing new, at least in principle. The very use of the term 'chromatic' for the musical scale, dating back to ancient Greece, linked the two: even then, some believed that a musical sound had a colour in the same way that it existed in the dimensions of pitch and time. Early colour diagrams imitated the harmonic and scalar relationships found in music, with their octaves and tetrachords. In the sixteenth century Giuseppe Arcimboldo wrote vocal music in which each individual line was associated with a particular colour. A hundred years later Louis-Bertrand Castel built an 'ocular harpsichord' intended to play colour sequences chosen from 144 possible hues, keys and wires operating slips of coloured paper in front of a light source –

a hundred candles in an early version. It took Jean-Jacques Rousseau to assert, in 1764, the reluctance of musical sounds to submit to individual definition by means of analogies with another form, whether in spoken language or colour. Undaunted, in 1786 J. L. Hoffman published a pamphlet on colour and harmony in which he linked the two types of chromatics by associating colours with instruments: yellow with clarinets, crimson with flutes, ultramarine with violins and violas, bright red with trumpets (one can only assume that no eighteenth-century trumpeter sounded like Miles Davis).

And yet every now and then a great writer could summon the image that captured music in a ray of colour. 'The lights grow brighter as the earth lurches away from the sun,' F. Scott Fitzgerald wrote in Nick Carraway's helplessly enraptured description of Jay Gatsby's parties at the mansion on Long Island Sound in *The Great Gatsby*, 'and now the orchestra is playing yellow cocktail music, and the opera of voices pitches a key higher.' And this, from earlier in the same passage: 'There was music from my neighbour's house through the summer nights. In his blue gardens men and women came and went like moths among the whisperings and the champagne and the stars . . .'

Blue gardens. Blue valentines. Blue kisses. Blue velvet. Blue and sentimental. I'm blue. Love is blue. Way to blue. Blue on blue (heartache on heartache). A nice word to say – and to sing, with its explosive initial double-consonant immediately softened, then succeeded by a long and shapely vowel. Born to be blue. Midnight blue. Almost blue. Blue moon. Blue angel. Blue train. Blue notes, of course:

the flattened thirds and sevenths of the blues. No colour has so saturated music over the last hundred years, while permitting so many shadings.

The Polish film director Krzysztof Kieslowski made a powerful connection in 1993 when he began his Three Colours trilogy with *Blue*, in which blue surfaces – swimming pools, blank television screens – echo the emptiness created in the life of a young woman by the death of her husband, a composer whose music permeates the film like an additional character. The themes of the trilogy are liberty, equality and fraternity. Or, to be more precise in the case of *Blue*, the lack of liberty, the encroachment on personal freedom, created by love – 'the prison created by both emotions and memory,' in Kieslowski's words. 'The colour's not decorative. It plays a dramaturgic role. The colour means something.' Another kind of blue, another kind of music.

Wassily Kandinsky, who was a practising cellist as well as the bridge from the Blaue Reiter movement to the Bauhaus, also heard the music of blue. 'Blue unfolds in its lower depths the element of tranquillity,' he wrote. 'The brighter it becomes, the more it loses its sound.' How uncannily similar that is to Miles Davis's celebrated remark when playing a Moorish melody during the recording of *Sketches of Spain*, the successor to *Kind of Blue*, in 1959. 'That melody,' the trumpeter told his collaborator, Gil Evans, 'is so strong that the softer you play it, the stronger it gets, and the stronger you play it, the weaker it gets.' Blue, the colour of heaven and of despair, of distance and intimacy, admits no easy resolutions.

4 Blue Moods

Conversations behind a Chinese laundry

The cool world was born between 1947 and 1949 in a basement room at 14 West 55th Street in midtown Manhattan. A place of exposed heating pipes and few furnishings, where the amenities stretched no further than a sink, a bed, a piano, a gramophone and a hot plate, it was reached by descending a half-flight of steps from the street and passing through the premises of the Asia Laundry. Goodness knows what the Chinese laundry workers or the first residents of the adjacent Rockefeller Apartments, a pioneering exercise in bright, bland international style, made of their neighbour Gil Evans, or of the hours and the company he kept during those years in the unlovely premises that could be regarded as the Bâteau Lavoir of modern music.

It was here, next door to Jules the barber and across the street from the solemn brownstone Fifth Avenue Presbyterian Church, that music changed its course. This was where introspection and understatement entered the equation, diverting jazz from its primary function as entertainment into a more self-conscious role. Here is where new and subtle ways were found to express emotional intensity. In this basement, a kind of music formerly stereotyped in the public mind as hot and hectic was purposefully cooled down and slowed down. In the process it became a matter of intellectual and, for some, spiritual inquiry. And from this room went out the ideas that altered not just jazz and its associated forms of popular music but much else besides.

The formation of two of the idiom's most popular groups, the Modern Jazz Quartet and Gerry Mulligan's famous piano-less quartet, the latter responsible for launching the career of the trumpeter Chet Baker, came about (in 1951 and 1952, respectively) as a result of the theoretical discussions that took place in Evans's apartment. The two great monuments of the late years of the idiom we call modern jazz, *Kind of Blue* and John Coltrane's *A Love Supreme*, represented a more highly evolved response to the same source of inspiration, their very disparity demonstrating the breadth of possibilities that had been revealed. The hushed intensity of *Kind of Blue* in turn fathered a new genre of meditative music-making (whose faintest ripples became known as New Age music), while Coltrane, rejecting understatement and ellipsis, imbued *A Love Supreme* with a form of passionate expression specifically directed towards the attainment of spiritual bliss. Between them, these two recordings influenced not just would-be imitators but countless musicians working in related fields.

At the time he moved into the apartment, Evans was an unknown arranger of music for the kind of big bands which, for the previous fifteen years, had provided the era's popular dance music. His early career as a bandleader in California had not been a success. Devoted to music, and rigorous in his study and preparation, he discovered himself to be unskilled and uninterested in the art of self-promotion. When he arrived in New York in 1941, it was to join the orchestra of Claude Thornhill, an ensemble which, thanks to the leader's fondness for adding French horns and extra woodwind to the trumpets, trombones and saxophones of the conventional jazz-tinged swing band, languished some way behind those of Benny Goodman and Artie Shaw in popularity. To Evans, however, Thornhill's liking for experiment offered a tonal palette whose richness and flexibility enabled him to combine his admiration of Duke Ellington and Louis Armstrong with a strong leaning towards the early twentieth-century European impressionism of Maurice Ravel, Gabriel Fauré and Manuel de Falla.

Under attack from post-war economic factors and from the distant pre-echoes of rock 'n' roll, the era of the big bands was already drawing to a close. Evans instinctively immersed himself in the sounds of the bebop revolution, whose headquarters were to be found on a strip of West 52nd Street between Fifth and Seventh Avenues. Only three blocks south of Evans's address, clubs such as the Famous Door, the Three Deuces and the Onyx provided the stars of the new music with excited audiences.

Some of those stars, notably Charlie Parker and the young Miles Davis, became accustomed to using the apartment, where the door was never locked, as a crash pad. For Davis, already a drop-out from the Juilliard Conservatory, and others it functioned chiefly as an informal salon, a place in which, day and night, a conversation took place about the future of music; to Parker, who lived there with Evans for several weeks, it also represented a convenient place to store the paraphernalia of heroin addiction. 'It had all the pipes for the building as well as a sink, a bed, a piano and a hot plate, and no heat,' Gerry Mulligan wrote, recalling the years when some of New York's most adventurous young musicians met regularly to talk and compare their ideas. Mulligan also lodged there for a while. 'It was an exciting time musically,' he continued, 'and everybody seemed to gravitate to Gil's place.' Later he added: 'That's when a lot of fruitful relationships started – there was the opportunity to hang out and talk for as long as we wanted. It was a kind of a *Who's Who*. And music was always the subject.'

One of the most significant exchanges of that short but intense era took place between Davis and George Russell. Born in Cincinnati in 1923, Russell had begun his career as a drummer but developed a deep interest in harmonic theory. In 1946, just as he was starting to make a reputation as an arranger, he wrote a piece called 'Cubana Be' for Dizzy Gillespie's big band. Devised as a feature for Chano Pozo, the brilliant and tempestuous Cuban conga player whom Gillespie was introducing to American listeners, it was based on a sketch by the trumpeter to which Russell added an introduction incorporating no harmonic movement at all. 'It wasn't based on any chords, which was an innovation in jazz,' Russell said. 'The whole concept of my introduction was modal . . .'

It was during a lengthy convalescence from a bout of tuberculosis in 1946–7 that Russell shared a conversation with Davis which took root but would not bear fruit for a decade. 'Miles sort of took a liking to me,' Russell told the musicologist Ingrid Monson. 'And he used to invite me up to his house. We'd sit down and play chords. He liked my sense of harmony. And I loved his sense so we'd try to kill each other with chords. He'd say, "Check this out." And I'd say, "Wow." And I'd say, "Listen to this . . ." I asked him one day on one of these sessions, what's your highest aim? And he said, "To learn all the changes." That's all he said. The more I thought about it, the more I thought there was a system begging to be brought into the world. And that system was based on chord-scale unity. The whole aspect of a chord having a scale – that was really its birthplace.'

While Russell immersed himself in the study of a system in which scales and modes would replace the prison of chord sequences, Davis's friendship with Gil Evans was yielding the first rewards of what would become a long-term collaborative friendship. Born in Toronto in 1912, Evans had spent most of the 1930s in California, serving his apprenticeship as a bandleader and arranger before moving to New York and attaching himself to Thornhill. At a time when most of his contemporaries were trying to ingratiate themselves with young American dancers, Thornhill quietly insisted that the audience should come to him. This attitude attracted considerable respect from his peers, but little enthusiasm from the public. The trademark of the Thornhill orchestra was a love of exotic texture linked to rhythms that could be described as passive, at least compared to those of bandleaders influenced by Fletcher Henderson, Count Basie and Duke Ellington. Even the bands of Benny Goodman and Artie Shaw annexed far more of the elements of hot jazz than Thornhill cared to borrow. His music was characterised by its concern for the creation of an almost static beauty: not the greatest of qualifications for a band-leader in a market dominated by rivals who competed to make their audiences dance.

As Thornhill's chief arranger, Evans became the man who refined the formula. His initial influence had been the music of Louis Armstrong – among the records he purchased as a teenager, the one that exerted the greatest impact on him was a 78rpm disc with the Armstrong orchestra's versions of 'Memories of You' on one side and 'You're Lucky to Me' on the reverse, recorded in Los Angeles in 1930 – but his deep love and knowledge of jazz ran parallel with a passion for the music of the French and Spanish impressionists of the early twentieth century, particularly that of Fauré and his pupil, Ravel, and de Falla. Although he did not discover his affinity for this music until after his arrival in New York, his immersion was swift and intensive as he spent many hours in music libraries studying recordings and scores. From these composers he learned how to use a palette of woodwinds and brass with special concern for unusual and often provocative combinations. Thornhill's line-up included two French horns and a tuba, while the saxophonists were required to double on various woodwind instruments. An Evans chart might end with a piccolo holding a double high C several octaves above a C held by a tuba, for instance. Or a theme might be stated by a pair of alto flutes, perhaps joined for the recapitulation by a tightly muted trumpet. It was a painterly way of making music, and far too refined to satisfy the requirements of dance-hall audiences, although it commanded the loyalty of a group of musicians of parallel temperaments; when Thornhill reformed his orchestra in 1946, after a four-year wartime hiatus, most of his personnel enthusiastically returned to the colours, including Evans.

'In essence, at first, the sound of the band was almost a reduction to inactivity of the music, to a stillness,' Evans told Nat Hentoff in 1957. 'Everything – melody, harmony and rhythm – was moving at minimum speed. The melody was very slow, static; the rhythm was nothing much faster than quarter notes and a minimum of syncopation. Everything was lowered to create a sound, and nothing was to be used to distract from that sound. The sound hung like a cloud . . .'

His early experiments included rearrangements for Thornhill of Tchaikovsky's *Arab Dance*, Mussorgsky's *The Troubadour*, Granados's *Spanish Dance No 5* and Yradier's *La Paloma*, but he often borrowed themes and motifs from those who inspired him in order to recast existing pieces or to begin the construction of new ones – and not merely because he was a painfully slow worker who often found life easier when he had pre-existing material to reshape, rather than invent his own from scratch. It was a process the English critic Max Harrison aptly called 'recomposition'. In the early 1960s, for example, the infectious ground bass figure from Ravel's *Pièce en forme de habanera* became the platform for Evans's celebrated 'Las Vegas Tango'.

Having followed the emergence of bebop with great interest, Evans also extended the Thornhill orchestra's range by producing arrangements of three tunes associated with Charlie Parker; the band recorded them in 1947, long before the new music had become familiar to a general audience, let alone accepted by dancers. In his versions of Parker's 'Yardbird Suite', 'Anthropology' by Parker and Dizzy Gillespie, and 'Donna Lee' by Parker and Miles

Davis, he attempted with considerable success to retain the fleetness and mobility of a small bop combo while deploying the tonal resources of a full orchestra. This adventure was no more likely to ingratiate the Thornhill orchestra with the ballroom public than its earlier strategies, but the leader went along with it, just as he had given in to his own desire to expand the band's instrumentation, thus increasing the payroll and the travel expenses at a time when the big-band business was becoming financially risky for all but the most successful attractions. Posterity will thank Claude Thornhill, even if his bank manager didn't. For it was when Gil Evans was searching for a lead sheet of 'Donna Lee' and permission to create a big-band arrangement of the tune that he met Davis, the twenty-one-year-old trumpeter with Parker's quintet and the tune's chief composer.

'I told him he could do it if he got me a copy of Claude Thornhill's arrangement of "Robbin's Nest",' Davis later recalled, proving that at least one young cutting-edge bebop musician was aware of the Thornhill orchestra's adventurous attitude. 'He got it for me, and after talking to each other for a while and testing each other out, we found out that I liked the way Gil wrote music and he liked the way I played. We heard sound in the same way.'

The timing was perfect. By the middle of 1948 Davis had grown impatient with Parker's personal and professional unreliability, as well as with the standard formula of bebop. He and Evans began spending a lot of time together in the West 55th Street basement, talking about music and discovering a common sensibility despite the twelve-year gap between their ages and the difference in the colour of their skin. They listened to Ravel and Fauré, and Evans introduced him to the ideas of John Cage and the innovations of Harry Partch, which expanded his horizons even if he was not about to espouse Cage's ideas on indeterminacy or Partch's use of self-created instruments. 'I could relate to his ideas and he could relate to mine,' Davis wrote. 'With Gil, the question of race never entered; it was always about music. He didn't care what colour you were. He was one of the first white people I had met who was like this. He was Canadian and maybe that had something to do with how he thought. He was just the kind of guy you love being around, because he would see things nobody else saw. He loved paintings, and showed me things I would never have seen. Or he would listen to an orchestration and say, "Miles, listen to the cello right here. How else do you think he could have played that passage?" He used to go inside of music and pull things out another person wouldn't normally have heard. Gil was a thinker and I loved that about him right away.'

Not without significance to the style-conscious Davis was the fact that Evans's diffidence and his narrow silhouette combined to create a naturally cool image, refreshingly at variance from the 'super-hip black musicians wearing peg-legs and zoot suits' who surrounded the trumpeter in his normal environment. Evans favoured a relaxed look of slender grey suits cut in the Italian style, with knit shirts. 'Here was this tall, thin white guy who was hipper than hip,' Davis remembered. And by the summer of 1948 they had worked out how to make music together.

Among the other regulars at West 55th Street were

Gillespie and Parker. But most of the regular circle were younger men – many of them composers, such as George Russell, John Benson Brooks, Gerry Mulligan, John Lewis and John Carisi, who shared an interest in looking for ways to incorporate the discoveries of bebop into a new orchestral language. They admired the swinging brass and reed sections of the Count Basie band, and they adored the adventurous textures created by Duke Ellington and Billy Strayhorn, but they were after something more modern in its attitudes, more allusive, more oblique, more asymmetrical, something that matched the way other art forms were evolving in order to meet the complex emotional demands of the post-war years: a blend of existential remoteness and urban agitation. And it was a group of younger musicians who were recruited to participate in the music of the Miles Davis Nonet, as it became known – a nine-piece band with which Davis and Evans would attempt to produce a scaled-down variant of the Thornhill orchestra, with additional input from musicians raised in the bebop idiom.

Max Roach, Davis's colleague in the Parker band, was the drummer. Gerry Mulligan and Lee Konitz, who had both worked in the Thornhill band with Evans, were the saxophonists. John Lewis and Al McKibbon, both formerly with Gillespie's big band, were the pianist and bassist. J. J. Johnson, another Parker alumnus, was the first-choice trombonist, but his temporary unavailability meant that a younger musician, Mike Zwerin, took his place. Junior Collins and Bill Barber came directly from the Thornhill band, on French horn and tuba respectively.

There was no doubt about Davis's status as the leader.

'He took the initiative and put the theories to the test,' Mulligan wrote. 'He called the rehearsals, hired the halls, called the players, and generally cracked the whip.' When the band made its first appearance, at the Royal Roost on Broadway in September 1948, it was under a very clear billing: 'Miles Davis's Nonet: Arrangements by Gerry Mulligan, Gil Evans and John Lewis.' The unusual decision to highlight the identity of the arrangers provided the clearest possible signal of the group's intention to concentrate on a novel approach to ensemble organisation.

'I was looking for a vehicle where I could solo more in the style that I was hearing,' Davis wrote. Bebop was too fast and frantic for his temperament. Whereas most bop trumpeters played as high as they could reach into the trumpeter's stratosphere, Davis seemed to 'hear' – in other words, to be more comfortable with – music in the middle and lower registers. (This turned out to be a slight misconception, since in later years Davis would show himself to be not only acquainted with but highly expressive in the instrument's upper levels, yet it was one he appeared happy to propagate.) He and Evans talked about how they wanted the music to sound, and Evans and Mulligan set about determining the instrumentation and the players they required. There were a few preliminary disputes over the personnel but in the end the combination of a thoroughbred bop rhythm section – Lewis, McKibbon and Roach – and a set of horns dominated by sonorities from the Thornhill orchestra gave them the blend and the balance they needed. The presence of Konitz and Mulligan ensured that the solos would never be cut from standard bebop material, while the rhythm section would not settle for the kind of stasis that damaged the jazz credentials of Thornhill's orchestra.

'Right now, ladies and gentlemen, we bring you something new in modern music,' the celebrated disc jockey and MC Symphony Sid Torin told listeners to New York's WMCA radio stations on the night the nonet made its first live broadcast from the Roost, where it was sharing the bill with the Count Basie orchestra. Davis later remembered that Basie had sat listening to the band every night. 'He liked it. He told me that it was "slow and strange, but good, real good".'

Basie's 'slow and strange' turned out to be perhaps the first definition of 'cool', the word with which the nonet became most closely identified, to the point where, after its handful of recordings had been collected on to a long-playing record, it was rechristened after the title of that album, becoming known as the *Birth of the Cool* band. Cool was, of course, the opposite of hot, the quality associated in the public mind with virtually all previous forms of jazz, from King Oliver's Creole Jazz Band to the Dizzy Gillespie Orchestra. 'Hot' meant trumpets and trombones using highly vocalised tones, and flamboyant drummers who kept the tempo and the temperature high. Only Lester Young, the great tenor saxophonist, proposed an alternative, preferring a light tone and fluid phrasing to the big sound and declamatory attack of his contemporary Coleman Hawkins, who had previously defined the language of the jazz saxophone. The sense of detachment that distinguished Young's playing made him, in a sense, the first modern jazz musician. And even when bebop came along, although its music was sophisticated and its hipster performers proud of their cool façade, it was essentially a hot music, built on the impact created by dizzying speed of thought and execution. 'Bird and Diz played this hip, real fast thing,' Davis wrote in one of the key judgements of the era, 'and if you weren't a fast listener, you couldn't catch the humour or the feeling in their music.'

The Miles Davis Nonet changed all that. Its sonorities were pure, its voicings open, the cadence of its music calm and smooth. Davis later said he had instructed Evans and Mulligan to create a band whose horns replicated the range of a choir: soprano (trumpet), alto (alto saxophone and French horn), tenor (trombone), baritone (baritone saxophone), and bass (tuba). André Hodeir, the French composer and critic, described the nonet as a 'chamber orchestra', and saw the inclusion of the French horn as symbolising an implicit rejection of the hot tradition. The lack of duplication of voices and the individual players' preference for comparatively light timbres gave the sound of the ensemble an airy clarity that immediately set it apart from anything previously heard in jazz. Its ballads, notably Evans's ethereal arrangement of 'Moon Dreams', were weightless reveries, while the up-tempo tunes, such as Evans's version of Davis's 'Boplicity' and Lewis's flying treatment of Denzil Best's 'Move', proposed a new kind of post-bop music, something more fleet and lucid – more *modern* – than the style invented by Parker and Gillespie. Unlike bebop, this wasn't confrontational music. Not only did it not care if you didn't like it, it affected not even to notice.

Inconveniently enough, Evans suffered one of his periodic

crises of productivity during the run-up to the Roost gig, which meant that although he had effectively set the tone for the band, only two of the charts were actually his. The repertoire also included arrangements by Lewis, Mulligan and Carisi. 'It did not seem historic or legendary,' Mike Zwerin wrote fifty years after that first night, long after he had metamorphosised from a trombonist into a Paris-based contributor to the *International Herald Tribune*. The nonet was never remotely a financial success, its life extending no further than two weeks at the Roost in 1948, a short stay at the Clique Club the following year, and a dozen 78rpm sides released by Capitol Records to some interest from critics but a general indifference from the public. Perhaps, though, there were other reasons for its lack of longevity. Many years later, Mulligan spoke to me of a conversation with Konitz in 1988 at Evans's memorial service, where four of the surviving members of the nonet participated in a recreation of the old music. 'Lee reminded me that it had become a very faction-ridden band,' Mulligan said. 'He said it was the only nine-piece band with eight cliques. At the time, I must say, I was so totally focused on the music that I hardly noticed.'

Musicians outside the band were also focusing on its intriguing sound, many of them coming to the conclusion that its innovations gave them an opportunity to update their own approach to music. By the time Davis ended a stay of several weeks in Europe, where he led a band with the pianist Tadd Dameron at the Paris Jazz Festival, and returned to New York in the summer of 1949, he discovered that 'white musicians who were copying my *Birth of the Cool* thing were getting the jobs'. When Mulligan moved to Los Angeles and formed his piano-less quartet with Chet Baker in 1952, the lighter, breezier approach came to be known as the West Coast Sound, and later as 'cool jazz'. Shelly Manne, Shorty Rogers, Bud Shank, Art Pepper, Marty Paich and Bob Cooper – all prominent in the LA scene – were significant figures in this new movement. But the phenomenon had its roots in the conversations between Evans and Davis and their friends in the apartment behind the Chinese laundry, acknowledged in 1954 when Capitol compiled the studio recordings into a ten-inch LP and gave it the title that has identified the nine-piece band and its music ever since. 'It was a wonderful time, a special time,' Mulligan told me, 'and the nonet grew directly out of that experience.'

Davis failed to capitalise immediately on the innovations he had sponsored, thanks mostly to an involvement with heroin which set in after his return from Europe. In Paris in the summer of 1949 he had made the acquaintance of the Left Bank set, forming particular friendships with the writers Jean-Paul Sartre and Boris Vian. He also fell in love with a twenty-two-year-old singer, Juliette Gréco, whose performances at the Tabou on the rue Dauphine had already made her an icon of Saint-Germain des Prés. She went to hear him at the Salle Pleyel, and remembered: 'To be struck by him, it wasn't necessary to be a scholar or a specialist in jazz . . . between the man, the instrument and the sound, there was such harmony. At that aesthetic level, it was pretty shattering. So I met this man, who was very young, as I was. We went out for dinner in a group, with people I didn't know. And there it was. I didn't speak English; he didn't speak French. I haven't a clue how we managed. The miracle of love . . .'

At twenty-three, Davis's social and intellectual horizons had been decisively broadened, and he experienced for the first time a life without racial prejudice, one in which he was accepted as an artist rather than an entertainer. But the lure of New York was too strong. Once he got back home to a world in which jazz musicians and black people had little status, he realised what he had left behind, and entered a period of addiction which lasted four years and included an arrest and a short stay in jail in Los Angeles. In the light of his subsequent development, however, it would be difficult to believe that this brush with the leading lights of the existentialist movement had not exerted a considerable influence on his view of himself as an artist.

There were many records and gigs during that period following his return from Paris, but it was not until a year after he had come off heroin, during a stay at his father's farm outside East St Louis in 1953, that he took the next step on the road to *Kind of Blue*. On Christmas Eve 1954 he led a recording session with an all-star quintet which gave evidence of a new command of space, authority and atmosphere in his playing. The version of 'Bags' Groove', a straightforward twelve-bar blues written around a single extremely catchy phrase by the vibraharpist Milt Jackson, displayed a clarity and an economy that were combined with the aloofness inherent in the trumpeter's playing to produce an effect of drama without rhetoric. Played at an unhurried medium tempo, the tune elicits a performance notable for its relaxed concentration. It was becoming evident that the fewer the notes Davis played, the stronger his impact: a revolutionary concept in a music where muscular athleticism had a value expressed when one horn player confronted another in what were known as 'cutting contests', a form of musical arm-wrestling popular in after-hours clubs.

This is when we start to hear the Miles Davis whose playing had such an impact on an entire generation of trumpeters, such as Booker Little, whose death from a blood disease in 1961, at the age of 23, robbed jazz of an important voice. 'Miles Davis minimised how much trumpet playing you could do as much as anybody could minimise it,' he said. 'But many people have a misconception about him. They say he can't play trumpet. But he's a fantastic trumpet player with a fantastic mind. He was one of the first guys around who didn't have to play every note in an A minor chord to give you the impression of an A minor chord, and to get the mood that the section needed.'

By now, too, Davis's characteristic open-horn tone had taken shape, that plaintive, hollowed-out sound which the critic Kenneth Tynan's nine-year-old daughter, listening to *Kind of Blue*, described to her father as the sound of 'a little boy who's been locked out and wants to get in'. When Davis inserted a Harmon mute into the bell of his trumpet, leaving out the stem that other players used to produce a wah-wah effect, he obtained a tight, drizzling sound even more powerfully evocative of mid-century alienation.

Where did Miles Davis's sound come from? From inside

Miles Davis, of course, once he had acquired the confidence to move beyond the realm of outside influence and to play himself. But Gil Evans told me of a conversation he'd had in the 1960s with Louis Armstrong, during which Armstrong mentioned that he thought Davis sounded like Buddy Bolden, the legendary pioneer cornetist from New Orleans. Bolden played with his band in the bars of Storyville during the early years of the twentieth century but was committed to an insane asylum in 1907, at the age of thirty. No recordings of him survive, although legend says that a wax cylinder was made in the late 1890s, but never found. 'Now that's historically fascinating,' Evans said, 'because Louis Armstrong was one of very few people who could have heard both Buddy Bolden and Miles Davis, and who could therefore be in a position to make the comparison.'

It might seem an odd comparison, since Bolden's chief musical characteristic was said to have been his enormous power. It was claimed, in one famous description, that on a clear night his playing could be heard on the far side of Lake Ponchartrain, fourteen miles away. Jelly Roll Morton said something similar: 'The whole town would know that Buddy Bolden was in the park, ten or twelve miles from the centre of town. He was the blowingest man ever lived since Gabriel.' How such playing could be compared with Davis's characteristic intimacy is hard to say, although it would be difficult to dispute Armstrong's claim, given the nature of its source. But listen, if you can, to Davis's version of the standard 'When I Fall in Love' from the *Live at the Plugged Nickel* set recorded by the trumpeter's quintet in a Chicago club in 1965: the sound of the trumpet seems rudimentary, almost bugle-like in its artlessness, and powerfully affecting. Tune out the rhythm section in your head, along with the knowledge that the melody was written (by Victor Young, for the film *One Minute to Zero*) not until 1952, and for a moment you could be listening to a man playing on the top of a levee by the Mississippi river more than half a century earlier.

The Christmas Eve session in 1954 also produced two long versions of 'The Man I Love' and another extended track, 'Swing Spring', said to have been based by Davis on a scale that he had heard Bud Powell practising. He never recorded it again but already, it seemed, his conversations with George Russell were exerting an effect on his thoughts about harmony.

Six months later, on 9 July 1955, Davis took part in the New York session that produced a ten-inch album called *Blue Moods*, recorded for Charles Mingus's fledgling label, Debut Records. Mingus's lawyer, Harold Lovett, had just bailed Davis out of Riker's Island prison in New York, where the trumpeter had been incarcerated for non-payment of alimony and child support. He needed money, and was paid only the union rate for the session, which featured a quintet completed by Mingus on bass, the trombonist Britt Woodman, the vibraharpist Teddy Charles and the drummer Elvin Jones playing restrained versions of four standards: 'Nature Boy', 'Alone Together', 'There's No You' and 'Easy Living'.

Possibly influenced by the reason for his participation, and by his up-and-down relationship with the volcanic

Mingus (with whom he would have an angry exchange in the pages of *Down Beat* later in the year), Davis never cared for *Blue Moods*. 'Something went wrong at the session and nothing ever really clicked, so the playing didn't have any fire,' he wrote many years later. 'I don't know what it was – maybe the arrangements – but something definitely went wrong.' A less subjectively involved listener might feel otherwise – that these careful arrangements and straightforward performances show a command and continuity of mood rare in jazz at the time, particularly in the early days of the long-playing record, when musicians had yet to get to grips with the idea of turning thirty or forty minutes of music into a coherent statement.

Although it never achieved much in the way of a critical reputation, *Blue Moods* certainly fulfilled the promise of its title. Its twenty-six and a half minutes of music are wistful, elegant, fragile, distilled, detached. Three of the arrangements are by Charles and the fourth ('Alone Together') by Mingus; none is formulaic and each has its own way of maximising the resources of the quintet (in the opening statement of 'Nature Boy', for instance, the vibes plays the theme over bowed bass, with the trumpet providing an obligato). In strict jazz terms Davis's solos throughout *Blue Moods* may not be his most adventurous or compelling, but the atmosphere is effectively sustained and overall the music has survived the years with distinction. Reviewing the album for *Down Beat* on its release that December, the critic Nat Hentoff awarded it a maximum score of five stars.

Blue Moods was following in the pioneering footsteps of Frank Sinatra's *In the Wee Small Hours*, which had been recorded four months earlier in Los Angeles and, thanks to a unity of mood ensured by the tightly focused choice of songs and by Nelson Riddle's exquisite arrangements, has come to be seen as popular music's first 'concept album'. Only a handful of years after the appearance of the twelve-inch, 33rpm microgroove long-player, someone had recognised the potential of a format which did not need to be treated as an opportunity to juxtapose a variety of approaches (fast–slow, happy–sad). Instead it could be used to create a unity of mood that might prove better suited to the needs of modern listeners. (Sinatra and Riddle followed up *Wee Small Hours* three years later, the year before *Kind of Blue*, with an even finer cycle of lovelorn ballads titled *Frank Sinatra Sings for Only the Lonely*, later nominated by the singer as his own favourite of all his albums.) Perhaps, then, *Blue Moods* was jazz's first concept album; for Miles Davis, it was certainly the start of something.

5 Blue Dawn

From the Third Stream to the *nouvelle vague*

Eight days after the *Blue Moods* session, on 17 July 1955, Davis made an appearance at the Newport Jazz Festival. Free from heroin for more than a year, he was ready to make a statement. Wearing a white tuxedo and a black bow tie and standing in the middle of a distinguished pick-up band containing the saxophonists Zoot Sims and Gerry Mulligan, with Thelonious Monk on piano and the Modern Jazz Quartet's rhythm team of the bassist Percy Heath and the drummer Connie Kay, he played Monk's 'Hackensack' and 'Round Midnight' and Parker's 'Now's the Time'. The highlight of a performance that announced his renewed vigour and replenished imagination was a wonderfully poised and inventive version of 'Round Midnight', alone with the rhythm section. He and Monk argued about the tune's harmonies on the way back to New York that night, but the critics were dazzled.

'I don't know what all those cats were talking about,' he said later. 'I played the way I always play.' But the evolution of his sound and the perception of a new sense of focus and assertiveness in his playing impressed a knowledgeable and influential audience, drawing the particular attention of George Avakian, a senior A&R man at Columbia Records. Avakian had approached Davis a year earlier, only to discover the existence of a contract between the trumpeter and

Bob Weinstock, the head of Prestige Records, a specialist jazz label. The deal was not due to expire until 1957.

Davis was all for committing himself to a new deal, even though it would not take effect until the old one ended, in order to leave the restricted world of small independent specialist labels such as Blue Note and Prestige and secure his presence on the roster of one of America's most illustrious and powerful record companies, whose vast marketing and distribution system would be made available to him. Avakian, however, was in no hurry. Not, that is, until that day in Newport. Then he got a move on and contacted Davis's new manager, Harold Lovett.

Meanwhile Davis had been experimenting with the personnel of his new band, a quintet. When they opened at the Blue Note in Philadelphia in April 1955, the line-up featured the tenor saxophonist Sonny Rollins, the pianist Red Garland, the bassist Paul Chambers and the drummer Philly Joe Jones. Rollins, a native New Yorker, had already been heard on some of Davis's Prestige recordings. Garland, from Dallas, Texas, had been on the New York scene for several years and was hired chiefly because he could play in a style that reminded Davis of Ahmad Jamal, the Chicago-based pianist whose elegant sense of space and imaginative treatment of standard tunes had impressed the trumpeter. Chambers, just twenty years old, had arrived in New York from his native Detroit only a few weeks earlier, and had already made a big impression with two quintets, one led by the pianist George Wallington and the other by two trombonists, J. J. Johnson and Kai Winding; his playing blended harmonic acuity with a middleweight tone and an insistent swing. Jones, nicknamed after his native Philadelphia in order to differentiate him from the Jo Jones who had propelled the Count Basie Orchestra during its 1930s heyday, was one of the fieriest of the generation of drummers coming up behind Kenny Clarke, Max Roach and Art Blakey, the bebop pioneers.

Unusually, Weinstock agreed to a proposal that Davis should be allowed to record for Columbia before the new contract took effect, as long as the results were not released until the original deal had expired and the switch had been made. As a result, Davis found himself recording, in a sense, at two different speeds. His Prestige albums, for which he was comparatively poorly recompensed, were recorded quickly at the independent studio of the engineer Rudy Van Gelder in Hackensack, New Jersey, and reflected the quintet's club performances in repertoire and mood.

By the time the quintet set foot in any recording studio, however, the personnel had already undergone one significant and lasting change. Rollins, wishing to rid himself of a heroin habit, followed Davis's example and removed himself from the New York scene (although, lacking a father with a farm, he had to sign himself into a hospital in Lexington, Kentucky). After trying and rejecting John Gilmore, a young member of the Sun Ra collective and therefore a believer in astral travelling and other interesting theories, Davis accepted Jones's recommendation of John Coltrane, a twenty-nine-year-old tenorist who had been born in North Carolina and raised in Philadelphia. Davis was dubious, since he remembered hearing Coltrane five years earlier at the Audubon Ballroom in Harlem, where, as a member of Dizzy Gillespie's band, he had been comprehensively outshone by Rollins. Clearly, however, Coltrane had made ground in the interim, although Davis was still somewhat irritated by his lack of interest in his appearance and by his persistence in asking questions about the music. Less off-putting, at least to begin with, was the fact that Coltrane was a heavy heroin user. So, after all, were Garland and Jones. In those days, bands often divided socially along the line between users and non-users. And, of course, no one was better placed than Davis to recognise how difficult it was for jazz musicians of that generation to avoid a temptation that was as close a companion as their instruments, and for many a more constant one than their wives or girlfriends.

Coltrane rejected the proposal of a job with the organist Jimmy Smith – a figure of growing popularity, whose offer represented a solid income but unchallenging music – in order to join Davis, a clear indication of his seriousness of purpose. The reshaped quintet played their first engagement at the Club Las Vegas in Baltimore in late September and recorded together for the first time a month later, at a session at Columbia's studios at 779 Seventh Avenue South in New York City, which yielded only one track for what would eventually be Davis's debut album for the label. In November, however, Davis returned with the quintet to the more familiar surroundings of Van Gelder's New Jersey studio to record, in a single day, the contents of what would be their debut LP for Prestige.

The first LP by the New Miles Davis Quintet, as it was billed, was released by Weinstock the following spring under the title *Miles*. They did not return to the studio until a year later, when – in what we can assume to have been a standard double session of six hours' duration – no fewer than a dozen pieces were recorded, enough for two complete twelve-inch albums, with a couple of tunes left over. Prestige would store up the material and release it over a period of years, taking advantage of the raising of Davis's profile that followed his promotion by a major label. His early Columbia sessions, however, were more painstaking affairs, since they represented the start of a campaign to take him out of the confines of the jazz world and to turn him into a celebrity of a different kind.

Very quickly, the quintet developed its own voice. 'Faster than I could have imagined, the music that we were playing together was just unbelievable,' Davis remembered, describing how it 'used to send chills through me at night, and it did the same things to the audience, too'. This was a time when small bands with individual identities were the principal vehicles for modern jazz. Some of them, such as Art Blakey's Jazz Messengers, the Horace Silver Quintet, the Gerry Mulligan Quartet, Charles Mingus's Jazz Workshop, the Dave Brubeck Quartet, Shorty Rogers and the Jazz Giants, Shelly Manne and his Men, the George Shearing Quintet, the Chico Hamilton Quintet, the Modern Jazz Quartet and the Max Roach-Clifford Brown Quintet (until Brown's untimely death in 1956), were the focal points of its popularity, their records mostly disseminated via the labels founded by a group of dedicated enthusiasts who became independent record producers – Alfred Lion and Francis Wolff of Blue Note, Bill Grauer and Orrin

Keepnews of Riverside and Prestige's Weinstock on the East Coast, with Lester Koenig of Contemporary and Richard Bock of Pacific Jazz in Southern California.

Blakey had been among the first to appreciate the importance of creating an identity for his group. 'Guys would throw together a band for one night and play standard bebop tunes, just stand there and jam,' he said. 'And people got tired of that. Everybody was just copying. There was no innovating going on. So we decided to put something together and make a presentation for the people. We stayed basically around New York, but we made some gigs in other cities. This helped the clubs and the whole scene because other guys would form real bands and start working.'

A few – mostly white – bandleaders, such as Shearing and Brubeck, secured contracts with bigger record companies, benefiting from the influence these concerns exerted over radio disc jockeys and network television producers. Their groups, a quintet and a quartet respectively, each developed an identifiable and highly congenial sound which the publicists and pluggers of Capitol and Columbia, respectively, could exploit to successful effect. Independent labels enjoyed the occasional minor hit in the album charts, such as André Previn's version of the *My Fair Lady* score on Contemporary, but had Shearing's 'Lullaby of Birdland' and Brubeck's 'Take Five', both of which became international hits, been released on small labels it is far less likely that they would have been heard outside the world of jazz. Nor would Brubeck have become the first jazz musician to appear on the cover of *Time* magazine, as he did in 1954.

So Miles Davis, if he were to become a star, had to have a band, and a band with a sound of its own. Unlike the nonet, the quintet had nothing unique about its instrumentation. Trumpet, tenor, piano, bass and drums was as conventional as it gets: the basic line-up of the bebop variants known as hard bop and post-bop, a reliable configuration responsible for innumerable forgettable sessions as well as many classic ones. But through his choice of sidemen and the projection of his own temperament, Davis turned this shop-worn format into something so fresh and distinctive that almost straight away he had a market leader on his hands.

The contrast between his trumpet tone and the sound of Coltrane's tenor was the most obvious identifying characteristic: here were two equal and opposite kinds of intensity, one seemingly detached and the other displaying a ferocious commitment. Where Davis played with his eyes open, aware of the world around him, Coltrane appeared to be on a mission to discover and reveal a passion deep inside. Where Davis's playing was economical to a degree previously unknown in modern jazz, Coltrane's improvising was marked by his desire to wring the material dry of every possible variation, to fill every unforgiving minute with sixty seconds' worth of notes. The alteration in atmosphere when one took over from the other was like a sudden change in the weather, and the difference in the response it encouraged from the rhythm section gave the quintet an even broader palette of colour and emotion.

Since their first recordings for Columbia had to remain in the can until the deal with Prestige ran its course, the first releases – the four albums titled *Miles*, *Workin'*,

Steamin' and *Relaxin'* – made their appearance on the smaller label. They revealed the group's adaptation of the post-bop style, one in which the use of space assumed a greater role. By contrast with the more hectically exuberant approach of the Roach-Brown Quintet or the Jazz Messengers, the Davis group never sounded unduly hurried. The propulsive Chambers and the fiery Jones could swing as hard as any of their contemporaries on bop warhorses such as Parker's 'Ah-Leu-Cha' and Dizzy Gillespie's 'Salt Peanuts', but they could also settle back into the kind of springy, loose-limbed two-beat grooves prescribed by the leader for use behind such standard ballads as 'Just Squeeze Me' and 'If I Were a Bell', tunes that also offered the opportunity for Garland's urbane block-chorded solos to put another, warmer and more approachable kind of lyricism into the mix.

Some of the group's salient characteristics, notably the pervasive and easeful sense of space, provided clear evidence of the attention Davis had been paying to the recordings of the trio led by Jamal, whose unorthodoxy was as pronounced in its way as that of Thelonious Monk, albeit offering a much gentler and less rigorous challenge to the audience. Born Fritz Jones, Jamal had a wonderfully delicate touch and a profound sense of musical architecture. A keyboard virtuoso, he nevertheless liked to leave holes in his music, both vertical and horizontal – he and his accompanists felt it unnecessary to fill all the available registers with sound, and they allowed their melodies to breathe. Davis borrowed the two-beat style and the use of tension-building ostinatos and rhythmic suspensions from Jamal, as well as several items from the pianist's repertoire of standards, notably 'The Surrey with a Fringe on Top', 'All of You', 'Love for Sale' and 'A Gal in Calico', with Jamal's arrangements more or less intact, and an original tune, 'Ahmad's Blues'. Critics had little time for Jamal, whose music they dismissed as at best merely decorative and at worst a kind of lounge jazz (it would take almost half a century for that term to lose its pejorative meaning), but Davis leapt to his defence. 'I live until he makes another record,' he said around this time. 'He doesn't throw his technique around like Oscar Peterson. Things just flow in and out of each other.'

For jazz composers in the early 1950s, a crisis loomed. Although bop had lifted improvisation to new levels of rhythmic and harmonic complexity, written material had failed to make a matching leap. Charlie Parker was still relying on thirty-two-bar standard tunes and the twelve-bar blues, which seemed an unsatisfactory state of affairs. The music was straining against seams which were both too constricting and too familiar.

The young pianist Paul Bley left Canada to study at the Juilliard Conservatory in 1950, and soon found himself confronting the same problem. 'Up until the fifties,' he wrote in his autobiography, recreating the frustration and uncertainty of those years, 'all jazz music was played on compositions that, if they weren't always popular songs, followed the song form itself. But this form is based on redundancy. If it takes a minute to play an AABA section, you've already played three redundancies in the first minute. To keep that up for fifteen minutes, with three As per minute, is a redundancy to the highest power. We all knew this in the 1950s, but we didn't know what to do about it. Improvisers had yet to concede that since the largest part of their performances was made up, the next natural step was to eliminate the disparity between the length of the written music and the length of the improvised music. If a score was going to give you two minutes of written music in a fifteen-minute performance, why bother? Especially if it was two minutes of written music that was harmonically full of repetition.'

One possible solution seemed to be an entry into the world of free improvisation, an approach tried (and quickly rejected) by the pianist Lennie Tristano, who recorded two wholly unpremeditated pieces, 'Intuition' and 'Digression', with his quintet in 1949. More promising to others was the idea of seeking an accommodation with the straight world, where compositional techniques were far more advanced and varied, offering the promise of a kind of intellectual credibility and dignity to which many of the new generation aspired. Miles Davis was no stranger to classical music, and hardly unique in that. In his early teens he had studied with the principal trumpeter of the St Louis Symphony Orchestra, whose concerts he attended, and although his time at Juilliard in 1944–5 had been truncated by his desire to immerse himself in bebop, his association with Charlie Parker – an admirer of Bartók and Varèse – would have silenced any doubts he might have entertained about the relevance to a jazz musician of an informed interest in classical techniques. And it was in 1956 that two former bandmates in the *Birth of the Cool* nonet, the pianist John Lewis and the French horn player, composer and conductor Gunther Schuller, founded the Jazz and Classical Music Society in order to explore the possibility of bringing the two idioms closer together.

This was the birth of the short-lived movement known as the Third Stream, an epithet devised by Schuller. It began with an album for Columbia titled *Music for Brass*, produced by George Avakian and including pieces by Schuller, Lewis, J. J. Johnson and Jimmy Giuffre. At Schuller's request, Davis took the role of featured soloist in Lewis's sombre 'Three Little Feelings' and Johnson's livelier 'Poem for Brass'. For this recording Davis took along a newly acquired flügelhorn, which he employed on both pieces. His playing was poised and confident, and the compositions represented honourable attempts to create a worthwhile synthesis, but there was something too self-consciously solemn about this music – brows were too furrowed, perhaps – and the movement as a whole failed to catch the public's imagination, although it went out in a blaze of glory in 1960 when the emerging saxophonists Ornette Coleman and Eric Dolphy appeared at a well publicised New York concert as the soloists in Schuller's 'Abstraction', which featured Coleman with a group including a string quartet, and 'Variations on a Theme of Thelonious Monk ('Criss Cross')' and a subsequent recording session, released as *Jazz Abstractions*.

One of the men loosely associated with the Third Stream movement was George Russell, who had been a regular participant in the conversations in Gil Evans's apartment in the late 1940s. Russell had shown such inclinations as early as 1948, when his composition 'A Bird in Igor's Yard', a transparent reference to Charlie 'Yardbird' Parker and Igor Stravinsky, was recorded by the band of the clarinettist Buddy De Franco. After Davis had stimulated him to undertake research into the modes that underpinned many ancient and non-Western genres, including European plainsong and other diatonic forms, Russell had developed a theory which he set out and published in a book titled *The Lydian Chromatic Concept of Tonal Organisation*, whose first edition appeared in 1953. Although the concept was not universally accepted, it influenced a number of the more adventurous young musicians and Russell himself used it as the basis for several interesting compositions.

The most ambitious of them was a suite titled 'All About Rosie', included alongside works by Mingus, Giuffre, Schuller and the classical composers Milton Babbitt and Harold Shapero on an album called *Modern Jazz Concert*, the result of a festival organised by Schuller at Brandeis University and released by Columbia in 1959 as a follow-up to *Music for Brass*. Featuring the young pianist Bill Evans, 'All About Rosie' is a complex and intricately worked piece which, while corresponding to a degree with the Third Stream's ambition to blend the formal structures of modern classical music with the emotional spontaneity of jazz, never falls prey to the flaws that often proved an insuperable handicap to such projects. Russell makes good use of the increased conceptual scope, avoids most of the movement's freshly minted clichés, and ensures that Evans has all the encouragement he needs to produce a brilliant improvisation in the up-tempo third section, a solo of great audacity and verve, far away from the pensive moods with which the pianist would later become associated.

Despite the failure of the Third Stream experiments to attract critical approval or a wide audience, George Avakian had glimpsed a possibility. Six years after the last of the *Birth of the Cool* sessions, Davis had sounded impressive in a setting more expansive than his normal small-combo environment. An idea had been set in motion.

The quintet, however, was thriving. With the powerful Shaw Artists agency working on Davis's behalf, bookings were plentiful. The Café Bohemia in New York, the Patio Lounge in Washington DC, the Pershing Room in Chicago, the Storyville in Boston and the Blackhawk in San Francisco were among their showcases in the first year of the band's existence. The release of their first Columbia album, *Round About Midnight*, helped build their reputation, and the individual musicians were beginning to establish identities of their own – particularly Coltrane, who had started making his own albums for Prestige, usually with members of the Davis rhythm section, and was exhibiting the early stages of a powerful originality.

But at the end of April 1957, after eighteen months of apparently steady progress, Davis sacked Coltrane and Jones. He was an ambitious bandleader who took his responsibilities seriously, and he had lost patience with their heroin-induced unreliability. Avakian's instincts about putting him together with a larger group had born fruit, and he spent May recording the tracks for *Miles Ahead*, the first of his three full-scale orchestral collaborations with Gil Evans. In June he went back on the road to present a new quintet, with Rollins returning and Art Taylor, who made a fine contribution to the *Miles Ahead* sessions, replacing Jones at the drum stool. The amended line-up was short-lived. After only two months Rollins left to form his own band, replaced first by the Belgian tenor saxophonist Bobby Jaspar and in October by Julian 'Cannonball' Adderley, an ebullient young altoist from Florida whose band, co-led with his brother, the cornettist Nat Adderley, had appeared opposite the Davis quintet at Café Bohemia in July. Taylor, too, was replaced before long, first – on Adderley's recommendation – by Jimmy Cobb, and then by the returning Jones, for the sake of whose dynamic propulsion Davis was once more prepared to overlook the occasional display of indiscipline.

Coltrane, meanwhile, used the time to make serious changes to his life and to his music. In mid-July he joined Thelonious Monk's quartet for a season at the Five Spot Café which lasted until mid-December. 'Monk is exactly the opposite of Miles,' he said. 'Miles didn't like to discuss things too much, and always seemed like he was in a bad mood.' Inspired by his new employer's fascinating compositions and by Monk's more open attitude, Coltrane's playing grew in richness and in confidence. Off stage, an experience he later described as a 'spiritual awakening' helped him conquer his heroin addiction. And just before Christmas, when Davis returned from a European tour, Coltrane would be back in the fold, his reservations suspended.

*

The commitment made by Columbia Records paid off in the final weeks of 1957 with the release of *Miles Ahead*, to a generally warm response. 'When Miles Davis signed with Columbia,' George Avakian wrote in a note on the album's sleeve, 'we found in each other a mutual interest in furthering the ideals of the nine-piece band. What direction this desire would take was uncertain, beyond the conviction that Gil Evans was the arranger we wanted.'

Almost equally significant was Davis's decision to abandon the trumpet in favour of the flügelhorn throughout the album, its warmer, richer tone helpfully emphasising tendencies already apparent in his sound on the smaller-bore instrument: a stylish elegance and an unruffled calm even at higher tempos. In avoiding the plummy sound often produced by other exponents of the flügelhorn, he made it seem as though, entering his thirties, he had finally stepped into his own skin. Selecting material from a variety of sources and moods, from the brassy, high-stepping 'Springsville', with which the album opened, to the closing jauntiness of 'I Don't Want to Be Kissed', via the graceful melancholy of Leo Delibes' 'The Maids of Cadiz', Kurt Weill's 'My Ship', Evans's 'Blues for Pablo' and J. J. Johnson's 'Lament', the soloist and his arranger had carefully constructed a suite in ten movements designed to encourage the aspects of Davis's playing that set him apart from the other trumpeters – the Kenny Dorhams, Bill Hardmans, Red Rodneys and Donald Byrds – who had sprung from the bebop era. Evans, building on his work with Thornhill and the *Birth of the Cool* nonet, used strikingly unorthodox instrumental groupings to create a set of musical micro-climates for his featured soloist. The ever-changing combinations of flute, oboe, bass clarinet, French horn and tuba came and went like clouds passing across a blue sky, their kaleidoscopic shifts of hue and density occasionally penetrated by the shafts and stabs of a conventional brass section of five trumpets and three trombones. This was not Third Stream music: it was something new. When Evans adapted a piece by Delibes, or borrowed motifs from de Falla's *The Three-Cornered Hat* for 'Blues for Pablo', he was achieving a transmutation to which even the term 'synthesis' did not do justice.

In *Down Beat*, Ralph J. Gleason noted the music's ancestry in Evans's work with Thornhill. Awarding the album a maximum five stars, he wrote: 'Miles's use of flügelhorn on this album does not in the slightest detract from his communication. Rather, it lends a certain spice to it. As he extracts from this sometimes blatant instrument all its mellowness and fullness . . . Miles's solos throughout have an almost ascetic purity about them. They are deliberate, unhurried, and almost inevitable in their time.' Many years later, the pianist Keith Jarrett – a member of Davis's band in the early 1970s – would remark: 'If Miles had never done any of those things with Gil Evans, he would probably never have lusted after that sound that he probably lusted after for the rest of his life.'

The punchy brass and the impeccably swinging rhythm team of Chambers and Taylor retained certain signature elements of conventional big-band music, but the greater proposition was one of a new degree of freedom in the organisation of large jazz ensembles. And, inevitably, the sheer beauty of this music aroused suspicions among certain critics who, sceptical of the influence of Ravel, Fauré and Evans's other impressionist favourites, thought it too exquisite to be true to the elements of the music's traditional essence. Albert McCarthy, the editor of *Jazz Monthly*, referred to its 'port-and-velvet' quality. (Such suspicions would be reinforced exactly fifty years later when 'The Maids of Cadiz' turned up as the background music to a promotional film for a new Ralph Lauren perfume, directed by Wong Kar-Wai.) As had happened in the case of the Modern Jazz Quartet, however, a wider audience paid no attention to such principled but misguided reservations. *Miles Ahead* was the first of Davis's recordings to find its way to a wider audience, one that responded instinctively to its prevailing air of modernity; to these listeners the introduction of its glowing sound-world, completely devoid of the clichés of the swing era or the agitation of bebop, into their domestic environments was the equivalent of having a Rothko print on the wall. Initially packaged with a cover photograph of a *soignée* white woman on the deck of a sailing boat, it quickly became the bestselling record of Davis's career to date. Later, infuriated that a white face should have been used to sell his music, he would have the cover changed to a picture of himself – playing a trumpet, misleadingly enough.

The most significant step in the progression towards *Kind of Blue*, however, was taken during that pre-Christmas trip to Europe on which Davis travelled without his band. He had barely disembarked from his transatlantic flight to Paris when Marcel Romano, the promoter of his brief tour, asked if he would agree to perform the incidental music for a film being made by a young director, Louis Malle, and starring Lino Ventura and Jeanne Moreau. Davis agreed, and began to work on sketches for the soundtrack to *Ascenseur pour l'echafaud* (*Lift to the Scaffold* – or, in the US, *Elevator to the Gallows*) while rehearsing with his specially assembled quintet.

One member, the expatriate drummer Kenny Clarke, was an old friend. A bebop pioneer, Clarke had deputised for Max Roach on the *Birth of the Cool* band's final studio session in April 1949 and been a member of the quintet co-led by Davis and the pianist Tadd Dameron that played at the Paris Jazz Festival the following month, sharing the bill at the final concert with Sidney Bechet and Charlie Parker. Five years later he had been the drummer on several of Davis's sessions for the Prestige label, including the one that produced the classic 'Bags' Groove'. The ensemble was completed by three gifted young French musicians: the pianist René Urtreger and the bassist Pierre Michelot, both of whom had accompanied Davis during a brief solo visit the previous year, and the twenty-year-old tenor saxophonist Barney Wilen. The tour was short – the Olympia concert was followed by engagements in Brussels, Amsterdam and Stuttgart, then by a return to Paris for a two-week season at the Club Saint-Germain – and not as successful as the promoter had hoped, but the soundtrack session turned out to be one of the pivotal events of Davis's career.

Freed from the need to produce complete performances and thereby from the conventional format of theme-solos-theme, and given something to work with outside the normal musical parameters of chords, melodies and rhythm, Davis used the occasion to make a huge conceptual shift. Malle had shown him a roughly assembled print of the film, and when Davis and his musicians convened in a darkened room at the Post Parisien studios at ten o'clock on the night of 4 December, the director screened loops of the sequences that he wanted the music to underscore while the quintet improvised on the few musical fragments which were all Davis had brought to the session. Malle would signal where to start and stop, and Davis would give a whistle to halt the band when they had played enough. 'He had given us very little to go on,' Barney Wilen remembered, 'so it was more or less an effort of collective spontaneity.' But there was more to it than that. 'Miles created a musical universe of such quality that the musicians who played with him often surpassed themselves,' René Urtreger said. 'They were practically forced to play at their best. I think there are certain musicians, even very famous ones, who never played better than they did with Miles Davis.'

In four hours they recorded almost an hour's music, in pieces ranging in length from two minutes to four minutes, although few of the pieces had the sort of structural framework that would have been required in a normal recording environment. 'It turned out beautful,' said Clarke, who had put the band together. 'Miles was very relaxed,' Michelot recalled, 'as if the music he was playing wasn't that important. He knew exactly what he wanted, and he also knew exactly what he wanted from us, which is very much to his credit. The session is characterised by the absence of specific themes, which was new for the period, especially for a soundtrack. Apart from one piece, which was based on the chords of 'Sweet Georgia Brown', we only had the most succinct guidance from Miles. In fact he just asked us to play two chords – D minor and C7 – with four bars each. That was new, too. The pieces weren't written to a specific length.'

Because the music was going to be used under the moving pictures and their associated dialogue, Davis needed to worry about nothing more than capturing and sustaining a mood. Development, in the usual musical sense, became irrelevant. It seems clear that the chance to strip the music of such conventions as beginnings and endings was highly appealing to him: it is easy to see how intros and codas would seem as superfluous in the Davis scheme of things as introducing individual songs, acknowledging applause or remaining on stage when other musicians were taking solos, none of which he felt obliged to do. The music would therefore be shorn of otiose and superficial gestures, reduced to its essentials. When something had been said, why bother wrapping it in pretty paper and tying it with a ribbon bow?

Nothing, really, could have been more modern. Twenty years later, with albums such as *Live Evil* and *On the Corner*, Davis would re-emphasise his lack of interest in Western formal structures, removing all sense of climax or resolution from the music, in which beginnings and endings were performed by the engineer's fader or the tape operator's razor blade, slashing across the music at apparently random points. The music had become a loop, a continuum, an infinitely sustainable mood into which the listener could come and go at will. And the culture of sampling and mixing, which grew up in the last twenty years of the century, was in some senses the fulfilment of the work he began with the soundtrack for Malle's film, in which fragments of music were deployed for effect, those fragments being as valuable, or as significant, as a complete performance. The director, in fact, selected the sections he wished to use, after Davis had returned to America.

When the soundtrack was first released as an album, soon after the appearance of the film in 1958, it became evident that a large amount of echo had been added to the instruments in the post-production process, presumably with the intention of making the sound more atmospheric. (A meticulously prepared reissue thirty years later included the entire session, including fragments and alternative takes, with the artificial echo removed.) Some of these pieces contain not just some of Davis's finest trumpet playing, in an unusually exposed setting, but an extraordinarily accurate foreshadowing of his preoccupations of the next thirty years. The skeletal piano and bass and lightly splashing cymbals accompanying the muted trumpet on 'L'assassinat de Carala' would have been perfect material for his quintet of the mid-60s, while the dry-toned tenor solos played by Wilen on the two takes of 'Le petit bal' could be a prototype of the discreet, laconic style invented by Wayne Shorter, a member of that great unit. The piercing high note with which Davis ends the unused second take of the piece known as 'Chez le photographe du motel' is a moment of sudden drama as thrilling as the epic climax of 'Solea', from *Sketches of Spain*. And above all, as we look forward to *Kind of Blue*, there is the sense that nothing matters except truth and beauty.

6 Six Colours (Blue)

Adventures in modality: from *Milestones* to *Porgy and Bess*

When Miles Davis reconvened his band for an opening at Chicago's Sutherland Lounge at Christmas 1957, it had grown into a sextet. With the newcomer Cannonball Adderley and the returning John Coltrane, the leader now had a three-piece front line offering far more scope than the old bebop quintet format, which had its roots in the founding partnership of Charlie Parker and Dizzy Gillespie. Adderley's rhythmically exuberant and naturally blues-based style provided an important extra dimension, an obvious complement to the approaches of Davis and Coltrane. Each of the three was an improviser of great character, whose signature was immediately apparent in a single phrase. The saxophonists Davis tried and rejected may have possessed equal or equivalent technical and intellectual virtues, but they lacked the element of personality that made the new sextet such a potent unit.

Although Sonny Rollins was a wonderfully sophisticated improviser, with a much admired gift for thematic elaboration, Davis knew that Coltrane represented the future. Whereas Rollins commanded respect and admiration, Coltrane inspired a response that could be measured in awe. And, for all the complexity of his work, Rollins was a 'jazz musician' in the most straightforward sense: he functioned within the idiom, with the materials at hand, and his solos were complex, highly sophisticated and beautifully developed variations on a theme, revealed in a widely noticed analysis by Gunther Schuller of the improvisation on 'Blue Seven', from the great 1956 album *Saxophone Colossus*. Impressing those already familiar with the language of jazz, such feats hardly reached out beyond them. Like Davis, however, Coltrane had something in his playing which seemed to transcend that sizeable but limited audience. His instrumental tone communicated directly with a broader constituency who, almost irrespective of their prior knowledge of the idiom, found themselves transfixed; again like his leader, his sound had a kind of human quality bearing no resemblance to the sort of vocalised effects hitherto popularised by the musicians of early jazz. He had a 'voice', and an unmistakeable one – although, as had always been the way with jazz, it was one that legions would eventually want to impersonate. His growing obsession with harmonic elaboration, an insistence on exploring not just every note of each chord but every note of each possible harmonic extension and substitution, led him into solos of sometimes inordinate length, and when Davis complained, the perpetrator plaintively observed that he just didn't know how to stop. 'Try taking the horn out of your mouth,' Davis retorted. But so commanding was Coltrane's sound that he was beginning to hold audiences spellbound – those, at least, who were not storming out, complaining that what he was doing constituted a kind of 'anti-jazz'. In time, Coltrane began to exude the aura of a man on a pilgrimage that was part musical, part spiritual – the quality which, after his death, led a group of adherents to form a church devoted to the worship of God through the memory of the late saxophonist.

Adderley was a more earthbound player, his instincts rooted in the southern soil of the blues. Like Coltrane three years earlier, he had another career option: an offer to join the quintet of Dizzy Gillespie. 'I figured I could learn more (with Miles) than with Dizzy,' he said. 'Not that Dizzy isn't a good teacher, but he played more commercially than Miles.' Although his own group would later become among the most commercially successful in jazz, Adderley's first impulse – like those of many young musicians of his generation – was to lead him in the direction of idealism, self-improvement and the development of the music. 'Musically, I learnt a lot with Miles,' he said. 'About spacing, for one thing, when playing solos. Also, he's a master of understatement. And he taught me more about the chords, as Coltrane did, too.' He also learnt, after an initial degree of uncertainty, that the scope of the blues was far wider than he had hitherto believed possible or proper. His playing with the Davis sextet, however, could be misunderstood. Some critics, perhaps unwilling to believe that such a group could exist without a single flaw, and possibly also resenting Davis's independent stance while unable to attack him directly on grounds of taste or execution, accused Adderley of superficiality, of being incapable of getting as far inside the music as his colleagues. The English critic Steve Voce, for example, used the term 'music-hall alto' to disparage his work with the sextet. But while it is true that Adderley was the least profound of the three horn players, the most florid and the most prone to produce a glib quotation from popular songs when he needed to insert a quick emergency stitch in a solo, during his time with Davis he also proved himself capable of rising to meet the challenge of experimental material without compromising his blues-based sensibility, his bouncy drive or his inherent feeling for melody. His solos increased the group's appeal by creating a sense of diversity, exploring another kind of intensity and adding a contrasting strand of colour to the ensembles as well as the solo sequence. His warm, ripe, broad-grained tone combined surprisingly well with Coltrane's austere, slate-grey sound in the harmonised saxophone figures that Davis could exploit when arranging some of his new compositions, often with the help of Gil Evans.

As they went into Columbia's East 30th Street studio in February 1958 to begin recording the tracks that would be issued as the album titled *Milestones*, the rhythm section was the tried and tested unit of Garland, Chambers and Jones, now in their third year together, give or take various impromptu or enforced breaks. It had become a perfectly balanced mechanism, characterised by Chambers's lithe swing and impeccable note-choice, by Garland's block-chorded solos and by Jones's use of what had become known as the 'Philly lick', a rimshot ticking off the fourth beat of each bar at medium and up tempos. The drummer would use this as a device to establish momentum and build tension before gradually breaking up the regular pattern with asymmetrical snare and bass drum punctuations which intensified the forward push.

Among the tracks to derive the greatest benefit from the use of the Philly lick was 'Milestones', the new album's title track and, after the Malle soundtrack, the most significant single signpost on the road to *Kind of Blue*. Recorded during the second of the album's two sessions, it represents the first full-blown attempt to replace chord patterns with cycles of scale-based modes. Leaping straight into its simple and extremely catchy theme at a brisk sixty bars per minute, 'Milestones' can seem deceptively conventional, not least because the piece lasts a mere five minutes and forty-two seconds and contains, besides its opening and closing theme statements, three solos packed with incident. Beneath its skin, however, something very different is taking place. Forty bars long, the tune is constructed in three parts: an opening sixteen-bar section based on the Dorian mode (a G minor 7th chord implying the scale of F major), a second sixteen-bar section based on the Aeolian mode (an A minor 7th chord implying a C major scale), and a return to the opening Dorian mode for the final eight-bar section. Harmonically, the sense is of a rise from the first section to the second (G minor to A minor, a whole step), followed by a settling back into a resolution. Rhythmically, the first and last sections are driven along by a propulsive walking bass line and a conventional triplet-based ride-cymbal pattern. For the second section, however, which is the equivalent of the eight-bar bridge in a standard thirty two-bar AABA Broadway tune, but is repeated to form a forty-bar AABBA sequence, Chambers omits the first beat of each bar, filling the remainder with a riff-like figure that gives the illusion of holding the rhythm in suspension as the drummer, driving ahead, occasionally varies the internal balance by moving the rimshot to the second beat of the bar.

Each of the three horn soloists is given two choruses, beginning with Adderley, whose fluid melodic invention conveys a sense of uncaged joy, alternating mercurial boppish phrases with broad scoops and soaring glides (and a passing quotation from 'Fascinating Rhythm'). Davis follows, and in its frequent changes of trajectory his solo is one of his most inventive as well as being among his loveliest; the contrast of his poise and economy with Adderley's fecundity is immediately striking, and his tone on the trumpet has acquired, perhaps through a sort of osmosis, much of the bloom that distinguished his flügelhorn playing throughout *Miles Ahead*. Set between the two saxophonists, the trumpet seems to glow with an extra lustre. Coltrane, the final soloist, leaps on the new freedom like a man liberated from a straitjacket, hungry for the chance to examine the implications of each harmonic unit without needing to observe a strict cycle of chord changes.

The absence of solo room for piano, bass or drums intensifies the air of concentration, of mission. This is a seamless display of the improviser's ideal state: relaxed intensity. Between them, the three soloists bring remarkable powers of distillation to bear on this new freedom. There were only two takes of 'Milestones', a piece that does not seem to have been played by the group before it entered the studio that day; the second take, which provided the issued master, is as close to unimproveable as makes no difference. (A trumpet fluff on the final theme statement may be taken as the unintended equivalent of the dropped stitch in the Persian carpet that is the weaver's humble acknowledgement of his human frailty in the face of Allah's perfection.) But perhaps the most telling impression left by this remarkable piece of music is the way each musician, in his own way, exploits the sense that, as the modes shift, the music is changing gear. No single chord change in a conventional sequence could exert this dramatic effect: the move from one scale to another not only adds another element of tension and release but raises or lowers the intensity. It gives the soloist time to ruminate while also exploiting the eternally fascinating responsiveness of the human emotions to harmonic change. And, having started without fanfare, the piece ends without ceremony but with enormous implications for the future: very unusually for a jazz record in the 1950s, it fades out, and the fade must have been an intentional effect, the staccato theme and Jones's rimshots slowly disappearing towards a horizon that seems infinite.

A few days later there was another harbinger of things to come in Davis's unexpected appearance as a star sideman on the Adderley-led session that produced a Blue Note album jauntily titled *Somethin' Else*. A single day in the New Jersey studio where Rudy Van Gelder had developed the label's characteristic rich, warm sound was enough to produce six tracks, five of which made up the original album, but this was no typical mid-50s blowing session. With highly sympathetic accompaniment from an ad hoc rhythm section of Hank Jones on piano, Sam Jones on bass and Art Blakey on drums, Adderley and Davis pushed beyond the normal parameters to produce a piece of work that took its place in the continuing evolution of the music.

The track that defined the album was a version of 'Autumn Leaves', originally a French *chanson* with a tune by Joseph Kosma and (in its original form, as '*Les Feuilles mortes*') a set of words by the poet Jacques Prévert. It was a piece that Davis may have heard sung by his former lover Juliette Gréco, whom he had seen again the previous year during his visit to Paris and who had recorded it with a swooning orchestral arrangement. Kosma's melody is made up of short ascending phrases which, taken in series, describe a gentle descent: a rare and exquisite example of a tune's form also reflecting the subject of its lyric, mirroring leaves briefly eddying in autumn breezes before floating to earth. At twenty-eight bars per minute, a tempo that could be described as a pensive stroll, the Davis/Adderley version is a little faster than Gréco's, its mood more bracing. Since this is a tune that would be a part of the trumpeter's repertoire for years to come, it seems fair to assume that he had a hand in shaping the striking arrangement. Its formal introduction begins with a sombre piano and riff, over which the horns shape a mournful harmonised phrase interrupted by four bars of staccato stabs over a Latin beat before the earlier motif returns, giving way to Davis's theme statement over a Jamalesque two-beat bass and Blakey's restrained brushes. Adderley's solo, a masterpiece of post-Parker alto playing, is filled with his characteristic touches, including asymmetrical clusters of double-time phrases, sudden arcs of broad melody and occasional dramatic trills, tied together by a glowing lyricism. Davis, using a Harmon mute to produce the little-boy sound that so affected Kenneth Tynan's small daughter, demonstrates the power of restraint, while Hank Jones laces a single-note line through the chords like a silver thread. Davis returns to restate the theme, which is followed by a piano cadenza and a coda formed from the bass riff of the intro, played much slower this time, over which Jones continues to improvise until the muted trumpet returns to bring the coda to an appropriately subdued close. In terms of shaping a performance and sustaining a mood, it is one of Davis's most effective pre-*Kind of Blue* recordings, and became deservedly popular.

Another of the album's tracks pointed even more clearly to the future, despite attracting less attention. On the face of it, Davis's 'Somethin' Else' is a twelve-bar blues with a theme based on a simple call-and-response between trumpet and saxophone. But it sounds subtly different, and on further investigation the album's annotator, the critic Leonard Feather, discovered that Davis had been playing games with the traditional blues format. In place of the usual harmonic progression he had substituted a far less predictable sequence consisting of two twelve-bar units, the first in the key of F and the second in the key of C, with several detours along the way, often involving flattened 5ths and 6ths and raised 9ths. The harmonic relationships between the two units made it sound as though the musicians were playing in two keys at once, offering them a greater range of options and lending their improvisations a teasingly unresolved air, while the structure of the changes removed any sense of inevitability. And yet, somehow, the listener was still aware of listening to a twelve-bar blues. This was Davis taking the core materials of his art and, thanks to the inspiration of such men as Gil Evans and George Russell, stretching them in new and stimulating ways.

In particular, Davis was making use of the materials Russell discovered after hearing, back in 1947, that the trumpeter's chief musical ambition was 'to learn all the changes'. Thinking about it, Russell decided that Davis had not meant it literally but was trying to indicate that he was searching for a new way to approach harmony. The composer embarked on research into the relationship between chords and scales that took him back to the ancient Greeks before leading him to a harmonic theory that would enable Davis to dismantle the harmonic boundaries within which jazz had enclosed itself. Out of this philosophy of tonality came 'vertical polymodality', in Russell's phrase: a means of expanding the number of notes available to improvisers.

'I began by thinking that every chord has a scale associated with it,' Russell said. 'When I played the first half of the (C) scale, I wondered why the F was where it was. The next four notes of the scale sounded much better – the first four seemed not in unity with the scale – they sounded closer to a G major chord. How was I going to tell musicians that if you have a C major chord, you can play a G major scale?'

Davis was the first to get the news, and quick to get the point. 'He [Russell] used to say that in modal music C is where F should be,' he wrote. 'He says that the whole piano starts at F. What I had learnt is that when you play this way, go in this direction, you can play forever . . . I saw all kinds of possibilities.' Gradually he was beginning to incorporate

Russell's discoveries into his everyday musical life, nudging his musicians towards a more relaxed relationship with their harmonic environment.

Gil Evans, who also shared conversations with Russell, had been thinking along similar lines, and the next Davis/Evans collaboration made it clear. Their variations on George Gershwin's music from *Porgy and Bess* were about as far away from the standard jazz-goes-to-Broadway adaptation (such as André Previn's treatment of *My Fair Lady* or Dave Brubeck's versions of various Leonard Bernstein show tunes) as could be imagined. Evans pushed even further beyond the conventional limits of jazz orchestration, retaining the spirit of Gershwin's songs but adding and subtracting as he saw fit.

'Summertime', for example, had its normal setting of sultry lushness surgically removed and replaced by the cool breezes of carefully voiced horn figures supporting the solo muted trumpet above the restrained medium-tempo swing of Chambers and Cobb. Evans made the tune sound even more like a blues than it already did, but a blues of extreme refinement, and for the trumpeter he provided a scale on which to base an improvisation that was both free-ranging and perfectly focused. A similar approach elevated 'It Ain't Necessarily So', Evans again deploying the background horn figures as if they were a pianist's left hand, providing spare harmonic support for a liberated soloist. Davis's wonderful two-chorus improvisation on 'Gone', accompanied only by Paul Chambers and Philly Joe Jones, makes a thirty-two-bar structure sound like a G-minor blues. These passages ventilated an album otherwise distinguished by orchestral writing of great richness and (reminiscent of the old Claude Thornhill approach) virtually no forward momentum, often requiring Davis to play a role almost analagous to that of a cantor or a muezzin, intoning sacred texts to an enraptured multitude.

It was shortly before the *Porgy and Bess* sessions began that the sextet made its first appearances with a new pianist. The final element of the group had fallen into place. Piqued that his leader had tried to tell him what to play on a tune called 'Sid's Ahead' during the last of the *Milestones* sessions, Red Garland had walked out. Davis ended up playing the piano himself on that track, but quickly turned his mind to the question of a replacement for a man whose playing he had come to see as too conservative and inflexible to suit the changes he was planning. It was George Russell who suggested Bill Evans, but Davis had been aware of the twenty-eight-year-old from New Jersey for some time; he knew that the cerebral Evans could adapt the Jamal approach and take it further.

A product of Welsh and Russian bloodlines, Evans had acquired a bachelor's degree in music via a scholarship to Southeastern Louisiana University before serving a 52nd Street apprenticeship with the bands of the guitarist Mundell Lowe, the clarinettist Tony Scott and the singer Lucy Reed. It was Reed who, in the summer of 1955, introduced Evans to Russell; early the following year Evans was part of the sextet that recorded Russell's *Jazz Workshop* album, a set of adventurous Lydian-inflected miniatures including one piece, 'Concerto for Billy the Kid', which functioned as a feature for the pianist. That summer an album called *The Touch of Tony Scott* featured a Russell composition called 'Aeolian Drinking Song', performed by a quartet including Evans: its structure abandoned chords in favour of a single scale. The pianist had certainly been properly primed for his new gig.

It began in April 1958 and a month later they were in the 30th Street studios, celebrating Davis's thirty-second birthday by recording four tracks: 'On Green Dolphin Street', 'Fran Dance', 'Stella by Starlight' and 'Love for Sale', which were released as one side of an album called *Jazz Track*, completed by the first US appearance of the music from *Ascenseur pour l'echafaud*. In these recordings, and in the sextet's radio broadcasts from the Spotlight Lounge in Chicago that year and their performances at the Newport Jazz Festival and the Plaza Hotel in New York, there are few signs of the formal developments Davis had initiated with 'Milestones' and 'Somethin' Else'. The band seems to be concentrating on integrating the soloists and the rhythm section, getting comfortable with each other on a club repertoire that still included the staples 'Two Bass Hit', 'Ah-Leu-Cha', 'Oleo' and 'Walkin'' alongside a selection of show tunes. Only in Evans's playing, a discreet, finely nuanced and highly personal blend of Lennie Tristano's close-voiced harmony clusters and Horace Silver's lean post-bop approach, was a change of emotional temperature becoming apparent.

By the time it came to fruition, however, Evans had already left the group, his formal resignation the product not of his already well-advanced heroin addiction but of an inability to ignore the resentment shown by some of Davis's fans towards the inclusion in the group of a white musician. Davis himself, although fully aware of his own blackness, was colour-blind when it came to collaborators: his musical soulmate, Gil Evans, was white, and he was more than happy to have his group's approach realigned by the other Evans's presence at the piano keyboard. 'Red's playing had carried the rhythm but Bill underplayed it and for what I was doing now, with the modal thing, I liked what Bill was doing better,' Davis would write. To accommodate what he called Evans's 'quiet fire', Davis had even been prepared to reduce the heat emanating from the other musicians, adapting the repertoire and the overall approach. Nevertheless in November, at the end of a two-week stay at the Village Vanguard in New York, Evans left the group, temporarily replaced by Garland pending the arrival of a permanent appointment, the Jamaican-born Wynton Kelly, who made his debut at Birdland on 1 January. A two-week engagement at the famous club on Broadway, around the corner from West 52nd Street, was followed by a fortnight at the Sutherland Lounge in Chicago, where they also played at the Civic Opera House on a bill with Thelonious Monk, Gerry Mulligan and Sarah Vaughan. And then, after a week at the Blackhawk in San Francisco, Davis was ready to return to the studio for the first of two sessions that would change music.

7 Interlude: Outside in Blue

Camus, Moravia, Mastroianni and the man with the Strand cigarette

'The modern mind is in complete disarray,' Albert Camus wrote in his notebook in the early 1940s, around the time that the publication of *L'Etranger* (*The Outsider*) was making him famous in France. 'Knowledge has stretched itself to the point where neither the world nor our intelligence can find any foothold. It is a fact that we are suffering from nihilism.'

How attractive this notion sounded to a generation growing up in Europe after the Second World War. The mass killing had stopped but a fog of philosophical confusion persisted. The fruits of reconstruction were making life easier without, for some, dispelling a sense of profound dislocation. Given *L'Etranger* to study at the age of fifteen, twenty years after its publication, I found the famous opening words of Meursault, the book's anti-hero, both unsettling and appealing: 'Mother died today. Or maybe yesterday; I can't be sure. The telegram from the home says: *Your mother passed away. Funeral tomorrow. Deep sympathy.* Which leaves the matter doubtful; it could have been yesterday.' Either way, Meursault doesn't seem to care very much.

Camus had read *La Nausée* (*Nausea*), the novel with which, in 1938, Jean-Paul Sartre effectively announced the birth of existentialism – 'the first media craze of the post-war era,' as Simone de Beauvoir would observe. Thirty-

three years old, a teacher in Le Havre and not yet political-
ly engaged, Sartre described the life of a historian of
approximately his age, living in a provincial town and overcome by feelings of meaninglessness and self-disgust, evident in a growing detestation of his work, books, his girlfriends and even physical objects. The protagonist, Antoine
Roquentin, tells himself: 'I tear myself from the window
and stumble across the room; I glue myself against the looking glass. I stare at myself, I disgust myself: one more eter-
nity. Finally, I flee from my image and fall on the bed. I
watch the ceiling, I'd like to sleep.' Roquentin is in the grip
of the phenomenon Sartre termed 'existential angst': a
dread of the essential absurdity and hollowness of the
world.

If Sartre's Roquentin was the first existentialist, Camus'
Meursault came to be seen as the harbinger of a couple of
decades of existential disengagement: some of it real, some
merely decorative. From *L'Etranger* to the Man in the Gray
Flannel Suit of Sloan Wilson's novel and the atmospheric
under-the-streetlight cover painting of Frank Sinatra's *In
the Wee Small Hours*, both of which made their appearance
in 1955, to the 1959 television advertisement for a new
brand of cigarettes featuring a solitary, raincoated man who
was 'never alone with a Strand', the isolated, enigmatically
disenchanted man became a curiously potent figure.

He was even at the centre of a publishing sensation created in 1956 when a non-fiction book called *The Outsider*, by
Colin Wilson, an unknown twenty-five-year-old English
writer, became an international bestseller. Wilson traced an
archetype connecting the work of Dostoevsky, Nietzsche,

Kafka, Lawrence, Hesse, Hemingway, Sartre and Camus. 'The Outsider's case against society is very clear,' he wrote, discussing Henri Barbusse's *L'Enfer*. 'All men and women have these dangerous, unnamable impulses, yet they keep up a pretence, to themselves, to others; their respectability, their philosophy, their religion, are all attempts to gloss over, to make look civilised and rational something that is savage, unorganised, irrational. He is an Outsider because he stands for Truth.'

In *La Noia* (which first appeared in English as *The Empty Canvas*, later as *Boredom*), published in 1960, the Italian novelist Alberto Moravia put these words into the mouth of his narrator, Dino, the young son of a rich family, who has abandoned his vocation as a painter: 'For many people boredom is the opposite of amusement; and amusement means distraction, forgetfulness. For me, boredom is not the opposite of amusement. I might even go so far as to say that in certain of its aspects it actually resembles amusement in as much as it gives rise to distraction and forgetfulness, even if of a very special type . . . The feeling of boredom originates for me in a sense of the absurdity of a reality which is insufficient, or anyhow unable, to convince me of its own effective existence . . . from that very absurdity springs boredom, which when all is said and done is simply a kind of incommunicability and the incapacity to disengage oneself from it.'

Such luxuriant self-examination was characteristic of the intellectual life of the 1950s. 'The Outsider is not sure who he is,' Colin Wilson wrote. 'He has found an "I", but it is not his true "I". His main business is to find his way back to himself.' The rise of psychoanalysis also had a part to play. 'Put away your Penguin Freud, Diana,' a piqued Miles Brand (played by Laurence Harvey) scolds Diana Scott (Julie Christie) in *Darling*, a John Schlesinger film that was released in 1965 but drew its tension from the contrast between a young 60s female and two men – the suave, amoral Brand and Robert Gold (Dirk Bogarde), an earnest man of letters – who were, in their very different ways, creatures of the preceding decade.

Conveniently, modern jazz – oblique, gnomic, somehow detached even when at its most intense – was available to provide the soundtrack to existential angst and its American counterpart, a natural synergy described by Jack Kerouac in a passage from *On the Road*, written in 1951 but not published until six years later: '"Where we going, man?" "I don't know but we gotta go." Then here came a gang of young bop musicians carrying their instruments out of cars. They piled right into a saloon and we followed them. They set themselves up and started blowing. There we were! The leader was a slender, drooping, curly haired, pursy mouthed tenorman, thin of shoulder, draped loose in a sports shirt, cool in the warm night, self-indulgence written in his eyes, who picked up his horn and frowned in it and blew cool and complex and was dainty stamping his foot to catch ideas, and ducked to miss others – and said, "Blow," very quietly when the other boys took solos.'

The American novelist John Clellon Holmes wrote in a magazine article in 1958: 'In the arts, modern jazz is almost exclusively the music of the Beat Generation, as poetry (at least until Kerouac's novel) is its literature. If the members of this generation attend to a wailing sax in much the same way as men used to attend to the words and gestures of sages, it is because jazz is primarily the music of inner freedom, of improvisation, of the creative individual rather than the interpretive group. It is the music of a submerged group, who *feel* free, and this is precisely how young people feel today.'

Not everyone was overjoyed, or thought it a good thing that jazz should so accurately reflect the confusions of the day. When John A. Tynan, *Down Beat*'s West Coast editor, reviewed the Miles Davis Sextet at Jazz Seville in Los Angeles during the summer of 1959 in terms that indicated his disapproval of the way the group presented its music, his words on John Coltrane in particular were intended to convey a wider concern. 'On the whole, the tenor man's contributions suggested superficially stimulating, lonely and rather pathetic self-seeking,' Tynan wrote. 'Is this truly the dilemma of the contemporary American jazz artist? One hesitates to believe it so.'

A different contemporaneous response to Coltrane came from the American poet and painter William Morris (a minor contemporary of Kenneth Rexroth, Lawrence Ferlinghetti and Kenneth Patchen), as he demonstrated in his poem 'cantiba high', also written in the year that *Kind of Blue* was recorded: *my helen my paris / you live today / with other eyes / your bodies still are golden / you listen to coltrane in the night / how like ulysses / his long horn moans from the black sea / coming through the black mist / black ships are counted by poets.*

While those words were being written, Federico Fellini

was at the Cinecittà studios in Rome, engaged in the production of *La Dolce Vita*, his seventh film. Its central character, Marcello Rubini (played by Marcello Mastroianni), is an elegant, affectless journalist who floats around the fringes of Roman society in beautifully cut dark suits and an English sports car, observant but unengaged and unjudgemental. Nino Rota provided a fine score for the film, whose musical content also included the sight and sound of the young singer Adriano Celentano performing a frenzied version of 'Ready Teddy' in an early nightclub scene, but the more fitting accompaniment to the late nights on the glittering Via Veneto and amid the concrete tenements of bleak suburban wastelands would have been tracks from *Kind of Blue*, which was released while Fellini was in the final stages of preparing the film for its premiere in February 1960, ahead of its triumphal screening at the Cannes film festival that spring. In a way, however, Mastroianni's portrayal needed no accompaniment: the character of Marcello Rubini already was the embodiment of the sound – spare, knowing, self-contained – of Miles Davis's trumpet in its late-50s glory.

In the wake of *La Dolce Vita* came Michelangelo Antonioni's great trilogy of *L'Avventura* (1960), *La Notte* (1961) and *L'Eclisse* (1962): a set of films in which existential angst met actors of powerful physical beauty (Mastroianni, Jeanne Moreau, Monica Vitti, Alain Delon, Lea Massari, Gabriele Ferzetti) amid fine modern architecture and exquisite interior decor shot in carefully shaded black and white, and in which a pervasive sense of non-communication was generally more eloquent than the dialogue. In his survey of post-war Italian cinema, Peter Bondanella described Antonioni's 'exceptional sensitivity to the philosophical currents of our times, his ability to portray modern neurotic, alienated and guilt-ridden characters whose emotional lives are sterile – or at least poorly developed – and who seem to be out of place in their environments. If the perfect existentialist film could be imagined, it would probably be the Antonioni trilogy . . .'

In cinematic terms, this was the birth of the cool: an established idiom encountering new feelings, new instincts, the modern dystopia. Antonioni's films often approached the condition of a new silent cinema, those silences becoming the terrain in which his characters fail or decline to connect. And what were Antonioni's famously unresolved endings if not a new way of seeing life to which the extended fade-outs of 'Milestones' and 'All Blues' provided a perfect aural correlative?

Miles Davis's dark Italian suits and his European sports cars made him stand out from the generality of jazz musicians in the 1950s. No doubt his visit to Paris in May 1949, when he met Sartre and Boris Vian and fell in love with Juliette Gréco, had broadened his cultural horizons as well as his fashion sense. Two thousand fans turned up to hear him play at the Salle Pleyel in the Faubourg Saint-Honoré. 'Bespectacled, goateed Parisians nodded bereted heads sagely at each exciting harmonic change, screaming and whistling their approval of every soloist,' *Melody Maker*'s Paris correspondent reported.

That was the night Davis met Gréco, then making a name for herself in the clubs of the Left Bank, and through her the leading existentialists of the time. When the tour was over, he remained behind in Paris. More than half a century later, Gréco remembered: 'Sartre said to Miles: "Why don't you and Juliette get married?" Miles replied: "Because I love her too much to make her unhappy." At that moment it wasn't a matter of infidelity [Davis was already married, with two children] or of behaving like a Don Juan; it was simply a question of colour. If he'd taken me back to America with him, I would have been seen there as a "nigger's whore".'

Davis never forgot his feelings for the young singer and actress, or how it felt to walk the banks of the Seine and sit in the Café de Flore on a spring evening. Something of the aroma of those weeks permeated his subsequent work, and not just in the addition of 'Les Feuilles mortes' to his repertoire. He recognised an affinity with that world, and it welcomed him as his music became deepened and enriched through contact with another sensibility, one that suffuses the conception of Kind of Blue.

And with his next album, the almost equally well loved Sketches of Spain, a little ink-sketched silhouette of a man in profile, playing a trumpet, appears on the front, as it would on the covers of Someday My Prince Will Come, Miles Davis at Carnegie Hall, Quiet Nights and Seven Steps to Heaven. This was Columbia's art department recognising the marketing value of his stance as the symbol of inner freedom, of improvisation, of the creative individual rather than the interpretive group, the man who said 'Blow' very quietly when the other boys took solos, the Outsider who stands for Truth.

Curiously, however, the Strand cigarette campaign was one of the most disastrous in the history of the British advertising industry. The public, it turned out, did not want to smoke a cigarette that reminded them of loneliness.

8 The Blue Moment

An Armenian Orthodox church with a three-second reverb

Creative musicians are often justifiably suspicious of the way their listeners invest emotional capital in specific recordings. To Bob Dylan, for instance, a song can exist in many versions, sometimes across several decades, and the one initially captured in the recording studio is no more than a fleeting snapshot of its early blooming. Listeners, however, tend to measure an artist's progress in the albums that are made available for sale, usually according to a schedule determined by a commercial plan; sometimes, too, they use the same yardstick to measure their own lives. I remember seeing the cover of *Milestones*, and hearing the title track, and feeling that my life had just been changed in some quite significant way. The same was true of the cover and contents of *The Freewheelin' Bob Dylan* a few years later. From such an instinctive affection can come the urge to force an artist to stop, to freeze his or her work at a certain time, the time best suited to our own needs. The artist, moving on, does not necessarily see it that way.

Quite a few of Miles Davis's albums possessed a documentary quality. A fair proportion, particularly those made by the first (1955–7) and second (1964–8) great quintets, offered a straightforward representation of what he and his band were up to in concerts and clubs at that particular moment. Most of *Milestones*, with the exception of the title track, answered that description. *Kind of Blue*, however, was something different. It may have taken much of its shape spontaneously in the studio, but the outline of that shape was the result of a premeditation that continues to reverberate in the responses of those in whose lives it occupies a special place.

In Herbie Hancock's words, Miles Davis approached the recording of *Kind of Blue* in the early weeks of 1959 looking for 'the spirit of discovery'. Focusing on the scalar approach proposed to him by George Russell and encouraged by Gil Evans, Davis wanted to see what would happen to his musicians if he cast aside an important armature from which his groups habitually benefited, that of the standard song form and the gestures that went with it. 'I wanted them to go beyond themselves,' he said.

Two other sources of inspiration were also giving him a specific impetus. The first came from a visit to a performance by Keita Fodeba's Les Ballets Africains with his then girlfriend, Frances Taylor, a dancer. There he heard not only a range of stimulating polyrhythms played by drummers from Guinea and Senegal ('they would do rhythms like 6/8 and 5/4,' he remembered, 'and the rhythm would be changing and popping') but also the distinctive sound of the kalimba, the African 'thumb piano' made out of a wooden box and strips of tin. The second source was a lingering memory of listening to gospel singers in the countryside on Sunday evenings during childhood visits from the family home in East St Louis to his grandparents' house in Arkansas. 'Those dark Arkansas roads,' he said, 'that's the sound I'm after.'

Davis was far from alone in wanting to explore these terrains. The arrival of Ray Charles as a force in popular music had brought many black musicians a greater awareness of their roots and a readiness to use the devices with which gospel music – and, to some extent, African music – created an emotional impact. Horace Silver's 'The Preacher' was a hit, as were Cannonball Adderley's 'Sermonette' and Johnny Griffin's 'The Congregation'. Art Blakey was showing an interest in working with African drummers whose cross-rhythms could overlay his own driving bop-derived style. Charles Mingus forsook his early attempts to blend bebop with modern classical music (expressed via such ensembles as Baron Mingus and his Symphonic Aires) to put together the compositions that made up an album titled *Blues and Roots*, full of church inflections and the collective polyphony that distinguished the earliest forms of jazz. The pianist Bobby Timmons gave his employer, Art Blakey, a tune called 'Moanin'' whose 'amen' chords made it a favourite with the Jazz Messengers' audience. Even the Jimmy Giuffre Trio's pastoral 'The Train and the River' seemed to speak to the same collective urge to revisit sources that might once have been thought to lack sophistication.

Given these imperatives, it was intriguing that Davis also had in his mind a determination to make the most of the potential he had discovered in his collaboration with Bill Evans, who had left the group three months earlier but now agreed to a temporary return. On the face of it, Evans would not have been the pianist most obviously suited to a project inspired by African music, or the blues. As Davis later observed, however, when reflecting on *Kind of Blue* in his autobiography, 'I was trying to do one thing and ended up doing something else.' That 'something else' was a realisation of his wish to get away from and go beyond the brash athleticism of bebop.

The first session was scheduled for half past two on the afternoon of Monday, 2 March. Irving Townsend, a Columbia staff producer, had booked the studio at 207 East 30th Street, a deconsecrated Armenian Orthodox church, for two consecutive three-hour sessions, the second of them to start at seven o'clock in the evening. As well as Evans, the entire working sextet was present – including Wynton Kelly, who had taken over as the group's pianist on New Year's Day. On his arrival at the studio, the new man, still feeling his way into what had become one of the most famous groups in jazz, was disconcerted to discover the presence of one of his predecessors. There had been no forewarning from Davis, who merely explained to Evans that he had invited Kelly to come along because there was one tune scheduled for the session to which his playing was better fitted.

One of the most unaffectedly lyrical pianists in the history of jazz (and the man after whom the distinguished New Orleans pianist Ellis Marsalis would name his first son), Wynton Kelly was perfectly capable of playing through the whole date. He would have found something to contribute even to the most delicate modal exercise. Davis, however, knew that he did not possess the special measure of distilled harmonic wisdom or the subdued luminosity of touch that Evans would bring to this very distinctive project. So the leader decided to make the first piece of the date a blues called 'Freddie Freeloader', the one to which he felt Kelly's playing was most appropriate.

Although Kelly, who was of Jamaican origin, was far more than just a blues player, he tended to suffuse even the Broadway songs in the group's regular repertoire with a strong blues feeling, and that was certainly what the leader was looking for on 'Freddie Freeloader'. Named after a well-known Philadelphia character who liked to hang around the band when they were in town, the tune is a hip-ster's anthem: a cool, finger-snapping twelve-bar piece, its two-note main motif transposed up and down according to the movement of the chords, so spare and epigrammatic in construction that Kelly is given ample space in which to insert a commentary from the sidelines before setting off on his own delightful solo, which he builds to a light-hearted version of the sort of block-chord climax associated with Red Garland. Davis's own solo presents a marvellous exam-ple of his approach to the blues: as with his playing on the title track of Adderley's *Somethin' Else*, he is locating the essence but avoiding any hint of a familiar phrase, and seeming to operate at one remove from the basic chords without creating the slightest sense of discomfort for the other players or the listener. He also shows off his gorgeous tone, with its newly acquired hint of flügelhorn richness. Coltrane follows, parading the intense style he had been mining in live performance, and the sequence is completed by Adderley, who digs into the soil of the blues with his usual lusty élan.

Already obvious is the benefit of working in this particu-lar studio and with its house engineers, their expertise at the placing of microphones and the judging of levels acquired from a long familiarity with the room's characteristics and the need to satisfy the requirements of renowned performers for a sound both faithful and distinguished. George Avakian, Davis's original champion at Columbia, had been among the working party that found the location for the company's new recording facility in 1950. Its unvarnished wooden floor and plaster walls and ceiling were purposely left untouched, as was a large drape that covered the back wall. Mitch Miller, Columbia's head of A&R, ordered that the floor should never be washed, in order to preserve its resonance (explaining that once the body of a fine violin has been cleaned, its tone is never the same). A control room was built into another wall so that the producers and engineers could survey the musicians from above. It was a room where large or small ensembles could dispose themselves as they felt most comfortable, and where the engineers' reluctance to use baffles or to equip the musicians with headphones meant that the process of recording proceeded in a relatively natural manner. Listening to each other at normal volume, in close enough proximity to be able to communicate by expression or gesture, the players could behave much as they would in a club or on a concert stage.

The studio's clientèle, all Columbia artists, was already varied and illustrious. Leonard Bernstein and the New York Philharmonic were frequent visitors. Tony Bennett had recorded his first hit, 'Boulevard of Broken Dreams', there during the studio's first year of operation. Glenn Gould made the first of his celebrated recordings of Bach's

Goldberg Variations there in 1955 (his 1982 recording would be one of 30th Street's last hurrahs). Johnny Mathis, Rosemary Clooney and the New Christy Minstrels were regulars. Irving Townsend, himself a musician and former bandleader, had produced two ambitious and historic recordings, Billie Holiday's *Latin in Satin* and Duke Ellington's *Black, Brown and Beige*, there in the previous year; well acquainted with the surroundings, he was able to put the musicians at their ease while monitoring both the performance and the quality of sound.

From the smooth, rounded ping of Jimmy Cobb's ride cymbal to the merest hint of hoarseness at the end of certain of Coltrane's phrases, the warm naturalness of timbre drawn from every instrument was enhanced by the inherent three-second echo of a room measuring a hundred feet high, a hundred feet wide and a hundred feet long. Further embellished by the subtle use of the signal from an echo chamber created from the concrete walls, floor and ceiling of an old storage room in the building's basement (although to nothing like the extent of the final version of the soundtrack to *Ascenseur pour l'echafaud*), this resonance was the equivalent of the gold leaf around an icon, and it would be much imitated as others sought to reproduce the imperishable glow emanating from *Kind of Blue*.

The second tune of the session turned out to be the one that, to many ears, most quickly identifies the album – not least because, when the album's five tracks came to be sequenced for release as a twelve-inch LP, it was chosen to lead off the first side. 'So What' continues the sound established with

'Freddie Freeloader' but, while retaining an essence of the blues, moves away from the structure into a world of improvisation built on scales. Evans and Chambers play its introduction, at first out of tempo, an ingenious miniature duet containing three separate motifs. It was almost certainly written by Gil Evans, who conducted an orchestrated version when it was performed by Davis's quintet and auxiliary horns on a CBS television programme, *The Robert Herridge Theatre Show*, a month after the first session, and two years later with a twenty-one-piece orchestra at Carnegie Hall. (Evans had written for Davis's smaller groups before: his neat arrangement of Monk's 'Round Midnight' led off the quintet's first Columbia album.)

The main theme is constructed on a call-and-response pattern familiar from gospel music. Immediately striking is the unusual decision to give the 'call' to Chambers's bass, the response (simulating a choir's 'amen') coming first from the piano and then from the three horns, tightly voiced and creating a finely grained texture. Not since Duke Ellington's 'Jack the Bear', written and recorded as a feature for the great Jimmy Blanton in 1940, had the bass been featured as the lead voice in such a prominent piece. Like 'Freddie Freeloader', 'So What' drops into a purring medium tempo; yet although there is only a marginal difference in the actual pace, the rhythm section's subtlety is such that the former, at thirty-three bars to the minute, sounds more leisurely than the latter, which is only a bar per minute faster but conveys a greater sense of forward movement. This may be due in part to the presence of Evans rather than Kelly; although the replacement is a less obviously swinging pianist, once the solos get started the timing and voicing of his chordal interjections create an intensity that brings its own kind of momentum.

The AABA pattern of each thirty-two-bar chorus resembles that of the forty-bar 'Milestones'; here the A section is based on a D minor 7th chord, played against a C major scale, while the B section again moves up a half-step to E flat minor, against a D flat major scale. Both of these harmonic combinations conform to the Dorian mode, again producing the sensation of accelerated motion as the mode moves up going into the seventeenth bar of each chorus, with the consequent feeling of relaxation as it falls back at the start of the twenty-fifth bar. By comparison with 'Milestones', which clocked in at sixty-two bars per minute, the slower tempo promotes a greater sense of relaxation without diminishing the intensity, and once again all the soloists – first Davis, succeeded by Coltrane and Adderley, with Evans to follow – produce work distinguished by a profound sense of architecture.

Nowhere on this album is there the impression, so prevalent in bebop and post-bop jazz, of notes simply being produced without any real internal rhyme or reason, simply in order to display technical prowess while fulfilling the demands of a set harmonic pattern. Now that the source materials have been pared to the minimum, and the setting of a medium tempo means that there is no obligation for the musicians to flex their muscles in a contest of athleticism, imaginations are sparked into vivid life. Davis's solo begins against an apparently inadvertent but superbly appropriate crash from Cobb's cymbal – perhaps the most famous single cymbal crash in all of jazz history – as the drummer switches from brushes to sticks; hanging and decaying over the first two bars of the improvisation, the shimmering sound provides a perfect platform for the trumpeter, who prowls the scales like a cat picking its way between windowsill ornaments, his peerless lyricism in full bloom. Coltrane begins with a similar concern for melodic invention before his harmonic obsession rises to the surface and he starts to turn the material to his own use, raising the pressure with incantatory figures that arise from a different kind of rhetorical urge. Adderley, by nature the most effusively voluble member of the group, meets the formidable intellectual challenge thrown down by his predecessors and leavens his intricate double-time runs with broad bluesy smears. Evans's solo, punctuated by the horns' 'amen' phrases, consists mostly of glowing block chords, very different in their use of close inner voicings, bordering on dissonance, from the more cheerful, bouncy variety patented by Garland and refined by Kelly.

'So What' is as energetic as *Kind of Blue* gets, and its air of restraint conditions the listener for the remainder of an album in which voices are never raised and the impact is created by deep emotions expressed within a framework of freedom and self-discipline. In that way, perhaps it speaks to some profound ideal of the human condition.

For all its air of laconic spontaneity, *Kind of Blue* had been the subject of greater forethought than any of Davis's earlier small-group recordings. He and Bill Evans had unfinished business, and at the heart of the project lay a collaboration that would lead to disputes over the attribution of some of the material on which the album was based.

One day at Miles's apartment on 10th Avenue, according to Evans, the trumpeter wrote down a couple of chord symbols – 'G minor and A augmented,' he said – and asked the pianist what he would do with them. This was the kind of question, intended as a stimulus, sometimes as a provocation, that Davis often asked his sidemen. 'I went home and wrote "Blue in Green",' Evans said many years later of a tune for which Davis received the sole composer's credit when the album eventually appeared, and for which the trumpeter and his estate have received the publishing royalties ever since.

At this distance it is impossible to untangle events that depended on reciprocal inspiration. We know that on 30 December 1958, barely eight weeks before the first *Kind of Blue* session, Evans went into a New York studio with a sextet led by Chet Baker to record a version of the standard 'Alone Together' prefaced by a four-bar intro perfectly pre-echoing the opening bars of 'Blue in Green'. But whereas 'Alone Together' was a thirty-two-bar Broadway tune, 'Blue in Green' turned out to be a ten-bar cycle of chords that folded back into itself, leaving the listener unaware of when the cycle was ending and starting again.

The composer Earl Zindars, a close friend of Evans, is quoted by the pianist's biographer, Peter Pettinger, as remembering that the tune was written in his apartment; it is also undisputed that on earlier occasions Davis had put his own name to another man's compositions, 'Four' and 'Tune Up' by the alto saxophonist Eddie 'Cleanhead'

Vinson. There must be a doubt over the nature of the melody itself, since on an aborted second take of the piece Davis opens with a line bearing only a tangential relationship to the one that emerges a few minutes later on the definitive version. A case can be made, too, for the claim that Davis's initial suggestion of the two chords may have been of a significance at least equal to whatever Evans made of them, and that the trumpeter's work on the recording was, in any case, the defining factor of a piece that would always have hovered in the uncertain area between composition and improvisation. When Evans recorded the piece in a trio version for his own album, *Portrait in Jazz*, the following December, it was credited to 'Davis-Evans'; half a century later, however, the *Kind of Blue* version remained ostensibly the trumpeter's property.

Played at a dead-slow tempo, the original version of 'Blue in Green' is a crystalline realisation of all the melancholy implicit in Davis's playing. Employing the tight, buzzing sound of a Harmon mute *sans* plunger, he appears to be revisiting the modus operandi of the Louis Malle soundtrack in order to create a piece of music existing only in its own moment, its own light, its own emotional space. Originally conceived as a feature for the trumpeter alone with the rhythm section, it was amended in the studio by an apparently last-minute invitation to Coltrane, who follows the first of Evans's two piano interludes with a solo that anticipates the austere beauty of his playing on his own much-loved *Ballads* album, recorded in 1961 and 1962. The supporting work of Chambers and Cobb, the latter swishing his wire brushes across the head of the snare drum with the lightness of a moth's wings, is almost subliminal; Chambers's attempt to double the tempo during Evans's second interlude is resisted as Davis returns for a final statement, the pianist and the bassist, using his bow for the only time on the album, providing an elegant coda to five and a half minutes of unsurpassed jazz balladry, with which the first session of *Kind of Blue* – and, as it would emerge in its twelve-inch, $33^1/_3$ rpm vinyl version, the album's first side – reached its conclusion.

In the fifty-one days between the two sessions, the sextet – with Kelly restored to the piano stool – played a week at the Apollo in Harlem (sharing a bill with Ruth Brown, Thelonious Monk and the orchestra of Johnny Richards), performed at a midnight concert at Loew's Valencia Theatre in Brooklyn and appeared – minus Adderley, who was suffering from a migraine, and plus the Gil Evans Orchestra – in the Robert Herridge programme, recorded at the CBS television studios, where their performance consisted of three pieces from *Miles Ahead* – 'The Duke', 'Blues for Pablo' and 'New Rhumba' – and 'So What', which allowed Davis, Coltrane and Kelly to stretch out, at a tempo just a couple of bars per minute faster than the recorded version, after the orchestra had played Evans's arrangement of the rubato introduction.

As individual recording artists, the members of the sextet were in demand. Kelly, Jones and Cobb recorded tracks for the Vee-Jay label, to be released as an album under the pianist's name, titled *Kelly Blue*. They also joined Adderley for a quartet album titled *Cannonball Takes Charge*, recorded in a single day for the Riverside label. Coltrane, who had just signed with Atlantic, invited Chambers to take part in his first session for his new label, alongside the pianist Cedar Walton and the drummer Lex Humphries, performing a couple of tunes that would later be re-recorded with other musicians and released under the title *Giant Steps*. Bill Evans, no longer a member of the working group, recorded an unusual two-piano album called *The Ivory Hunters* with Bob Brookmeyer, better known as a trombonist. And on Thursday, 16 April the sextet began a two-week season at Birdland, on Broadway between 52nd and 53rd Streets.

They had already played almost a week at the club when they reconvened at the 30th Street studio on Wednesday, 22 April for another session, again starting at half past two and this time scheduled to last three hours. No more time than that, it was felt, would be necessary to complete the recording of *Kind of Blue*.

It is hard to imagine, fifty years later, how the musicians could have plunged straight into a piece as intense as 'Flamenco Sketches' on an ordinary midweek afternoon, at a time when Manhattan's office workers would have been returning from their lunches and getting back to the day's duties. Inside the studio, however, time must have lost its meaning.

The only one of the album's five tunes to have been given two complete takes, 'Flamenco Sketches' had its origins in a conversation between Davis and Bill Evans on the day before the first session. While they were working through various ideas for the album, Davis mentioned his liking for a tune by Evans called 'Peace Piece', which had evolved while the pianist had been doodling with Leonard Bernstein's 'Some Other Time' (written in 1944 for the show *On the Town*) and found himself entranced by the opening two chords. One of several solo piano recordings made in December 1958 and released as part of the album *Everybody Digs Bill Evans!* the following February, 'Peace Piece' lasts a few seconds short of seven minutes and is an essay in harmonic stasis at very slow tempo, a themeless meditation on the simple repetition of those two chords.

It was Davis's idea (and here the question of who was the true composer rears its head once again) to begin with those two chords, C major 7 and G9, but then to move them through a series of modes by giving the soloists a sequence of five scales through which to proceed at their own speed. The scales in question were C Ionian, A flat Mixolydian, B flat Ionian, D Phrygian and G Dorian. The particular properties of the fourth of those modes, bringing an unmistakeably Moorish accent to each individual improvisation, may have inspired Davis's title.

The five scales, as transposed for E flat alto saxophone, can be seen in a photograph from the session, written on a scrap of manuscript paper and held in place on Adderley's music stand alongside a pack of Newport filter cigarettes by a tub of Bufferin headache pills and his mouthpiece cover, which partially obscures the first and fifth of them. Such minimal source material and yet, within the nine minutes and twenty-six seconds of the second and final take, so great an outpouring of invention.

Davis begins, again with the Harmon mute, at his most piercingly lyrical, occasionally relaxing the pressure and allowing his tone to soften. His improvisation lasts just under two minutes, and the subtlety of inflection and intonation evoke a remark made by another, younger trumpeter a couple of years after *Kind of Blue*'s appearance: 'There are a lot of notes between notes,' Booker Little said a few weeks before his death in 1961. 'They call them quarter-tones. They're not really quarter-tones but notes that are above and below A440 [standard concert pitch]. I think these notes have much more emotion if used correctly than the A440 notes. This is something Miles employs a lot and I doubt if he even thinks about it.'

So powerful is the impact of Davis's solo that the eight-second hiatus between the end of his improvisation and the start of Coltrane's is one of the most powerful anticipatory spaces in jazz, the rhythm section discreetly treading water before the tenor saxophonist, reverting to the first of the scales, enters for the start of an improvisation that matches the leader's for the patience of its pacing and even outdoes it in fidelity to the subtext of the harmonic material. When the tenorist's two minutes of carefully repressed drama end in a gently curling downward phrase, Adderley again supplies a leavening of joy to the prevailing astringency, adding a flush of colour without disrupting the overall scheme. Evans's invention is reminiscent of Debussy: a mysterious sequence of lightly clotted chords drifting above Chambers's nimble-fingered and wonderfully constructive commentary before Davis returns to telescope the scales into a brief concluding statement. In terms of a message to the future, 'Flamenco Sketches' was *Kind of Blue*'s unfiltered moment: full strength, pure essence.

'All Blues', the last of the five tracks to be recorded, was my introduction to *Kind of Blue*, thanks to Willis Conover and the Voice of America's *Jazz Hour* one night when the Cold War was nearing its zenith, and a thousand hearings later it retains every ounce of the impact it made coming through the speaker of a valve radio in the family kitchen. Originally conceived as a 4/4 tune, in which form it would have conformed even more accurately to Davis's reported description of it as a slowed-down 'Milestones', it was modified in the studio to 6/8 time, which – in combination with its seesawing vamp – immediately gave it a unique lulling quality.

This was the track on which Davis intended to evoke the haunting sound of the kalimba, the African thumb piano. If that was impossible, given the means at his disposal, the alternative solution provided the piece with one of its signatures. A rolling tremolo sustained by Bill Evans all the way through the theme choruses of this twelve-bar blues in G minor lends 'All Blues' an exotic air – it might almost have been played on another African tuned percussion instrument, the marimba-like balafon – even before the two saxophones enter to play the palindromic background vamp figure which would normally have fallen to the pianist. Paul Chambers responds to Davis's demand for him to maintain an almost unvarying ground bass figure – much harder work than the usual quarter-note 'walk' – while Jimmy Cobb swishes his brushes under the theme. Eased out by Davis's muted trumpet, this is a line of breathtaking simplicity delivered with such exquisite timing that it seems to be floating on a cushion of air. Together, the six instruments combine to create a statement of understated yet utterly compelling refinement.

While the leader is removing his mute from the bell of his trumpet in readiness to begin his improvisation, Cobb again switches deftly from brushes to sticks: first his right hand, which transfers the flowing *ching-chinga-ching* beat to the ride cymbal, and then his left, which – as Davis gets under way with a variation on the theme that sounds like a subdued fanfare – starts to tap out well-spaced punctuation on the tautly tuned snare drum in response to the soloist's terse phrases.

The interplay between Davis and Evans on this track is even more remarkable. Taking over the simple vamp from the horns, the pianist gradually breaks it down, adding upper voicings and little staccato syncopations in the ninth and tenth bars – the place in the structure where the harmonies are suspended and the tension momentarily released. At times, as the trumpet solo proceeds, Evans's extraordinary touch combines with the close voicings of his chords to make it seem as though he is strumming the instrument (perhaps this was one of the qualities that attracted Duane Allman, whose version of the tune, titled 'In Memory of Elizabeth Reed', became one of the Allman Brothers Band's most popular concert numbers in the early 1970s).

After an appropriate pause to allow the echoes of Davis's deliberations to die away, Adderley produces a solo in which heart-on-the-sleeve romanticism and sudden bursts of intricacy are nicely juxtaposed, all beautifully shadowed by Evans, who lightens his background figures to match the altoist's mood. With the entry of Coltrane, ushered in by Cobb's light press-roll, the tone darkens again: here the tenorist almost lets go of the composure he has maintained throughout the sessions, ending one phrase with an abrupt honk before engaging in flurries that recall his inclination to exploit every possible permutation of every chord. By pushing against the limits of the prevailing ambiance, yet staying just within its furthermost boundaries, he raises the tension of an otherwise relaxed piece in a way that justifies Davis's belief in assembling an aggregation of contrasting personalities.

Evans's solo begins with a limpid line marked by blues inflections before he splays broken arpeggios across the beat, followed by more of those tightly voiced chords. The horns return with the bedrock vamp (Coltrane so close to the mike, and playing so quietly, that you can hear the spittle against his reed), Davis stabbing out a stuttering single-note figure over the saxophones and the piano tremolo as, borrowing another trick from 'Milestones', the tune fades out, disappearing into a haze of its own creation.

Released in the United States on 17 August 1959, *Kind of Blue* received generally respectful reviews. Of the two major jazz magazines, one missed the point: *Metronome*'s reviewer scolded Davis for restricting himself to an ever smaller range and for 'taking no chances at all'. *Down Beat*'s anonymous critic, however, offered an opinion that would be shared by hundreds of thousands, and the prescience of his five-star review is worth quoting in full:

This is a remarkable album. Using very simple but effective devices, Miles has constructed an album of extreme beauty and sensitivity. This is not to say that this LP is a simple one – far from it. What is remarkable is that the men have done so much with the stark, skeletal concept.

All the compositions bear the mark of the Impressionists and touches of Béla Bartók. For example, 'So What' is built on two scales, which sound somewhat like the Hungarian minor, giving the performance a Middle Eastern flavor; 'Flamenco Sketches' and 'All Blues' reflect a strong Ravel influence.

'Flamenco' and 'Freddie Freeloader' are both blues, but each is of a different mood and conception; 'Sketches' is in 6/8, which achieves a rolling, highly charged effect, while 'Free-loader' is more in the conventional blues vein. The presence of Kelly on 'Freeloader' may account partly for the difference between the two.

Miles' playing throughout the album is poignant, sensitive and, at times, almost morose; his linear concept never flatters. Coltrane has some interesting solos; his angry solo on 'Free-loader' is in marked contrast to his lyrical romanticism on 'All Blues'. Cannonball seems to be under wraps on all the tracks except 'Freeloader', where his irrepressible joie de vivre bubbles forth. Chambers, Evans and Cobb provide a solid, sympathetic backdrop for the horns.

This is the soul of Miles Davis, and it's a beautiful soul.

Curiously, however, the album was released in a form that barely did it justice, riddled with flaws for which Irving Townsend must take the blame. This was the former band-leader's only studio involvement with Davis (he and Teo Macero would jointly supervise the recording of Rodrigo's *Concierto de Aranjuez* for *Sketches for Spain* at the 30th

Street studio later in the year), and as Columbia's designat-
ed A&R man it was his job to oversee every aspect of the
album's production. Whereas George Avakian had ensured
that *Round About Midnight*, *Milestones* and *Porgy and
Bess* had been delivered to the disc jockeys, the magazine
reviewers and the stores in a form that would command
attention, with evocative cover photographs (by Marv
Koner, Dennis Stock and Roy De Carava respectively) that
could do nothing but assist the growth of Davis's image as
a pre-eminent figure in contemporary jazz, *Kind of Blue* had
a comparatively subdued appearance. The cover close-up of
Davis, taken by Jay Maisel at the Apollo Theatre some
months earlier, was hardly inspired, although Don
Hunstein's black-and-white back shot on the back of the
jacket, depicting the trumpeter relaxing on a stool during a
Columbia session, was absolutely right. But it was in the
printed details that Columbia's art department let Davis
down, making references to 'Julian Adderly', 'Wyn Kelly'
and 'James Cobb', these versions provided, according to
Ashley Kahn's invaluable investigations, in a memo sent by
Townsend to the label's art department. Worst of all was the
confusion over the titles on the second side, which listed
'Flamenco Sketches' followed by 'All Blues': a reversal of
the true order which pushed many people (the *Down Beat*
reviewer among them) into making inaccurate references.

How that last error arose can be inferred from the facsim-
ile of the handwritten original manuscript of Bill Evans's
thoughtful sleeve note, included in the lavish fiftieth
anniversary set, where he describes 'All Blue' (*sic*) as 'a
series of five scales, each to be played as long as the soloist

wishes until he has completed the series', and 'F. Sketchs' (*sic*) as 'a six-eight, twelve measure blues form that produces another mood through a few modal changes and Miles Davis's free melodic conception'. Clearly the pianist had transposed the two titles but, with spellings corrected, this was how they appeared when the record was released. On Columbia's internal documents, too, the tracks were listed first correctly and then incorrectly. The error was eventually rectified, but not before many listeners had hard-wired the wrong connections. Again, Townsend's relatively fleeting involvement with Davis was probably behind the inability to sort out this rather important error before *Kind of Blue* was presented to the public. It was Macero, taking over responsibility for Davis's recording career when Townsend was transferred to the company's West Coast office in the summer of 1959, who asked for the mistakes to be corrected.

An equally remarkable flaw was not uncovered for more than thirty years: the first side of the album, comprising the three tracks recorded at the 2 March session, had been mastered at the wrong speed and the versions to which the world had been listening were about a quarter-tone sharper and almost infinitesimally faster than their true values. Columbia's practice was to use two tape recorders at every session, one being devoted to making safety copies which were sent immediately to the company's vaults. Each machine was regularly checked and adjusted. On this occasion, however, the 30th Street studio's primary Ampex three-track machine was running fractionally slow, which meant that when the tape was played on a properly calibrated machine it ran slightly faster, pushing up the pitch of the instruments and the tempo of the pieces. The error was corrected with Columbia's MasterSound audiophile CD release of 1993, and in every subsequent reissue around the world. Those with the sharpest ears claimed to be affected by the difference, including Bill Evans's biographer, Peter Pettinger, who wrote that it 'subtly affects the loping intensity of the first two numbers and intensifies the languorous atmosphere of "Blue in Green".'

It might be remembered, however, that in the days when everyone listened to vinyl recordings, few listeners outside broadcasting studios regularly, if ever, used a stroboscopic card to check and adjust the accuracy of their hi-fi equipment. In that sense, music was often listened to at the wrong speed. And no minor imperfections could hinder the progress of *Kind of Blue* into the world.

9 Blue Waves

John Coltrane and Bill Evans: quartet and trio

The recording of *Kind of Blue* marked the end of something for its participants – Bill Evans would never record again with Miles Davis, Cannonball Adderley or John Coltrane, for example – but the beginning of much else. At the close of the 1950s and the dawn of a new decade all three of the principal sidemen would form their own highly successful groups; even the rhythm section eventually struck out on its own, benefiting from its members' association with the trumpeter.

First, however, the sextet experienced a slow process of disintegration. As Columbia began the process of preparing *Kind of Blue* for release, the group completed its season at Birdland before moving on to the Sutherland Lounge in Chicago and the Blackhawk in San Francisco. At Jazz Seville in Los Angeles, during a July engagement, Coltrane announced his immediate departure; his short-term replacement, Jimmy Heath, was flown from New York. But Heath, an old colleague of Davis, was on parole to the authorities in Philadelphia, his home town. After being reminded by the police that he had to remain within a sixty-mile radius of the city, he was forced to withdraw. Coltrane returned later in the month for a final stay with the band, lasting nine months and encompassing a European tour the following spring.

It was during a return engagement at Birdland in August that, while standing outside the club between sets after seeing a white woman acquaintance into a cab, Davis was assaulted by a policeman and a detective and taken to the 54th Precinct police station, where he was booked for disorderly conduct and held overnight. Pictures of the musician with blood from a head wound spattered on his pale jacket were published in newspapers around the world. Bailed by his manager the next day, Davis had to wait until mid-October to have the charges dismissed by a panel of three judges, who ruled the arrest illegal. Until then, however, his cabaret card was revoked by the New York Police Department, meaning that he was unable to perform in the city's nightclubs. Meanwhile Adderley and Coltrane shared the leadership in order to fulfil the Birdland gig, while Nat Adderley filled in for the leader.

Cannonball Adderley left for good in September, and a *Down Beat* review of the sextet's opening at Jazz Seville in the summer provides an interesting portrait of this historic group in its final phase. 'In his first appearance on the West Coast for over two years,' John Tynan wrote, 'Miles Davis presented not a group but a very good rhythm section backing three star soloists. Not only were all six musicians not on-stand together during any set on opening night, but there was no ensemble playing to speak of and, when the group was reviewed, Cannonball laid out completely during two consecutive sets. The character of the sextet's engagement – for a reputed $2,500 a week – threw into razor-sharp focus the question of night club entertainment vs. untrammeled expression by jazz artists of varying maturity.

While there can be no questioning the validity of the instrumentalists' right to express themselves in the jazz art, the debatable point remains of social responsibility to an audience paying through the nose to hear and see them . . . For all the showcasing of the frequently brilliant soloists, one yearned to hear ensemble performances by these three horns of established merit. But apparently nobody had eyes – or the musicians were not prepared to offer such fare.' Tynan admitted that the audience had not shared his reservations, but had responded to the music with 'much palm-beating'.

The critic's description, however, shows that Davis had gone beyond the neat, carefully textured ensembles heard in the studio recordings of 'Milestones' and 'All Blues' into the world suggested by 'Flamenco Sketches', in which the business of the day was about the soloist getting to grips with a minimum of pre-selected base material. The tensions within the group can be glimpsed in Tynan's assessment of Coltrane's improvising: the tenor saxophonist, he said, 'communicated a sense of inhibition (sometimes even frustration) with his calculated understatement and contrived dissonance.' Adderley, by contrast, was commended for his 'compulsive strength and vigorous attack'.

That strength and attack were on plain view in the quintet the altoist formed the instant he left Davis's employment. Together with his brother Nat on cornet, Bobby Timmons on piano, Sam Jones on bass and Louis Hayes on drums, Adderley constructed a unit blending the energy of bebop with a passionate directness that found expression in the cadences of what was becoming known as 'soul jazz'.

Signed to Riverside Records by Orrin Keepnews, the label's co-owner and A&R head, they discovered that audiences at only their second engagement, at the Jazz Workshop in San Francisco, were reacting with particular enthusiasm to a Timmons tune called 'This Here', a compendium of funky phrases rooted in the emotional trigger mechanisms of gospel music. Adderley called Keepnews in New York and asked him to record the group during the engagement. Riverside had never recorded on the West Coast, and live recordings were in their infancy, but the spontaneous decision was made and the result, taped over two nights, produced not just a hit album, *The Cannonball Adderley Quintet in San Francisco*, but, in an edited version of 'This Here', a very popular 45rpm single.

This was a group with undisputed jazz credentials but also an ability to please crowds emanating from the leader's personal characteristics. 'Julian was one of the most completely alive human beings I had ever encountered,' Keepnews would write. 'He was a big man and a joyous man. He was a player and a composer and a leader, and when someone else was soloing he was snapping his fingers and showing his enjoyment, and before and after the band's numbers he talked to the audience. (Not talking *at* them or just making announcements, but really talking *to* them and saying things about the music – some serious, some very witty.)' The contrast with Davis's leadership could hardly have been more apparent. Adderley had managed to take the materials of bebop and infuse them with an unreflective zest harking back to Louis Jordan and the Harlem jump bands of the pre-bop era.

Having established a durable template, the group went on to further success with other compositions of similar nature, including Nat Adderley's 'Work Song' and 'Jive Samba', and Cannonball's own 'Sack o' Woe'. Each of these tunes was distinguished by what a pop musician would call a 'hook': a single memorable phrase. Towards the end of the 1960s Adderley would hire a young Austrian pianist who gave him a composition called 'Mercy Mercy Mercy', which made even greater capital out of the traditional gospel inflections and gave the group their biggest hit of all; a year or so later that pianist, Joe Zawinul, would contribute 'In a Silent Way' to Miles Davis's repertoire and play keyboards on the sessions that produced *Bitches Brew*, thus performing a key role in the trumpeter's next major change of direction.

During the weeks between the two *Kind of Blue* sessions, John Coltrane had spent a day in Atlantic's studio on West 57th Street working with Paul Chambers, the pianist Cedar Walton and the drummer Lex Humphries on two compositions that would form part of his own major project. One, 'Naima', was a luminous ballad dedicated to his first wife; it would become a jazz standard. The other, 'Giant Steps', was destined to give its name to an album that both established John Coltrane as a major jazz artist and brought an important phase of his career to a conclusion.

Coltrane rejected the results of that first session, but with *Kind of Blue* out of the way he was back at Atlantic on 1 May, this time with Tommy Flanagan on piano and Art Taylor on drums, to produce six of the seven tracks that would make up *Giant Steps*, one of the key albums of jazz history. Not until December, however, when the Davis band had just finished another three-week stint at Birdland, did he return, this time with the familiar rhythm section of Kelly, Chambers and Cobb, to complete the album by creating the definitive version of 'Naima'.

In itself, the tune 'Giant Steps' summarised this phase of Coltrane's development, strongly influenced by what he had learnt about modes and scales through his time with Davis but filled with a resolve to adopt a different approach to those discoveries. Running restlessly through a rapid harmonic sequence involving a cycle of major thirds, it forms a test of the improviser's agility and wits, a formidable technical challenge that is repeated, with variations, in other pieces on the album, such as the jet-propelled 'Countdown'. In temperament, these tunes are closer to the oblique structures devised by the bebop pioneers with the mischievous intention of throwing their would-be imitators off the scent than to the more relaxed intensity developed by Davis when he espoused the use of modes.

For Davis, the substitution of scales for chords enabled the music to decelerate and embrace a great spaciousness. Complexity would now be distilled. To Coltrane, however, each set of harmonies represented a conundrum to be overpowered rather than resolved: his solution was to try to play every possible extension of, and substitution for, every chord in the form of a flood of arpeggio-based runs, usually executed at maximum velocity. (There is a famous story about his participation in a session for George Russell's large-scale work *New York, New York* in 1958, when the composer invited Coltrane to take a solo and handed him a Lydian scale on which to base his improvisation. Coltrane held up the session by going off into a corner and working out his own harmonic substitutions.) For a while, a great melodist disappeared beneath what the critic Ira Gitler famously called Coltrane's 'sheets of sound'.

And yet *Giant Steps*, which became and remains a text-book challenge for saxophonists, was the end of the line for the approach on which Coltrane had been working since he joined Davis. In recordings from a series of concerts during their final European tour in the early weeks of 1960 it is possible to hear Coltrane's agonising struggle against the walls of harmonic constraint. As he abandons conventional phrase-forms in favour of lower-register honks and tentative multiphonics, his acute unease is all too apparent. The sound of a man trying to break down walls is thrown into even more uncomfortable relief by the conventional approach of the rhythm section, whose members continue steadily along their established path as though nothing unusual were happening. Davis, too, was made uneasy by tenor solos that had the sophisticated audience in the Olympia music hall, Paris, whistling and hooting. To his great credit, he never withdrew support from the explorer at his side. Coltrane, whose facility would have enabled him to delight Davis's listeners with the minimum of effort, was a man constitutionally incapable of taking the easy option. Once you had played all the notes in all the chords, he was asking, what was left? *Kind of Blue*, as it happened, had provided the answer.

The combination of exotic scales and the kind of harmonically simple 6/8 vamp played by Chambers under 'All Blues' formed the basis of Coltrane's next move, along with the polyrhythms that Davis had heard played by the Guinean and Senegalese drummers of Les Ballets Africains but which he had not been able to translate into the music of the sextet. Elvin Jones was not the first drummer Coltrane tried while assembling the components of his new quintet – the bop veteran Roy Haynes and the talented young Pete La Roca had been among the candidates – but he was the only one who demonstrated a new way of adding forward momentum to the motionless see-sawing modes that a new pianist, McCoy Tyner, and a succession of bassists were providing as the platform from which the saxophonist could launch his extended improvisations.

Coltrane was encouraged in a desire to push forward into his own territory by hearing the music being made by the Ornette Coleman Quartet at the Five Spot in New York during November 1959, in which all restrictions of conventional melodic and harmonic structure had been blown away in favour of a kind of naturalistic expressionism. The 'new thing', as the jazz avant garde of the early 1960s would be known, had yet to take shape, but Coleman and the pianist Cecil Taylor were nudging it into being and Coltrane saw the opportunity to break the chains of convention. He left Davis's group for the last time when they returned from Europe in mid-April 1960 and opened with his new own quartet at the Jazz Gallery in New York on 3 May.

Now he was featuring the soprano saxophone alongside his customary tenor, having heard the creative use to which this recherché instrument (familiar in jazz only through its use by Sidney Bechet and, occasionally, Johnny Hodges) was being put by Steve Lacy, a former Dixieland musician who had become a student of Monk and a protégé of Gil Evans. Acquiring his own instrument, Coltrane practised assiduously before unveiling it in public. Unlike Lacy, he produced a thin, piping sound immediately reminiscent of the double-reed instruments of India and North Africa. He had been listening to the music of Ali Akbar Khan and Ravi Shankar, masters respectively of the sarod, an eighteen-stringed lute, and the better-known sitar. Khan's *Music of India: Morning and Evening Ragas* had been released in 1956, followed a year later by Shankar's *Three Ragas*, enabling Coltrane to study and absorb an idiom in which modes are associated with particular times of day or seasons.

Six months after the quartet's debut he found the ideal vehicle for this new sound when, with Tyner and Jones, and with Steve Davis on bass, he recorded one of the unlikeliest of all jazz hits: a revised version of Richard Rodgers' 'My Favourite Things', from the score of *The Sound of Music*. To Coltrane, the childlike simplicity of the melody – in two sections, major and minor, which enabled him to shift between two modes in the manner of 'So What' or 'Milestones' – provided ideal material for his new approach, which incorporated the findings from his own assiduous research into the music of other cultures. The tune could also be laid over his own version of the 6/8 pulse used in 'All Blues', a metre particularly well suited to the propulsion provided by Jones's circling rhythms. Prefaced by Tyner's dark, hypnotic two-chord vamps, the tune is turned by Coltrane into a lengthy incantation in which he could pursue his obsessions without feeling constricted either by chronological or harmonic barriers.

'My Favourite Things' was the fruit of Coltrane's experience with the thinking that went into *Kind of Blue*, and it established a pattern for his work, both on record and in person. Very soon the quartet was gathering crowds whose reactions ranged from scorn through scepticism to complete acceptance of a music that seemed to exist beyond time or specific culture. The term 'jazz workshop' had been used in other contexts, notably by Charles Mingus and George Russell, but this really was such a thing: every night the quartet played, Coltrane seemed to be involved in a process of continuous and – despite the occasional prolixity of the results – rigorous research into possibilities without end. It was a strenuous business, for players and listeners alike. Coltrane's own solos were lasting anything between fifteen minutes and half an hour. Jones, in particular, needed a boxer's physique to keep pace with his leader, as did some listeners, even those attempting to overcome their own hesitancy.

'That ugliness, like life, can be beautiful is the most surprising discovery one makes after attempting to meet the challenge offered by John Coltrane,' Whitney Balliett wrote in the *New Yorker* in the spring of 1961. 'Coltrane's playing allows the listener no quarter. It belabours him, it hounds him, it stares him down. Coltrane is an inventive, impassioned improviser who above all traps the listener with the unexpected. His style, to be sure, is still unfinished. His tone is bleaker than need be, many of his notes are useless, and his rhythmic methods are frequently just clothes flung all over a room. In addition, Coltrane, unlike such colleagues as Sonny Rollins and Ornette Coleman, has not yet learnt what to leave out.'

More obvious traces of exotic influences were apparent in the Atlantic recordings that followed the initial surprise hit, notably the Spanish-tinged 'Olé', a version of an Iberian folk song also framed by Coltrane in that mesmerising medium-tempo 6/8, its reduced harmonic basis under-pinned by the twin double basses of Reggie Workman and Art Davis (one pizzicato, the other arco). An album called *Coltrane Plays the Blues* demonstrated the saxophonist's new conception in its evolutionary phase, and makes an interesting complement to *Kind of Blue* in so far as both albums represent radical extensions of the basic musical and emotional material of the blues.

It was when he signed a contract with the Impulse label in 1961 that Coltrane took the final leap to pre-eminence among his contemporaries. Under the supervision of the producer Bob Thiele, his new recordings were lavishly packaged in gatefold sleeves with excellent photography and striking design. A subsidiary of ABC, Impulse made the same kind of effort to project Coltrane's image as a trend-setter that Columbia had made with his former bandleader; the reward came in a series of albums that stretched the boundaries of jazz in ways of which Davis could never have dreamed. It is perhaps a sign of the mood of those times as well as of the producer's vision and integrity that Thiele made no effort to modify Coltrane's working practices in order to create recordings more palatable to a wide audience; instead he encouraged the artist to give expression to the full range of his instincts.

The elaborate arrangements for an eighteen-piece orchestra of the three pieces recorded in May and June 1961 for the album *Africa/Brass*, Coltrane's first release on Impulse, demonstrated Thiele's readiness to invest in the saxophonist's future. The composition 'Africa' made a spiritual and practical genuflection to the source via Jones's rolling polyrhythms, the whooping of French horns (orchestrated by the multi-instrumentalist Eric Dolphy, whom Coltrane had met in Los Angeles several years earlier), and the feeling that the saxophone soloist was finding his way through the undergrowth of a steamy jungle. Here, too, was an early example of explicit Afrocentricity at a time when African nations were achieving independence from their former colonial masters, and an implied statement of solidarity with the burgeoning civil rights movement at home.

Coltrane went further in all these directions – notably, in respect of the civil rights struggle, with 'Alabama', a stately lamentation written in the aftermath of the September 1963 bombing of a Montgomery, Alabama church in which four black children perished – but nothing drew his attention more than the principles and practices of Indian music. The version of 'Greensleeves', the old English folk song, heard on *Africa/Brass* is also cast in the 6/8 metre that suited the partnership of Jones and Coltrane so well, allowing them to create a running dialogue analogous to the interplay between Shankar's sitar and Alla Rakha's tabla drums heard on the records the saxophonist had been studying intently. Coltrane was also making frequent use of two basses to create a drone replicating the function, if not the sound or the precise effect, of the tambura in Shankar's music.

Impulse's positive attitude to Coltrane's career was evident in the decision to record him live at the Village Vanguard, on Seventh Avenue South in New York, in the first week of November 1961. Thiele and his engineers were present on four nights to capture Coltrane at the height of his new powers, fronting not just his regular group – in which Reggie Workman and Jimmy Garrison had replaced Steve Davis, sometimes alternating and sometimes playing together – but a handful of extra musicians. One of them, Eric Dolphy, had joined the group for the recording of one of the last Atlantic albums, *Olé*, and had become a semi-permanent addition, playing alto saxophone, bass clarinet and flute. The oboe and contra-bassoon of Garvin Bushell and oud and tambura of Ahmed Abdul-Malik were present to add colour and texture to the sound. Bushell, born in 1902, had played with such figures from earlier jazz eras as the bandleader Fletcher Henderson and the New Orleans trumpeter Bunk Johnson. The Brooklyn-born Abdul-Malik, who had played bass in the Thelonious Monk Quartet alongside Coltrane at Carnegie Hall in 1957, was of Sudanese descent and had been pioneering the fusion of jazz and North African music since the middle 1950s. Like the saxophonist Yusef Lateef (born William Evans), he had a friendship with Coltrane which incorporated discussions on the findings of their various musical researches.

The first of two albums Impulse released from these

nights in the small West Village club was titled *Live at the Village Vanguard*, and it created a furore thanks mostly to the inclusion of a sixteen-minute track called 'Chasin' the Trane'. Occupying one complete side of the vinyl LP, it consisted of an unbroken tenor saxophone solo, accompanied only by Garrison's bass and Jones's drums, with no theme or structure except the adoption of a slightly-faster-than-medium 4/4 metre and the loose suggestion of a blues tonality. Otherwise Coltrane was free to do whatever he wanted: to howl, to squeal, to blow split notes, to worry at phrases until he had shunted them into some sort of order.

Shock greeted this exposition of a relentless, almost desperate urge to leap into the infinite; outrage, too. The scene had been set by the *Down Beat* critic John Tynan, who reviewed the group at the Renaissance Club in Hollywood and remarked: 'I heard a good rhythm section . . . go to waste behind the nihilistic exercises of the two horns . . . [Coltrane and Dolphy] seem bent on pursuing an anarchistic course in their music that can but be termed anti-jazz.' That last phrase soon became a stick with which to beat Coltrane, and in April 1962, as the controversy reached its height, *Down Beat* published a cover story, titled 'John Coltrane and Eric Dolphy Answer the Jazz Critics', in which the magazine's editor, Don DeMichael, elicited the defence of the two men to the charge of unleashing anarchy on the jazz world, and in particular to the accusations that their performances went on too long.

'They're long,' Coltrane explained, 'because all the soloists try to explore all the avenues that the tune offers. They try to use all their resources in their solos. Everybody has quite a bit to work on. Like when I'm playing, there are certain things I try to get done and so do Eric and McCoy. By the time we finish, the song is spread over a pretty long time. It's not planned that way. It just happens. The performances get longer and longer. It's sort of growing that way.'

He admitted that self-editing was sometimes necessary in order to accommodate the scheduling requirements of nightclubs, where two bands usually alternated sets lasting forty or forty-five minutes. 'But when your set is unlimited, timewise,' he concluded, 'and everything is really together musically – if there's continuity – it really doesn't make any difference how long you play.'

In terms of what was to follow, the critics were wrong and the artist was right. By seizing the opportunity presented to him when Miles Davis introduced open-ended structures to replace the tyranny of chorus-repetition, Coltrane could be said to have licensed the performers and performances that would form the very disparate cornerstones of music in the closing decades of the century: such works as the speaking-in-tongues euphoria of Albert Ayler's 'Bells' (1964, nineteen minutes and fifty-five seconds), the shimmer and twitter of Terry Riley's *In C* (1968, 42:01), the relentless junkie paranoia of the Velvet Underground's 'Sister Ray' (1968, 17:55), the full-on European free improvisation of Peter Brötzmann's 'Machine Gun' (1968, 17:13), the cosmic cowboy wanderings of the Grateful Dead's 'Dark Star' (23:18 in the 1969 *Live/Dead* version), the psychedelic systems music of the Soft Machine's 'Facelift' (1970, 18:54), the solitary meditation of Keith

Jarrett's *Köln Concert* (1975, 66:05), the live version of Richard Thompson's sombre 'Calvary Cross' (1975, 13:27), Television's glassy 'Marquee Moon' (1977, 10:40), Funkadelic's acid-disco masterpiece 'One Nation Under a Groove' (1978, 11.26 in the extended mix), all the way through twelve-inch mixes, jam bands, process compositions and trance music to the work by La Monte Young whose title begins 'The Base 9:7:4 Symmetry in Prime Time When Centered Above and Below the Lowest Term Primes in the Range 288 to 224 . . .', installed at the Dream House on Church Street in TriBeCa (1993 to the present day).

With Coltrane, however, it wasn't just about length. Almost anyone could have decided that it was a good idea to let solos go on for half an hour. The combination of hallucinogenic drugs, Andy Warhol and James Brown would have seen to that. But Coltrane possessed another quality, something that had nothing to do with strategic decisions. His playing glowed with a sense of spirituality that reached out to new listeners in large numbers.

It had been there in his early days with Miles Davis, it had intensified during his time with Thelonious Monk, and it started to shine through when he began making his own recordings for the Prestige label. His treatment of Broadway standards – ballads like 'You Leave Me Breathless' or 'Violets For Your Furs' – seemed to come from a different planet than the one occupied by previous generations of great jazz tenor saxophonists such as Coleman Hawkins, Lester Young, Ben Webster, Dexter Gordon or Sonny Rollins. With his gaunt, anthracite tone and his roiling, jagged phrases, Coltrane exuded a sombre majesty that went beyond considerations of idiom. Many found the sound alone utterly compelling.

The launch of his own band enabled him to make the most of his ability to transfix a sympathetic audience. Before long Coltrane wasn't just attracting fans, he was creating acolytes. Those long solos were like internal dialogues, the public expression of the private discourse of a man arguing with himself in order to solve the problems of existence. This was a hieratic music, dedicated to some cause above and beyond the normal business of nightclubs and concert halls. Coltrane became jazz's equivalent of a great preacher, a man with a gift for holding audiences spellbound as he recited truths and insights.

One of the pieces on *Live at the Village Vanguard* was called 'Spiritual'. It began with the soprano saxophone delivering a gospel-like melody over a rubato accompaniment before dropping into the group's favourite modus operandi: a gently rocking 6/8 and a two-chord vamp, ready to be infused with the passion that would lead to a series of ecstatic climaxes, with the crash and batter of Jones's drums driving Coltrane to such extremes of emotion that the saxophone no longer seemed an adequate vehicle for their expression.

'Spiritual' turned out to be just a foretaste of Coltrane's growing interest in using his music as a vehicle for religious expression. Foreshadowing the sort of searching that would occupy tens of thousands as the decade went on, he was scanning Christianity, Islam, Buddhism, Sufism, Judaism, the Kabbalah, the occult and everything else he could get his hands on for answers and solutions. Coming from a devout Methodist family background, he did not follow the path of many of his contemporaries who converted to Islam but used the armature of Christianity as a basis for his own personal faith in an all-embracing divine creator. 'I believe in all religions,' he told Nat Hentoff. His goal, he said, was 'to uplift people, as much as I can. To inspire them to realise more and more of their capacities for living meaningful lives. Because there certainly is meaning to life.'

Beat-generation atheists and hippie pantheists alike had no problem with the source of Coltrane's inspiration. What they heard in his music, in the midst of a largely post-religious society, was the clear and timelessly affecting expression of humanity's yearning for grace and otherness.

The three pivotal works of his mature period were, for him if not for all the musicians who shared his journey, expressions of his faith. The first and most spectacularly successful, recorded in 1964, was called *A Love Supreme* and is generally seen as standing only a half-step below *Kind of Blue* in the pantheon of post-war jazz. A suite in four parts, *A Love Supreme* is an explicitly devotional work, the titles of its individual movements – 'Acknowledgement', 'Resolution', 'Pursuance' and 'Psalm' – indicating the sense of a spiritual journey contained within the thirty-three-minute work. Here the group that became known as the 'classic quartet' – completed by Tyner, Garrison and Jones – reached the zenith of its achievement: after three years together, the internal mechanisms were perfectly balanced and had yet to show signs of fatigue. The material is so well focused and so evenly distributed throughout the duration of the work that it never suffers even momentarily from the sometimes prolix repetition of vamps that affected some of their performances. Coltrane performs as if in a state of grace, his tone shining with a new radiance, even in moments of hoarse urgency. He is still the earnest searcher, but with a new serenity and clarity of purpose.

He could not stand still, however, and a year later *A Love Supreme* was followed by *Ascension*, in which he made a statement of common purpose with the new generation of free-jazz players. A single piece originally divided to fit the two sides of a vinyl LP, *Ascension* lasts thirty-eight minutes in the form in which it was originally issued (an earlier take, released subsequently, is two minutes longer) and is performed by an eleven-piece group including some of the young musicians making names for themselves in the downtown coffee houses and lofts that nurtured the New York avant-garde jazz scene, notably the saxophonists John Tchicai, Marion Brown, Archie Shepp and Pharoah Sanders. Coltrane's generosity to younger players was legendary; some of his contemporaries criticised him for his willingness to share the spotlight with those who had yet to approach his level, although he clearly drew energy from the presence of members of jazz's next wave.

In one sense, *Ascension* is a belated but wholeheartedly positive response to Ornette Coleman's *Free Jazz*, a thirty-six-minute recording from 1960 in which eight musicians – a double quartet – were largely given their heads over a regular metre. Five years later, Coltrane supervised a new-wave blowing session in which solos emerge before being engulfed by the improvising ensemble. Tyner's piano brings a measure of equal temperament to bear on the heterophonic mix, and it is sometimes said that the piece tends towards the modes associated with a B-flat minor blues. Coltrane's opening solo is a fervent expression of his belief in the new freedom, and his younger colleagues eagerly follow suit with varying degrees of success.

Ascension has always divided opinion. It was the only Coltrane album that John Lennon could remember hearing, and he hated it enough to take it off before the needle had reached the end of side one. In a thoughtful reassessment of Coltrane's playing career, the American critic Ben Ratliff achieved a useful summing-up. '*Ascension* is not a success in particular,' he wrote. 'It is hard to get around the tremulous chaos of the group sound, not to mention the many moments of a band whose members are not in sync with one another, reaching points where they might as well stop, but don't. Instead it is a success in general, a paradigm.'

It was certainly influential. A whole style of what became known as 'energy playing' grew up among musicians who had heard it. Peter Brötzmann's *Machine Gun*, one of the key works of the European avant garde, could hardly have existed without *Ascension*. The saxophonists Evan Parker, Willem Breuker, Mike Osborne, George Khan, Trevor Watts, Elton Dean, Gerd Dudek, Alan Skidmore, Dudu Pukwana, the trumpeters Manfred Schoof and Mongezi Feza, the trombonists Albert Mangelsdorff, Paul Rutherford and Nick Evans, the pianists Misha Mengelberg, Keith Tippett and Fred Van Hove, the bassists Buschi Niebergall, Harry Miller, Jean-François Jenny Clark, Johnny Dyani and Peter Kowald, the drummers Han

Bennink, Paul Lovens, Louis Moholo, John Stevens and Tony Oxley – all were among those affected by its sound and process. Night after night in London in the late 1960s and early 1970s musicians gathered in small places – an Oxford Street basement or the top room of a pub in a southern suburb – to play without adopting any form of advance preparation, relying only on their instincts and their ability to interact with each other.

It was a risky form of music-making and it succeeded in frightening away a whole generation of listeners who might have arrived in the hope of being able to call themselves jazz fans, but it was also an undertaking of stupendous courage and nobility. For a very short time, when the musicians of such adventurous rock groups as the Soft Machine and King Crimson made common cause with young jazz musicians, it seemed that the attention of a large audience might be a possibility. Keith Tippett, for example, appeared on BBC Television's *Top of the Pops* show with King Crimson in 1970, shortly before filling the Lyceum Theatre for a concert by his fifty-piece group Centipede, which included King Crimson's Robert Fripp and the Soft Machine's Robert Wyatt alongside a squadron of free improvisers. But those hopes were short-lived. Attention moved elsewhere and the children of *Ascension* were forced to devise alternative means of securing their audiences, with varying degrees of success.

The successor to *Ascension* was called *Meditations*, another suite whose subtitles indicated the nature of the work: 'The Father and the Son and the Holy Ghost', 'Compassion',

'Love', 'Consequences' and 'Serenity'. For this recording, made in November 1965, the quartet had been joined by Pharoah Sanders and by a second drummer, Rashied Ali. (Sanders, the first of the new recruits, had been with Coltrane a month before the recording of *Meditations*, participating in a piece called *Om*, which begins with the expanded group intoning the sacred Hindu syllable of the title and goes on to incorporate chants from the *Bhagavad Gita*.) The folkish nature of the themes, the abandonment of a regular metre in favour of free rhythms and the sometimes frenzied interplay of the two saxophones were indications that Coltrane had been listening closely to the work of Albert Ayler, who had arrived in New York the previous year and had been acclaimed as the next significant figure in the avant garde. Ayler's album titles – *Spiritual Unity, Bells, Spirits Rejoice* – indicated a congruence with Coltrane's theological direction, and the older man appeared to view his musical methods as a means with which to refresh his own means of expression. Coltrane and Sanders both played percussion instruments on *Meditations*, a further indication of the leader's desire to thicken the rhythmic base.

The addition of Sanders and Ali created controversy since in terms of technique and experience neither was considered to be within measuring distance of the incumbents. Nor were the arguments confined to critics and audiences on the periphery. Elvin Jones, indeed, was rendered so uneasy by Ali's presence that, four years after beginning the journey via which the quartet became one of the handful of leading jazz groups, *Meditations* was his last studio recording with the group before his departure early in 1966. Sanders's style, which veered from a guttural writing to a priestly wail, appeared to have a considerable effect on his leader's approach to his instrument: the owner of the most distinctive tenor saxophone sound in the world suddenly became difficult to distinguish, at times, from the newcomer.

Sanders and Ali stayed with Coltrane until the leader's untimely death from liver cancer in July 1967 at the age of forty, participating in the series of live and studio recordings – *Kulu Se Mama*, *Live in Japan*, *Stellar Regions*, *Interstellar Space*, and *The Olatunji Concert* – which remain a puzzle to many of those most intimately affected by his earlier work. Increasingly stripped of narrative coherence in favour of a restless quest for spiritual resolution, with passages of great lyric beauty (such as the final movement of *Meditations*) separated by long stretches of furious free blowing, they seem likely to resist plausible analysis for some time to come.

Curiously, Eric Dolphy typified the significant element of jazz that did not fall under the spell of *Kind of Blue*. Dolphy was one of Coltrane's greatest friends, and his contribution to the Village Vanguard sessions is always stimulating but without really fitting into the group's overall approach. His playing represented an alternative tendency, one that grew more directly from bebop.

His compositions and his solos, particularly on bass clarinet, were angular and unpredictable, elliptical and often unresolved. The composition known as 'Miles' Mode', played twice during the Vanguard sessions and credited to Coltrane but believed to have come from Dolphy's pen, is a brief theme constructed from a two-bar twelve-tone row which is immediately repeated in retrograde motion: one of serialism's standard techniques. A single four-bar statement leads directly into improvisations based on the Dorian mode (hence the title), but the theme's leaping intervals have a flavour far more characteristic of Dolphy's highly personal melodic sense than of Coltrane's. Dolphy's harmonic instincts led him to prefer oblique chromaticisms that often made it seem, when he was elaborating on a familiar tune, as though he were playing in a distantly related key.

Ecstasy was not his goal. He was after a purely musical resolution. For all his fondness for filling his solos with twisting rivers of notes, there was an inner austerity and a rigour about Dolphy's music that set him apart from Coltrane's outpourings. His ear for creative dissonance would have made him a wonderful partner for Thelonious Monk (whose tunes were part of his repertoire), and perhaps it is no coincidence that among his finest recordings are two albums in which he performs the music of highly individualistic pianist-composers who often appear to be flirting with bitonality: George Russell's *Ezz-thetic* and Andrew Hill's *Point of Departure*.

Russell may have functioned as the midwife of modal jazz, but the music he made for himself sounded nothing like *Kind of Blue* or the developments that followed from it. The series of sextet and septet albums he made for Riverside in the early 1960s – *Stratusphunk*, *Ezz-thetic*, *The Stratus Seekers* and *The Outer View* – as well as a remarkable concert recorded at Beethoven Hall in Stuttgart in 1965 with a septet including Don Cherry, were demanding in a way that

Kind of Blue or even *A Love Supreme* were not, at least if the listener chose to opt for an easier listening experience. Like his earlier Jazz Workshop pieces, they were carefully constructed, with great attention to detail, and tough to play: spiky, brainy, often shot through with unsettling dissonance, and a wonderful challenge to the creative soloist. The Stuttgart concert includes a 25-minute suite in which a series of jazz standards – 'Bags' Groove', 'Confirmation' and 'Round Midnight' – are subjected to the Lydian concept, with results that are sometimes startling and highly rewarding.

Other composers and leaders believed that the future lay in more complexity, not less. Usually they were musicians with early training in classical music, such as André Hodeir, the French critic and composer whose 1950s recordings for Vogue and Savoy, with both French and American musicians, still sound exceptionally thoughtful and fascinating. In 1964 David Mack, an English composer, recorded an album titled *New Directions* in which all the compositions are based on the techniques of serialism, to which the soloists are encouraged to adhere. Don Ellis, a young trumpeter who distinguished himself on several of Russell's Riverside albums and later led a popular big band which won a hippie following for its exploration of Indian rhythms and tonalities, recorded twelve-tone pieces with his trio and quartet in the early 1960s. These men have no real heirs today.

In a series of brilliant recordings for Blue Note throughout the 1960s, and then again in a brief resurgence before his death in 2007, the pianist Andrew Hill created pieces that bent the angles of Monk's compositional approach into new and intriguing shapes. *Black Fire*, *Judgement*, *Smoke Stack*, *Compulsion* and *Time Lines* are works of great depth and originality. Adhering to jazz's most exigent intellectual traditions and with no room for compromise, they are still listened to and admired for their combination of humanity and ascetic rigour.

Hodeir, Mack and Ellis, however, share the fate of the original Third Stream composers, who are remembered only by the small number of listeners for whom the music's value tends to increase in proportion to its complexity and degree of difficulty, and to whom the Davis/Coltrane approach represented an unacceptably easy option.

Bill Evans turned thirty in August 1959; he spent the summer moving between club and studio gigs as a sideman with Tony Scott, Jimmy Giuffre, Chet Baker and Lee Konitz. It was at a recording session with Tony Scott in October that he found himself teamed with Scott LaFaro, a twenty-three-year-old bassist, and the drummer Paul Motian. LaFaro, born in Newark, New Jersey, had gone out on tour with the Buddy Morrow band at the age of seventeen, and had played in Los Angeles with Harold Land and Barney Kessel before hitting the road again, first with Chet Baker and then with Benny Goodman. Motian, a year younger than Evans, was from Long Island. He had taken part in Evans's very first recording session, for the bandleader Jerry Wald, four years earlier, and they had played together in Tony Scott's group before Evans invited the drummer to participate in his first album for the Riverside label, *New Jazz*

Conceptions, in 1956, with Teddy Kotick on bass (Sam Jones and Philly Joe Jones would provide the support for its successor, *Everybody Digs Bill Evans*, two years later). In between the sessions for *Kind of Blue*, Evans and Motian had shared the bandstand at the Village Vanguard as part of a quintet led by Konitz and Warne Marsh.

Neither Motian nor LaFaro was with Evans when the pianist began his new career as the leader of a trio with a three-week engagement at Basin Street East, a nightclub on East 49th Street in New York, opposite the Goodman orchestra. The bassist and drummer on opening night, both recommended by Miles Davis, were Jimmy Garrison and Kenny Dennis. But the club's treatment of the trio was so poor that both men left within the week, to be followed by a succession of replacements – 'four drummers and seven bass players, or something like that,' Evans remembered – before LaFaro and Motian arrived to give birth to a group that would change the way piano trios go about their work.

Evans had no interest in the old model of 'piano with rhythm accompaniment', as the labels of 78rpm records used to have it. A few of his predecessors, notably the bebop pioneers Bud Powell and Thelonious Monk, had encouraged their drummers, in particular, to play a more prominent and creative role in the music, drawing a particularly strong response from Max Roach and Art Blakey. Ahmad Jamal's sense of space, so greatly admired by Davis, allowed a trio to breathe in a different kind of way and brought out the contributions of his colleagues. By and large, however, two-thirds of the membership of most piano trios simply kept time and supplied a reliable harmonic foundation.

Displays of inventiveness were discouraged, at least while the pianist was holding forth.

What Evans wanted was a group in which all three members shared an equal creative interest, a conversation between three voices. The pianist's name might be on the flyers and the marquee, and the drummer's solos might be few and far between, but each musician would be free to use his imagination to enrich and direct the music. In Motian, whose work he knew well, and LaFaro, a young virtuoso, he found the ideal accomplices, and over a period of twenty months they would bring into being a form of jazz which sacrificed none of the music's strengths while raising levels of spontaneous interplay to new heights.

Barely a month after their first tentative steps at Basin Street East, they were in the studio to spend a day recording the nine tracks that made up an album titled *Portrait in Jazz*. The first chorus of the opening track, 'Come Rain or Come Shine', is enough to suggest that something different is happening here: Motian's light brushwork supports nothing less than a dialogue between piano and bass, Evans's probing single-note lines and close-voiced chords entwined in the sinewy bass figures with which LaFaro moves far beyond a conventional walking four-to-the-bar pulse. As the track progresses, the collective process loosens up to allow Motian to join the evolving debate. His contribution does not feature the kind of asymmetrical punctuation that characterised the work of a Roach, a Blakey or a Philly Joe Jones; instead it creates the sense that he is lightly nudging the tectonic plates of the performance. An even more remarkable initiative occurs in 'Autumn Leaves', the second track, in which

Evans and Motian stop playing in order to allow LaFaro to begin an unaccompanied solo, only to join him for a passage of a genuine three-way invention, full of counterpoint and counter-rhythms, each musician listening hard to the others. The album also featured a gorgeous dead-slow version of 'When I Fall in Love', in which all the components of the later ballad-playing approaches of Keith Jarrett and Brad Mehldau can be heard, particularly (in Jarrett's case) an octave shift in the second chorus, followed by a sudden burst of free-flying invention in which Evans's right hand tears away from the prevailing solemnity, creating dazzlingly inventive shapes that bear only the most tenuous relationship to the supporting material before the pianist switches tack to produce a strange passage of gothic left-hand tremolos. 'Blue in Green' appears as the closing track, but is already clear that while Evans has not bound himself to the new orthodoxies of modal jazz, he has incorporated many of its principles into his work, his inquisitive ear lending harmonic freshness to the most familiar standard tunes, buttressed by LaFaro's lightness of touch, flexibility of movement and astonishing imagination.

Portrait in Jazz was well received, but it would be more than a year before the trio returned to the studio. The time between was spent on tour, mostly in clubs, and their evolution is available for inspection on a bootleg recording which preserves several tunes played at Birdland between March and May 1960. The growth is readily apparent, particularly in Motian's more assertive contribution to the up-tempo pieces, and also in the way LaFaro has become even more of an equal lead voice, frequently exploiting the upper register and making his instrument sing out in a way then matched only by Charles Mingus. And those who accused Evans of emotional frigidity should have heard the trio's version of 'Speak Low', its origins closer to the driving bebop of Bud Powell and Hampton Hawes than to the intricacies of Lennie Tristano, the master of the cool school.

The trio's second studio album, *Explorations*, was recorded in February 1961, again in a single day. Despite Orrin Keepnews's recollection that Evans had a headache and was arguing with LaFaro over a topic that had nothing to do with music, the date is a perfect exposition of the progress they had made since *Portrait in Jazz*. A version of a Miles Davis tune called 'Nardis', written three years earlier for a Cannonball Adderley date on which Evans had played, demonstrates how the trio could now move as three separate meshing parts to create a single unity, full of suspensions and digressions resolved in ways both surprising and elegant.

This was, however, merely an appetiser for what was to come in the summer. On Sunday, 25 June 1961 Keepnews and a sound engineer set up their equipment in the Village Vanguard to capture the trio in action before an audience. The club had been the group's home for much of the year. Evans loved the forty-year-old Steinway piano, and appreciative audiences had been packing the little basement room. This would be the last day of that particular engagement, and they would be playing five sets: two in the afternoon and three in the evening, potentially giving the producer plenty of material from which to select the tracks for an album.

In the end two and a half hours of music were recorded and two albums were released, the first titled *Sunday at the Village Vanguard* and the second *Waltz for Debby*. Between them, they reset the bar for piano trios. Avoiding tunes that had been previously released, Evans made an interesting selection of standards and originals, including two pieces by Scott LaFaro and two by Miles Davis. Everything sounded at once perfectly synchronised and as if it were being played for the first time.

Davis's 'Milestones', the modal prototype of *Kind of Blue* and itself an example of perfection in its original form, had been covered many times – by the Gerald Wilson Orchestra and the Slide Hampton Octet, among others – and with varying degrees of sensitivity, but Evans, LaFaro and Motian turned it into the finest up-tempo example of the degree of interplay they had established in a year and a half of working together. Using the suspensions built into the composition, and taking unprecedented advantage of the mobility and intimacy of the trio format, they play wonderful rhythm and harmonic games with each other. LaFaro holds back the beat a fraction with his triple-stops on the opening sequence before supporting the eight-bar bridge with a variation on Paul Chambers's original riff and then plunging into a fantastic variety of inventions that converse with Motian's chattering kit on the one hand and with Evans's spare, sparkling piano on the other. Sometimes the bass slows down against the beat to such dramatic effect that it seems almost to send the music into reverse, only to leap into life again, spurting forward as if to race the other instruments to the next signpost. LaFaro's lengthy solo, a brilliantly intricate invention spanning the instrument's registers, is at the centre of a masterpiece: the sheer swing of the trio as they come out of his improvisation is staggering, making nonsense of claims that this group played nothing more than effete chamber-jazz. LaFaro takes the coda, too, the other instruments falling away as he spirals off until brought to earth by the bizarre laughter of a customer with a ringside seat and other things on his mind.

It was with one of LaFaro's own tunes, however, that the trio set music off in a new direction. 'Jade Visions' is an entirely appropriate title for a four-minute tone poem that starts where 'Blue in Green' left off and pushes ahead into uncharted territory: a piece so subtly conceived that it exists seemingly without melody, metre or harmonic scheme, simply unfolding according to its own logic. It would be wrong to call it a ballad, since that suggests a set of familiar conventions. In the context of the musical conventions of 1961 it could be said that 'Jade Visions' created its own little self-contained universe as LaFaro's resonant double-stops are echoed by Evans's right-hand figures and coaxed along by the gentle hissing and shushing of Motian's brushes on skin and cymbal. So unfamiliar was the mood it evoked that the second of two performances of the tune ends without anyone in the room realising; there is a pause, and then LaFaro runs his fingers across the open strings of his bass, apparently checking the tuning. This pungent yet weightless music has simply evaporated.

These were the last notes they would play together. The following Sunday night LaFaro was driving back to his parents' home in upstate New York when his car ran off an unlit road and hit a tree. He was killed instantly, aged twenty-five. Evans, heartbroken, could not bring himself to sit at a piano for the rest of the year.

Sunday at the Village Vanguard came out to a rapturous response in September 1961, followed six months later by *Waltz for Debby*. By then Evans had summoned enough energy to reform the trio, he and Motian joined in February by a new bassist, Chuck Israels. An extremely gifted player, Israels had recorded with Cecil Taylor and George Russell; in any other trio he would have made an impact, but comparisons were inevitable.

Evans spent the years until his death in 1980 making wonderful music with a succession of gifted bassists (including Gary Peacock, Eddie Gomez and Marc Johnson) and drummers (Larry Bunker, Jack DeJohnette, Marty Morell and Joe LaBarbera), but the unit of 'Milestones' and 'Jade Visions' was irreplaceable. 'What gave that trio its character was a common aim and a feeling of potential,' the pianist once said. 'The music developed as we performed, and what you heard came through actual performance.' Discipline and freedom, he said on another occasion, had to be mixed very sensitively if they were to achieve their ambitions. 'I believe all music is romantic, but if it gets schmaltzy, romanticism is disturbing. On the other hand, romanticism handled with discipline is the most beautiful kind of beauty. And I think that kind of combination was beginning to happen with this particular trio.'

Beginning to happen, he said. Bill Evans became one of the most copied musicians in jazz, yet it may be that none of the thousands of piano trios to have plied their trade around the world since he, Scott LaFaro and Paul Motian completed their last date at the Village Vanguard has come close to matching the racetrack inventiveness of 'Milestones'. 'Jade Visions', on the other hand, opened the door to a world in which generations of musicians would wrap their listeners in layers of pellucid lyricism and softly glowing texture.

10 Blue Horizon

Enter minimalism: La Monte Young and Terry Riley

Back in February 1959, a twenty-three-year-old pianist and composer was completing his master's degree at the University of California in Berkeley when he heard Miles Davis's sextet at the Blackhawk, a club on the corner of Turk and Hyde Streets in San Francisco's Tenderloin district. It was the group's last public appearance before the first of the two sessions that would produce *Kind of Blue.*

'I was very tuned in to what was going on in the jazz world in those days,' Terry Riley said half a century later, invited to recall the days when he was emerging from his studies and taking the first tentative steps on the path to becoming a founding figure of the minimalist movement and the source of a range of inspiration for the next generation. 'I was a closet jazz pianist – I played in clubs and so on, and I would always go to hear Miles or John Coltrane or Thelonious Monk when they were in San Francisco. I felt that what was going on in that particular realm was something I was also reaching out for, and that was to tune into modality.'

As a student and as a performer, Riley was involved on an intellectual and practical level with the new atonality of the European composers Karlheinz Stockhausen, Pierre Boulez and Luigi Nono, whose discoveries moved on from the twelve-tone serialism of Arnold Schoenberg, Anton Webern and Alban Berg in the first half of the twentieth century. Nevertheless he was experiencing a sensation of discomfort. 'Being an American, it didn't quite feel like it did it for me. So I was very interested in what they [the Davis group] were doing, because out of a kind of simplicity they were creating a very complex music and depending very much on the performers to do it. As a composer, Miles picked people who could realise his ideas – and not only that, but bring something of their own personality to them. He seemed to select personalities for particular pieces. He had a very specific way of working, which I found tremendously interesting, where the composer presents ideas and then lets the piece blossom out of the creative effort of the group. I wanted to do something like that myself during those days.'

The Blackhawk, he remembered, was an archetypal jazz joint. 'You couldn't see across the room for the smoke. It had a low ceiling and it was always densely packed when Miles was in town. His performance method interested me a lot. I was really taken with the fact that there was a kind of informality and yet a highly structured thing going on. He would often play with his back to the audience and when he got through with his solo he'd walk over to the bar. The other musicians were playing but he was always paying attention to what was going on. What I remember, too, was the very interesting way that the musicians worked together. It was highly disciplined but at the same time it felt very free. It wasn't constrained by the discipline. And, of course, it was some of the greatest playing that was being done by any performers anywhere, in any field.'

Soon afterwards Riley began playing with a rehearsal

band whose repertoire featured 'So What' and 'All Blues' from *Kind of Blue*. Their members included a young saxophonist, Jon Gibson, who would go to spend forty years as a key member of the Philip Glass Ensemble; a drummer, Peter Magadini, who later wrote books on polyrhythmic theory; Al Bent, a trombonist who went on to record with the vibraphonist Cal Tjader; and another saxophonist, Mel Martin, who became a stalwart of the Bay Area jazz community and organised big bands for Dizzy Gillespie, Benny Carter, Freddie Hubbard and McCoy Tyner. 'We'd meet once or twice a week,' Riley said, 'and we were playing Miles charts, Ornette Coleman charts, Coltrane charts. I was very into this and around 1963 I wrote a piece called "Tread on the Trail", which was kind of inspired by that whole idea.'

Riley had responded immediately to the realisation that Davis (with the help of Gil Evans and George Russell) was slowing down the music's harmonic movement. 'I was very interested in that, and of course what it really points to is the longer form. When you get into modality, you can make pieces of great length because there's a stasis in the music which doesn't make the performer restless to go on somewhere; you're just living in this beautiful modal environment. So I was very interested in the possibilities of the modal form. At this time I'd also become interested in the music of India and North Africa, Arab music, where of course the tradition for thousands of years has been modality and the musicians have very sophisticated ways of dealing with it. I don't know how aware of this Miles was, but he must have heard something.'

At Berkeley he came into contact with La Monte Young, another student of composition, theory and counterpoint. Born in Idaho in 1935, the same year as Riley, Young had spent his student years in Los Angeles, where he played the alto saxophone in jazz groups with such young musicians as Eric Dolphy, Don Cherry and Billy Higgins, who were destined to be among the most influential figures in the avant-garde wave that burst over jazz at the end of the 1950s. 'La Monte had a very serious affair with jazz before he came to UC Berkeley,' Riley said. 'He was influenced by Coltrane, for sure, and of course the modal direction of Coltrane became so strong and all the permutation he found in scalic movement was also something that La Monte had tried to mine in his own music. He had a big debt to Coltrane but his playing was also unique and original – it was as different from Coltrane as, say, Ornette's is.'

By the time Riley met him, however, Young was 'easing out of jazz' and towards the exploitation of sounds closer to those that had permeated his childhood in Idaho. 'The very first sound that I recall hearing was the sound of the wind blowing through the chinks and around the log cabin in Idaho where I was born,' Young wrote. 'I've always considered this among my most important early experiences. Since I couldn't see it and didn't know what it was, I questioned my mother about it for hours. During my childhood there were certain sound experiences of constant frequency that have influenced my musical ideas and development: the sound of insects; the sound of telephone poles and motors, sounds produced by steam escaping, such as my mother's tea kettle and the sound of whistles and signals from trains;

and resonations set off by the natural characteristics of particular geographic areas such as canyons, valleys, lakes and plains. Actually, the first sustained single tone, at a constant pitch, without a beginning or end, that I heard as a child was the sound of telephone poles – the hum of wires.'

Young had studied dodecaphony at Los Angeles City College and his study of Webern led him to conclusions that created an interest in what he called 'long-tone music', already reflected in early compositions such as *for Brass* (1957) and *Trio for Strings* (1958), but it was surely those earlier sonic affinities, drawn from landscape and environment, together with the equally influential use of psychotropic drugs (including mescaline and marijuana), that helped draw him away from the formalistic complexities of serialism and modern jazz towards the blues in its most unadorned forms and the drones used in Indian and North African music, where long tones and clusters – either implied or stated – were the keystones.

'He was a very good blues player and he showed me ideas about the blues that I hadn't considered before,' Riley said. 'The blues can be a modal form, too, and of course with Miles it really did turn into that, so it almost becomes a whole performance on the I chord, or with the IV chord implied. So when I really started to get interested in blues, that pulled me further towards modality.' Riley also wrote his own long-tone piece for string quartet, based on the sound of foghorns drifting from the waterfront up to his apartment on Protrero Hill.

In 1959 Young won a scholarship to study with Stockhausen at the Darmstadt composers' institute in Germany, where he met John Cage; as a result of that encounter, a conceptual element involving playfulness and indeterminacy entered his work, to be combined with his existing preoccupations. Some of his new pieces dispensed with all recognisable musical material, such as *Poem for Chairs, Tables, Benches, etc*, which consisted of instructions to move furniture around for twenty minutes. On his return he used a Berkeley travel scholarship to settle in New York, where he became involved with the Fluxus group of conceptual artists, who were also heavily influenced by Cage; his next group of pieces included *Composition 1960 No 7*, in which two notes – B and F sharp – are to be held 'for a long time', and *Composition 1960 No 10*, with its single instruction: 'Draw a straight line and follow it'.

In San Francisco, Riley had been experimenting with tape recorders, using methods borrowed from Stockhausen but to very different effect; his first tape piece, *Mescalin Mix* (1960–2), was a low-tech adaptation of *musique concrète* using sounds from various sources, including laughter and explosions, along with manipulation of tape speed by hand. He included Young, just back from Germany and about to leave for New York, among the performers on *Two Pianos and Five Tape Recorders* (1960), recorded live in the Berkeley concert hall. Tape interested him as a means of composing, he said, 'because it was a way to do something a little bit farther out than just writing pieces and it was doing something like sculpture – you could build on it and you could listen to it. Then again, you didn't have multitracking: everything was mono, so the only thing you could do was sound-on-sound, which generates a lot of distortion very quickly.' Rather than representing a technical handicap, that distortion would become a primary element of the process. The methods he was developing, he said, 'liberated sound as a texture to manipulate'.

In 1962 he went to Europe, spending time in Spain and Morocco before basing himself in Paris, where he earned a living by playing piano in an artists' bar in the Place Pigalle and in a band that performed for floor shows at US Air Force bases. In Paris he ran into a playwright friend from San Francisco, Kenneth Dewey, who invited him to provide the music for a play called *The Gift*, to be performed at the Théâtre des Nations in Paris for three nights that summer. Through Dewey he gained access to the electronic music workshop at ORTF, the French national broadcasting company, where one of the engineers introduced him to the technique of running a loop of tape between two machines, one on 'record' and the other on 'play', to create a build-up of sound. Riley called it 'time-lag accumulation technique', and it was to become one of the most significant discoveries in modern music.

The story of Dewey's play was that of something – the gift – being passed on from one actor to another, with a minimal amount of written dialogue and a lot of scope for improvisation. Dewey had been in Rome, working with the Living Theatre troupe, and some of the actors accompanied him to Paris, where he invited Riley to create music that would become part of the presentation.

Only a day or two before meeting the playwright, Riley had bumped into the trumpeter Chet Baker in a pool room on the rue Pigalle, adjoining the booking agency on which both men were dependent for work. At this point in his career, aged thirty-four, Baker was already a very tarnished idol. After his successes of the 1950s, when he was regularly being named the world's top trumpeter in magazine readers' polls, he had been brought low by what would prove to be a lifelong addiction to heroin. The cool, clean hipster with high cheekbones and a spotless white T-shirt captured for album covers and publicity photographs by the camera of William Claxton was already a bruised and crumpled relic of his former self. Eighteen months earlier, Baker had been released from jail in Lucca, Italy, after being convicted of narcotics offences. Reluctant to return to the United States, where he had fallen so far from fashion as to be virtually invisible and was despised by a large proportion of the jazz community, who believed that he had done little more than plagiarise Davis's early style, he remained in Europe, moving from gig to gig and picking up rhythm sections as he went. After meeting and marrying an English dancer in Italy, he tried to settle in London but again fell foul of the authorities; arrested on a charge of receiving stolen cocaine, he was deported to the country of his choice, which turned out to be France, where a small audience was still in thrall to what remained of his boyish good looks and his air of poetic dissipation. After being fired from a gig at the Blue Note, a smart club on the Champs-Elysées, he was hired by Le Chat Qui Pêche, a Left Bank dive, where he remained for several months. When Riley asked him to join the cast of *The Gift*, and to help him provide the music, he agreed.

The wealthy Dewey had hired a country house outside Paris for the actors and production staff, with a barn in which preparations and rehearsals began. Riley would spend his days at the ORTF studios, working on tapes which he would take to the château to play to the actors. At first Baker was severely unsettled by the unfamiliar environment; a musician who had grown up playing standard tunes was being thrown into an artistic environment in which the rules were being made up as the production took shape. Once Dewey had explained what was going on, however, he made an effort to participate.

'Chet said, "Far out, man. Far out. This is some far-out shit,"' Riley recalled. 'To begin with he thought it was kind of a crazy idea, because the whole project was quite avant garde for the time, and he wasn't prepared for that aspect of it, having to be a musician and also an actor. It was quite daunting for him in the beginning, but then he seemed to really like it.'

Riley's method was to record Baker and then to bring his recently acquired studio techniques to bear on the tapes. The first piece was a slow blues duet for trumpet and double bass, followed by a version of 'So What', the lead track of *Kind of Blue*, performed at the request of Riley, who had heard the group play it at Le Chat Qui Pêche. Riley cut the tape into loops of different lengths and re-recorded them on top of each other to form a layering effect. He added the voice of one of the actors, speaking a line from the play, and snatches of sound previously used in *Mescalin Mix*.

'The idea was that this would be built into layers of sound that they could improvise within the play,' he said.

'Sometimes the tape music could be going on by itself. Sometimes a musician would come in and improvise with it. Or at other times the whole band would improvise and we'd fade out the tape. When we actually did the performance, we had one tape recorder playing on stage. It could be picked up and moved around by the actors as a prop. It was destroyed on the last night of the performance. One of the actors was picking it up and throwing it on the floor and saying "What an experience!" each time he'd thrown it down. It survived the first few times and kept playing.' Typically, Baker failed to show up for the opening night and Riley had to understudy his role as the bandleader, using a lavatory plunger as a prop in place of a trumpet.

Released on compact disc forty-five years after it was recorded, the music for *The Gift* tends to come as a revelation to those who imagine that such techniques as looping, sampling and modifying recorded sounds belong to later eras, to such idioms as dub reggae, electronica and hip-hop. The opening duet for trumpet and bass, a prowling slow blues, sounds uncannily like some of the prophetic work on Miles Davis's *Ascenseur pour l'echafaud* soundtrack, particularly in the strikingly lavish use of echo on Baker's horn, until, very quickly, Riley's looping strategies come into play, making the listener feel as though he or she were walking through rooms filled with mirrors: the sort of effect that film-makers would recreate in visual terms to simulate disorientation once the influence of LSD visions had made its way into mainstream cinema. As the layers build up, particularly when Riley is isolating and multiplying Baker's unaccompanied trumpet, the result resembles one of Giovanni

Gabrieli's vaulting antiphonal works for brass choir, removed from the balconies of St Mark's Church in Venice and relocated to a psychedelic funhouse.

Riley's next project made his reputation. One evening in the spring of 1964, a few weeks after his return from Europe, he was sitting in a San Francisco city bus on the way to his rent-paying gig as a ragtime pianist in a waterfront bar, the Gold Street Saloon, when the outline of a piece that was to alter the future of music took shape in his mind. 'You know,' he said, 'a lot of times when you're writing a piece, you're trying to get an idea going and you're trying various things, and finally something will gel. With *In C* I was sitting on the bus, looking at the people on the sidewalk, and I just heard the whole thing, as if it had been presented to me from the heavens. I haven't had that experience many times in my life. So after work I rushed home and jotted it down.'

What he heard and jotted down was the idea for a series of fifty-three short musical figures, to be performed in sequence by a group of players – any number of them, using any kind of instruments – who could choose their moment of entry and the number of times they repeated each motif before moving on. The sequence started with three ornamented Es in the treble clef, progressing to other note-combinations that are sometimes more complex, sometimes even simpler (the thirtieth is a plain dotted semibreve C), and cover a range of two octaves. Despite the considerable interpretative freedom, however, there were guidelines from the composer: a group of thirty-five players is optimal, although it can be larger or smaller; it is important not to hurry through the figures but to listen to the other players and to find ways of interlocking with them; they should not race ahead or lag behind but try to stay within two or three figures of each other; they should exploit the extremes of the available dynamic range but attempt to raise and lower the overall volume together; if some chance combination seems to be working, by all means stick with it for a while; and an average performance time of between forty-five minutes and an hour and a half suggests that each figure should be repeated for somewhere between forty-five seconds and a minute and a half, or longer. A footnote advises the performers to practise the figures together in order to ensure that they are being played correctly, and in strict rhythm. Transposing any of the figures up or down an octave is also permitted. And Riley adds: 'The group should aim to merge into a unison at least once or twice during the performance. At the same time, if the players seem to be consistently too much in the same alignment of a pattern, they should try shifting their alignment by an eighth note or quarter note with what's going on in the rest of the ensemble.' When a player reaches the end, he or she should repeat the final pattern until the rest have also got there, at which point a series of crescendos and diminuendos permits the performers to fall silent as they wish.

One of the key elements of the work was the last to be added. It is easy to imagine the fifty-three figures floating in and out of each other in a rather woozy way, like clouds overlapping at different altitudes. But it was one of the musicians involved in its world première who provided the device that pinned the piece down and bound it into its characteristic form, without compromising its spirit. Steve Reich, a twenty-eight-year-old drummer and composition student who had moved from his native New York, where he had studied at Juilliard, to Mills College in San Francisco, had met Riley a few months earlier. Reich had studied with Berio at Mills, acquiring a thorough under-standing of twelve-tone theory and technique, but his inquisitive ears were leading him in other directions: in par-ticular towards the Coltrane quartet, which he saw on more than fifty occasions, usually at the Jazz Workshop, and towards the West African polyrhythms which found an echo in the work of Elvin Jones.

It was Reich who suggested that figures of which *In C* consisted should be performed over an unvarying ostinato created by even quavers (eighth notes) played on the top two Cs of the piano keyboard. Performed by Reich himself on a Wurlitzer electric piano at the first performance, this turned out to be the binding agent that brought the piece into sharp focus, particularly to ears dismayed by serialism and atonality. The combination created a shifting mosaic of sound, its density and textures constantly in flux. But, cru-cially, it had a consonance that, for all the formal challenges it contained and the uncertainties inherent in its superstruc-ture, made it essentially attractive to a listener's ear. *In C* would become one of the key works of Californian mini-malism, but the austerity of its underpinning (that ham-mered ostinato) was relieved by the richness of a stream of sound ebbing and flowing as the figures overlapped. Demanding on paper, in practice *In C* required only goodwill on the listener's part to yield its novel pleasures; no knowledge of the history or the theory of the twentieth-century avant garde was required.

The piece received its first performances, in versions lasting around ninety minutes, at the Tape Music Centre on Divisidero Street in San Francisco on 2 and 6 November 1964. For the première Riley wore orange trousers and a purple bow tie; the audience of about five hundred was similarly attired. 'It was sort of the beginning of the psychedelic dress-up era,' the composer Morton Subotnick, a friend and colleague, remembered. A policeman loitering outside was invited in and disabused of his suspicion that drug-taking and nude dancing were going on. The ensemble included the saxophonists Jon Gibson (soprano) and Sonny Lewis (tenor), Stan Shaff and Phil Winsor on trumpets, Subotnik on clarinet, Pauline Oliveros on accordion, Mel Weitsman on recorder and trumpet, and five keyboardists: Jeannie Brechan, Warner Jepson, James Lowe, Ramon Sender and Reich.

There were few follow-up performances until four years later, when Riley led a group of musicians from the New Music Centre at the State University of New York in Buffalo through *In C* at Carnegie Recital Hall. That aroused the interest of John McClure, the director of Columbia Records' Masterworks series, who arranged for Riley and the ensemble to record it as part of a series called *Music of Our Time*. Under the supervision of the young composer David Behrman, it was recorded with appropriate care in Columbia's midtown studio at 49 East 52nd Street, with the principal engineering duties performed by the pipe-smoking veteran Fred Plaut, who had performed the same role on the two *Kind of Blue* sessions at East 30th Street. 'I remember Fred had a kind of banker-ish air,' Riley said. 'It seemed odd that he was involved in this kind of project – he was much in demand for classical sessions.'

Handsomely packaged, as befitted the Masterworks series, its gatefold sleeve presented across its exterior panels a nicely suggestive graphic illustration by Billy Bryant depicting clouds passing beneath empty staves. On the inside the fifty-three musical figures faced an explanatory note by the producer, giving a brief biography of the composer and an outline of the work. 'The quality of the music,' Behrman wrote, 'depends on spontaneous interaction within the ensemble. A good performance reveals a teeming world of groups and subgroups forming, dissolving and reforming within a modal panorama which shifts, over a period of about forty-five to ninety minutes, from C to E to C to G.'

Given a subtle prominence on the front of the jacket was a quote from a review written after the work's first public performance four years earlier, demonstrating the prescience of the *San Francisco Chronicle*'s music critic, Alfred Frankenstein: 'You feel that you have never done anything all your life but listen to this music and as if that is all there is or will ever be . . .' The back carried an enthusiastic endorsement by a different kind of critical voice: that of Paul Williams, a rock critic well known to the readers of *Rolling Stone*, the counter-culture magazine set up in San Francisco only a year earlier and already influential among a new community of listeners hungry for innovation. 'All right, so let's say that what we have here is a "trip",' Williams wrote, 'a voluntary, unpredictable absorbing experience, one which brings together parts of one's self perhaps previously unknown to each other. Is this a pleasant trip, this business of being an audience to this performance? Yes, I believe it is . . .' He concluded: 'The stuff here is close enough to the basics of what music is to be listened to and appreciated with no musical background of any sort. It's kind of like not necessarily knowing if you dig ballet, but definitely liking the way the girl across the table moves her hands. No preconceptions, you just dig it. Welcome in.'

This first recorded version of *In C* was performed by a group consisting of Riley on soprano saxophone plus ten young musicians from Buffalo playing trumpet, trombone, flute, oboe, bassoon, clarinet, viola, vibraphone, marimba and piano. At this distance it is easy to spot the name of Jon Hassell, a twenty-seven-year-old Memphis-born trumpeter who had received his masters' degree from the Eastman School of Music in Rochester, New York and then spent two years studying under Stockhausen in Cologne before arriving in Buffalo to take a doctorate in musicology.

The recording was built up through overdubbing. All eleven musicians performed a first version of the work, with the piano dropping out for the second recording and the piano plus three others for the third, the remaining performers synchronising their playing to the earlier tracks through the use of headphones. The sound of the music in this recording is clear and bright, defined more by the high woodwind and the tuned percussion instruments than by the brass or the bassoon, and tending towards the kind of tintinnabulation associated with the characteristic timbre of the Balinese and Javanese gamelan ensemble, already a favourite with the sort of adventurous young composers and intrepid listeners who bought albums on the Folkways and Nonesuch Explorer labels (particularly the latter's *Music from the Morning of the World* and *Golden Rain*, which brought Indonesian music to a Western audience in the 1960s).

Gradually the reputation of *In C* spread. Toru Takemitsu in Japan and Cornelius Cardew in England supervised performances. Five years after the album's release, a younger composer named Walter Boudreau, struggling to establish a performing group called l'Infonie in Quebec City, came into possession of a copy and responded immediately to its propositions. 'Remember that these were the "hard" structural-complex-serial years where one had to come up with the most complicated scores and scientific explanations in order to make up for the lack of music that was so evident in the twelve-tone chain-gang extravaganzas,' Boudreau wrote. 'So, yes, this piece was like a breath of fresh air, badly needed, sort of an oasis before moving on to other musical perspectives.' L'Infonie's psychedelic big-band version, recorded in 1970, bears evidence of the presence of musicians trained in jazz, rock and classical music among a very different line-up, including four trumpets, four trombones, five saxophones, electric guitar, bass guitar, four percussionists, a story-teller and two painters. 'We were all young and making our way in the music world,' their leader wrote. 'Levels of performance were hazardous, if not uncontrollable.' The raw enthusiasm of their performance, with its clattering and yowling surges and occasional

Dadaist touches, was hardly impaired when, with five of the fifty-three figures still to go, their tape ran out.

Subsequent versions – and there would be several – opted for different timbral approaches, including heavy-metal guitars. Gradually the work became so celebrated, so firmly embedded in the canon of modern music, that in 1990 Riley supervised a twenty-fifth anniversary concert in San Francisco in which the piece was played by a thirty-one-piece ensemble including Henry Kaiser and Riley's son Gyan on guitars and the entire Kronos Quartet, among other old friends and associates. Taken at a slightly reduced pace, this version has a more languid, less insistent air.

After the world première of *In C* in 1964, Riley moved back to New York, where he found La Monte Young, who had installed himself there four years earlier. Having left Berkeley on a fellowship to study with John Cage at the New School, Young was writing pieces that showed the increased influence of the sustained tones that had attracted him in childhood. Coltrane's soprano saxophone playing had persuaded him to switch from alto to sopranino (another E flat instrument). Riley, too, had started playing the soprano saxophone. Both men had listened to Coltrane's work on the instrument in modal pieces such as 'My Favourite Things', 'Olé' and 'Afro Blue', and the horn's distinctive piping, reedy sound seemed the perfect voice through which to channel the growing impact of Indian music.

'I started playing soprano,' Riley said, 'when I was working with Sonny Lewis in San Francisco – I guess this was about the time I wrote *In C* – and I wrote these patterns out for Sonny to play and I recorded them and then put them through different delay processes. This was right after I'd worked with Chet Baker, and I really wanted to continue this kind of work with modal music and delays. They were done for Sonny Lewis but I decided that I couldn't do it with another player, I really had to learn to play the saxophone in order to get what I wanted out of the music. It was too hard to give direction and I wanted it to be coming from a spontaneous place in myself as I was performing, to actually develop the piece compositionally. That's why I ended up learning to play the saxophone. I got a few lessons from Jon Gibson and then I just taught myself.'

But Riley had not relinquished his interest in tape-enhanced music. The first album to appear under his name, released in 1966 (two years before *In C*) by the deceptively titled Mass Art label in an edition of a thousand copies, was called *Reed Streams* and included two pieces. The first, 'Untitled Organ', is a twenty-minute performance in which small figures are repeated with minor variations and permutations, overlayed to produce time-shift effects, prefiguring many performances by Riley in the late 60s and early 70s, often delivered as all-night concerts, which went under the title of *Poppy Nogood and His Phantom Band*. In the second piece, 'Dorian Reeds', Riley unveils his work on the soprano saxophone, again using his time-lag accumulation system to build layers of sound from simple circular phrases.

Other equally significant pieces were going unheard by the world at large. In 1965 he produced *Bird of Paradise*, built around an almost subliminally brief snatch of

'Shotgun', an R&B hit on the Soul label, a Motown subsidiary, by the tenor saxophonist Jr Walker and his All Stars. Two years later there was *You're Nogood*, based on a medium-tempo boogaloo-soul song of that name from an album by the Harvey Averne Dozen. Neither of these pieces was released on record at all until the innovations they proposed had long been absorbed into the mainstream.

Whereas Walker's 'Shotgun' is represented by a fragment that could be identified only by those intimate with the original record, Averne's 'You're No Good' is heard almost in its entirety in Riley's twenty-minute version, its components extended, repeated and distorted while more or less retaining the original pulse. At a pinch, and with a bit of creativity, you could dance to it, which was no coincidence since it was created at the behest of an unusually enlightened discothèque owner in Philadelphia who had enjoyed one of the first of Riley's all-night keyboard performances at the city's College of Art. So here we have the ancestor of the twelve-inch disco mixes that, a decade later, were being created by a new generation of pop producers – the likes of Tom Moulton, Larry Levan, Shep Pettibone and Frankie Knuckles – who remixed and added length and instrumental breaks to popular tracks by such artists as Sylvester, Evelyn 'Champagne' King and Gloria Gaynor in order to satisfy the requirements of dancers from New York's Studio 54 to London's Embassy Club.

It was in New York that La Monte Young created his Dream House, a setting for experiments with continuous sound and light, in which his Theatre of Eternal Music performed extended drone pieces. Among the pieces he created during that era were 'The Second Dream of the High-Tension Line Stepdown Transformer', which in its recorded form consisted of eight muted trumpets playing drones for seventy-seven minutes, and 'The Well Tuned Piano', a piece lasting several hours and played on an instrument tuned to just intonation: minimalist in materials, if maximalist in scale. In 1966 he created 'Drift Studies', a piece in which two sine-wave drones created intervals according to his precise calculations.

Young had been joined by John Cale, a twenty-one-year-old prodigy who had played viola in the National Youth Orchestra of Wales, graduated from Goldsmiths College in London and in 1963, on the recommendation of Aaron Copland, received a scholarship to study with Iannis Xenakis at the annual summer school in Tanglewood, Massachusetts. Before leaving Goldsmiths in the summer of 1963 he had organised a concert of new music at which he performed a piano piece by Young titled 'X for Henry Flynt'; this involved the player linking his hands and smashing both forearms on the keyboard, then repeating it X number of times (the precise number of repetitions being at the player's discretion). As the dissonances and harmonics from the grand piano filled the hall, the more vociferous members of the audience rose up and tried, without success, to separate the pianist from the instrument (not the last time Cale would provoke his listeners into a heated response). At the same concert, Cornelius Cardew played Young's 'Piano Piece for David Tudor No. 2'; both were billed, almost certainly with accuracy, as first British performances. During his time at Tanglewood later that summer Cale attempted to write a piece for all eighty-eight pianos kept at the academy, some of which he planned to float on barges on a nearby lake; not surprisingly, the idea went unrealised.

When the course ended Cale made straight for New York, where Young invited him to join Marian Zazeela, Terry Riley, the violinist Tony Conrad, the percussionist Angus MacLise and Young himself in the Theatre of Eternal Music, then engaged in rehearsals in the composer's loft on the Lower West Side. Young was on the brink of forsaking the saxophone; by the summer of 1964 he and Zazeela were contributing their voices to music which consisted of extended explorations of the properties of drones, made easier by the presence of violin and viola. Conrad bowed double-stops, playing two strings at once, while Cale filed down the bridge of his instrument in order to be able to play three strings simultaneously. Both instruments were amplified through contact microphones to the brink of distortion, and together they created a harsher version of the harmonic build-up provided in Indian music by the fingers and strings of a tambura, a resemblance heightened by MacLise's drumming, which was heavily influenced by a study of the techniques of the tabla and other Eastern percussion.

In a downtown milieu in which musicians, poets and film-makers mixed easily and collaboratively, Cale also found himself in close proximity to the Fluxus group of artists, a cross-media collective inspired by Dadaism and encouraged by Cage, in whose activities he had shown an interest while at Goldsmiths. Its loose and floating membership included Young and Riley, George Brecht, Nam June

Paik, George Maciunas, Yoko Ono, Joseph Beuys, the free-jazz saxophonist Peter Brötzmann and Gustav Metzger, the inventor of auto-destructive art. Within a year of Cale's arrival the Theatre of Eternal Music began playing in public, performing a series of Young's drone pieces, including 'The Tortoise: His Dreams and Journeys' and 'The Tortoise Droning Selected Pitches from the Holy Numbers for the Two Black Tigers, the Green Tiger and the Hermit', each lasting several hours.

In 1965 the group made a recording at Young's home, released thirty-five years later. 'The Day of Niagara' by the Dream Syndicate is a half-hour extract from a longer piece devoted entirely to the pursuit of the drone, the timbres and relationships shifting as individual voices enter and leave. Young, famously protective of his output, objected strongly to its release on the grounds that it came from a defective copy of the original recording and was, in any case, merely an excerpt from a greater whole which had yet to reach fruition. Yet notwithstanding the eighteen months of research and rehearsal that apparently went into the ensemble's performances, it has urgency, intensity and spontaneity; it manages to suggest the spirit of ragas, of the gamelan, of Zen chants, of the Coltrane quartet at its wildest, and of the experiments with feedback conducted by the Who's guitarist, Pete Townshend (a former art-college student and an admirer of Metzger), in such early recordings as 'Anyway Anyhow Anywhere' and 'My Generation'. There is virtually nothing to 'The Day of Niagara' except a drone; yet it contains multitudes.

*

Over on the Lower East Side, sharing an apartment at 56 Ludlow Street, Cale and Conrad also began a series of collaborative experiments, occasionally incorporating MacLise and the composer and saxophonist Terry Jennings, some of which they recorded. These, too, were exposed to the light four decades later, in a series of discs assembled by Conrad and released under Cale's name: *Sun Blindness Music*, *Dream Interpretation* and *Stainless Gamelan*. The influence of Cage is apparent in an untitled piece for prepared piano, while that of Young looms over the violin and viola drones of the twenty-minute 'Dream Interpretation'. But they were listening to rock 'n' roll records together, and in the early weeks of 1965 they attended a party at which they were introduced to Terry Phillips, the owner of Pickwick Records, who was looking for a band to promote a record he had made with an aspiring songwriter named Lou Reed. 'The Ostrich', Reed's attempt to exploit the craze for songs promoting new dances, was as basic a piece of rock 'n' roll as could be imagined, its guitar-playing so rudimentary that it almost qualified as a drone. This made it easy for Cale, switching to guitar, and Conrad, strapping on a bass guitar for the first time in his life, to provide backing for Reed's voice and lead guitar; they were joined on drums by Cale's friend Walter Di Maria, a percussionist and composer who had as little experience of playing rock 'n' roll as they had themselves, and rather less interest. Appropriately, they called themselves the Primitives.

Perhaps Cale's 'Summer Heat', recorded in 1965 and preserved on the *Sun Blindness Music* CD, comes from this period: the Welshman strums a single chord on an electric guitar for just over eleven minutes, letting the strings ring and allowing the combination of harmonics and the amplifier's distortion to create the illusion of a whole battery of instruments. Cale seems to be testing the possibilities of both his instrument and himself: the hard, aggressive strum would suffuse the music he was about to make.

Although the Primitives was a project that lasted no longer than the few weeks it took to determine that 'The Ostrich' was never going to fly, Cale and Reed established a rapport that was maintained in rehearsal sessions with Conrad, in which MacLise replaced Di Maria. Reed, a former English student at Syracuse University, had studied with the poet Delmore Schwartz and was writing lyrics in which Cale perceived a genuine originality, even though the folkish tunes to which they were set struck him as banal. The pair of them were travelling on the subway when they bumped into Sterling Morrison, a former college classmate of Reed, who added his guitar to their rehearsals. As the band coalesced, several names – the Warlocks, the Falling Spikes – were tried and rejected. Within weeks Conrad had removed himself from the group when he left the flat he shared with Cale, where he was replaced by Reed. After MacLise decided to pursue his own directions, they also acquired a new percussionist: Maureen Tucker, the sister of a friend of Reed. Gradually Cale cut down his time with Young and the Theatre of Eternal Music project, and by July he and his new partners had also settled on a permanent name, taken from a paperback found by Conrad in a New York City gutter: the Velvet Underground.

11 Dark Blue

The Velvet Underground: how art came to the discothèque

To hear *The Velvet Underground and Nico* in the early months of 1967 was to be grabbed by both arms and pulled forcefully through the doors of perception. Drugs were not a necessity. Even to ears prepared by John Coltrane, Albert Ayler, Cecil Taylor, Ravi Shankar, Bo Diddley and a first sight of Jimi Hendrix, this was something very different and, to those of an inquisitive disposition, extremely enticing.

I first saw their name in a copy of the *Village Voice*, where they were praised by the critic Richard Goldstein, whose approving words – this time from a piece in the *New York World Journal-Tribune* – were reprinted on the sleeve of that first album: 'The whole sound seems to be the product of a secret marriage between Bob Dylan and the Marquis de Sade.' He loved them, in fact. And so did I. Not because Andy Warhol had provided the cover art and become their sponsor, although that was certainly an intriguing factor (his name was equal in size to theirs on the cover – although not on the version released in Britain, where a single sleeve replaced the gatefold for reasons, presumably, of cost: the back cover became the front, the celebrated 'Peel slowly and see' banana disappearing entirely). Not because the words of their songs offered a delicious flirtation with evil, or because they were fronted on several songs by an ice-cold blonde German named Nico who was described in the credits, with ultimate cool, as a *chanteuse* – the first time the term had been used in rock 'n' roll, and possibly even outside France at all – and called, in another press cutting, 'another cooler Dietrich for another cooler generation' (they should have given the English counter-cultural journalist John Wilcock of the *East Village Other* a royalty for that irresistible come-on). The main attraction was the music itself, which contained passages that seemed to sum up everything modern music could be or was going to be. And that, in large part, was thanks to the man with long dark hair and a long dark face pictured on the sleeve and credited with playing electric viola, piano and bass guitar.

In the city in the English Midlands where I lived in the 1960s we had what was known as an 'alternative' bookshop, bravely stocking not just the British underground publications *International Times* and *Oz* but imports from the United States and elsewhere, which is how I got to read the *Voice*, the *Other* and John Sinclair's *Changes* while also buying the English edition of the Cuban revolutionary government newspaper *Granma* and the poems and essays of LeRoi Jones. That shop was a gateway to a world in which I felt at home.

Naturally, the Warhol connection did the Velvet Underground no harm. They had made a demo tape in the Ludlow Street loft before they met him, and before Maureen Tucker's arrival, including 'Venus in Furs' (sung by Cale in a British folk-rock style), 'I'm Waiting for the Man' (sung by Reed in a Greenwich Village folk-rock style) and 'Heroin'. Cale took it with him on a trip to London, but could raise no interest. He did, however, buy a selection of British 45s to take back and play to his band mates, including the Who's 'My Generation' and the Small Faces' 'Whatcha Gonna Do About It'. The result was immediate. No more folk-rock for the nascent Velvet Underground. In came the energy of distorted guitars and amplified viola. And, not coincidentally, the weird negative energy of Maureen Tucker's anti-drumming.

'Rock 'n' Roll: Everybody's Turned On' was a *Time* magazine cover headline in the spring of 1965, and by the end of that year Andy Warhol had decided that he was not going to be left out. Already familiar with Cale's participation in La Monte Young's projects, he heard the Velvet Underground accompanying underground film shows at various downtown locations. Then one of his *soi-disant* 'superstars', the poet and scene-maker Gerard Malanga, was invited by the underground film-maker Barbara Rubin to attend their first real gig, at the Café Bizarre on West 3rd Street in the Village, and ended up dancing on the stage. He was back the next night with Paul Morrissey, Warhol's manager, in tow. The following night Warhol himself showed up, with a group of acolytes. They included Nico, the German model and singer who had played a small part in Fellini's *La Dolce Vita* and had appeared on *Ready Steady Go!* to promote a single released on Immediate, the fashionable British record label run by Andrew Oldham, the Rolling Stones' manager, before becoming a recruit to the *dramatis personae* assembled at the Factory, Warhol's headquarters on East 47th Street.

It was a natural fit. In two crucial respects, the Velvet Underground were the only possible group for Warhol. First came songs reflecting their interest in the sort of transgressive activities that characterised the activities at the Factory. Second came the use of repetition and the acceptance of what the straight world would see as boredom, ennui or *la noia*: an existential angst apparently stripped of meaning. The incessant hammered piano figures and unvarying rhythm beds, not so distantly related to the pulse of *In C*, could be seen as analogues of the multiple versions of the same image (Elvis, Marilyn, car crashes, electric chairs, etc) churned out by the silkscreen printers working at the Factory. And the drones, derived from Cale's work with Young, echoed the endless, eventless dreamscapes of Warhol's films: *Empire*, *Sleep*, and so on. The members of the Velvet Underground were as capable of hanging around the Factory in a state of suspended animation as any would-be actor or poet. And from their point of view the most significant aspect of the relationship was this: if the Velvet Underground were going to pursue a career based on demolishing the unwritten rules and conventions of rock 'n' roll, then Andy Warhol would be the last person in the world to discourage them.

He invited the group to the Factory, where he offered to be, in effect, their patron: to manage them, to give them financial backing and to make them the centrepiece of a multimedia spectacle. The only catch was that he and Malanga wanted Nico to sing with them. Reservations were expressed, examined and set aside, equipment was purchased, songs were written for Nico, rehearsals were held, more expensive drugs were acquired and in March 1966 the Exploding Plastic Inevitable opened a three-week season upstairs at the Dom, a former Polish social centre on St Mark's Place in the East Village. In the separate downstairs room the attraction was Tony Scott, the clarinettist who had helped launch the career of Bill Evans and had recently released an album called *Music for Zen Meditation* (a follow-up, *Music for Yoga Meditation and Other Joys*, would appear a year later).

Around four hundred people made it upstairs on opening night, to be confronted by the Velvet Underground and Nico, plus lights, films (Warhol's *Couch* and *Vinyl*), the on-stage dancing of 'superstars' Gerard Malanga and Mary Woronov, and – between sets – a sound system that occasionally played three records at once. From the balcony, wearing a leather jacket and shades, Warhol surveyed the scene. In a sentence that summarised one of the pivotal moments of rock history, John Wilcock concluded his approving *East Village Other* review: 'Art has come to the discothèque and it will never be the same again.'

In March they began work on their first album, at the old Scepter Records studios in New York, where they recorded ten tracks in either one or two days, depending on which surviving member's testimony is to be believed. 'Produced by Andy Warhol', the sleeve would eventually boast, but at Scepter the musicians were left alone with the studio's regular engineer, who briskly discouraged them from attempting more than one take on any of the songs. In April they travelled to California, where they received an unfriendly welcome from the hippies at the Fillmore Auditorium before moving on to Los Angeles, where they re-recorded three tracks at TTG Studios in Hollywood with the aid of Tom Wilson, a genuine record producer. Wilson was used to experimentation; he had supervised records by John Coltrane and Cecil Taylor for his own Transition label before moving on to work with Bob Dylan on *Another Side*, *Bringing It All Back Home* and *Highway 61 Revisited*; he was also the man who, by adding electric instruments to Simon and Garfunkel's hitherto unadorned 'The Sound of Silence', had created one of the earliest folk-rock hits.

Back in New York, Wilson recorded a final track with the group: 'Sunday Morning', with its pretty-pretty glockenspiel and gentle melody, seems to have been a fairly transparent attempt to create a soft-rock hit single and was chosen to open the album, although Reed's lyric belied its chintzy surface. The band members would later complain that they were not given enough studio time and that Wilson was a relatively uninterested presence. They had even greater cause for dissatisfaction when the release was held up until March 1967, a year after recording had begun and more than six months after it had been completed. The sleeve art had to be retouched and reprinted when a dispute arose over the rights to a photograph of Eric Emerson, another of Warhol's superstars, projected behind the group on stage in a photograph that formed part of the rear jacket. Then Verve Records, the label to which Warhol had sold the album, decided to give first priority to the promotion of another Wilson-produced album: the debut of its other 'alternative' group, California's Mothers of Invention, whose *Freak Out!* was released in 1966. That alone may have been enough to foment the Velvets' long-standing dislike and distrust of the West Coast.

The delay did nothing, however, to diminish its impact on those susceptible to such music at such a time. The flaws in the production only enhanced its mysterious appeal. Clashing dissonances, questionable intonation and a strangely blurred sound on certain songs differentiated it from everything else in the hectic world of mid-60s popular music. Even amid the kaleidoscope of recent and contemporaneous work that included Bob Dylan's *Blonde on Blonde*, the Beatles' *Revolver*, the Beach Boys' *Pet Sounds*, the Four Tops' 'Reach Out, I'll Be There', James Brown's 'Papa's Got a Brand New Bag', *The Hums of the Lovin' Spoonful*, Jefferson Airplane's *Surrealistic Pillow* and the Jimi Hendrix Experience's *Axis: Bold As Love*, the Velvet Underground's music stood entirely apart.

As Brian Eno said years later, not very many people heard the Velvet Underground's first album but each one who did was inspired to go out and form a band. I was past the band-starting days by then, having failed a couple of years earlier in a mission to get up from the drum stool and graft a free-form alto saxophone solo loosely approximating the style of Ornette Coleman (and using a white plastic Grafton instrument just like his) on to the Bo Diddley beat that the rest of the band, temporarily minus their drummer, were trying to play to an audience of increasingly disconcerted mod dancers. But the message of *The Velvet Underground and Nico* could hardly have been clearer. Lou Reed, John Cale, Sterling Morrison, Maureen Tucker and Nico were proposing nothing less than a new way of thinking about rock 'n' roll – even better, a new way of turning it into art music without calling on the services of a George Martin to graft string quartets and Bach trumpets on to polite pop songs.

Was John Cale the first man to recognise an affinity between the harmonically reduced music on which he had been working with La Monte Young and Terry Riley and the playing of such early rock 'n' roll guitarists as Link Wray and Bo Diddley? Cale had certainly been attracted to rock 'n' roll from an early age, while pursuing his apparent vocation as a gifted young classical musician; now he recognised an opportunity to merge his interests, and the apartment on Ludlow Street became, in its way, the equivalent of Gil Evans's West 55th Street pad almost two decades earlier.

Had Lou Reed not met John Cale in 1965, it seems highly unlikely that he would have found a context in which to play the guitar solos that punctuate the album: his sudden immersion in the world of downtown artists made possible the snaking Coltraneish effort on the urgent 'Run Run Run' and the fractured atonal playing that distinguishes 'European Son (To Delmore Schwartz)'. Nor would certain of his most striking early songs, such as 'All Tomorrow's Parties', 'Heroin' and 'Venus in Furs', have received the sort of settings that made them stand out.

As it happened, Reed was a fan of avant-garde jazz. In his student days he had hosted a college radio show that he titled *Excursions on a Wobbly Rail*, after a track on one of Cecil Taylor's early albums. And the way the Velvet Underground was set up allowed him to make a connection between that influence and his love of rock 'n' roll, just as Cale brought the influence of contemporary classical and experimental music. John Coltrane and Ornette Coleman were about to meet La Monte Young and Terry Riley, on ground established by two young men with an eye on a very different audience.

Cale hated jazz. In the early days of the Velvets he had tried to persuade MacLise not to use conventional ride-cymbal patterns to carry the rhythm. He particularly adored the playing of Maureen Tucker, MacLise's replacement, because it was the opposite of 'hip' and 'swinging'. And Tucker's playing became the most obvious symbol of the difference between the Velvet Underground and every other rock group in the world in 1967.

Most drummers of the time, whatever the style of band in which they played, were interested in developing their technical prowess. A lot of them worshipped Buddy Rich, who was supposed to have the fastest hands and feet of them all. The more thoughtful admired Max Roach or Elvin Jones – or Tony Williams, who broke the hearts of a generation of young drummers in 1963 when, aged sixteen, he was hired by Miles Davis and turned out to be a virtuoso beyond compare. (Tony Williams had broken my heart, too, although the fan in me recovered fairly quickly.) Because of this overriding interest in technique, most drummers didn't have much time for someone like Ringo Starr, who ignored the textbooks and made up his own highly effective style. But Tucker took drumming very much further away from the realm of tutors and rudiments.

Perhaps she didn't mean to. She was said to admire the polyrhythms of Babetunde Olatunji, the popular African drummer, and the thunder of Bo Diddley's classic records. But, as the first post-Ringo drummer, Tucker played with an attitude that not only showed no interest in technical proficiency but actually ignored the backbeat, the very pulse of popular music. Whether she intended it or not, she became the first drummer in jazz, blues, soul music, rock 'n' roll or any of their associated forms to show no interest in anything related to the old concept of 'swing', a form of momentum that was jazz's clearest sign of its origins in African culture, and which passed into rock 'n' roll's bloodstream in a modified – and vastly simplified – form. If Louis Armstrong's Hot Five, the Duke Ellington Orchestra and the Miles Davis Sextet swung, then so, in their different ways, did Elvis Presley's band, the Rolling Stones and the Motown rhythm section. Maureen Tucker was either unwilling or unable to conform.

Invited by other members of the group to do something unorthodox, she replaced the usual practice of marking time on a ride cymbal or a hi-hat with a thudding tom-tom beat that was a distant cousin – but only distant – to the more primitive forms of R&B. She took the pedal off her bass drum, sat it on its side, and played it with a felt-headed mallet. She played standing up, like a classical percussionist – or like drummers in the earliest days of rock 'n' roll, posing for a publicity photograph or an album cover with nothing more than a snare drum and a pair of sticks alongside their fellow band members. With Tucker there were no licks, no tricks. She played what each song required, in a completely original way. In juxtaposition with everything else going on in the group, it was devastatingly effective.

Sterling Morrison may have remained the least prominent member of the group, and happy to be so, but he too was amenable to new directions. Cale spoke of his 'meticulous nature – he would work on parts, especially on the bass.' Sometime during the very early days of the Velvet Underground he and Cale recorded the piece eventually released under the title 'Stainless Steel Gamelan', ten minutes of arpeggios plucked in a striding rhythm above and below the bridge of an electric guitar, combined with the use of a Cembalet, a cheap electronic keyboard. The non-stop pealing combines the bell-like sonority of a genuine gamelan with the stern metronomic effect of the pulse from *In C*, and looks ahead to the striking arrangement of the Velvets' 'All Tomorrow's Parties', in which the binding agent of a modern classical work found a pop-music application.

The Velvet Underground were moving away from a total reliance on chord-based songs into the area of modes and drones, and they knew exactly what they were about. 'That theory about the blues La Monte had, about how all the basic chords could be played together – that was a basis for the Velvet Underground,' Cale said. 'If they were three-chord songs, I could just pick two notes on the viola that really fit for the whole song. It would give a dream-like quality to the whole thing.'

Almost every track on *The Velvet Underground and Nico* proposed its own separate and novel direction. The Beatles were doing that, too, with *Rubber Soul* and *Revolver*, but the Velvets offered surprises right from the start: those who had heard something about the band's reputation were taken aback straight away by the soft-voiced, deceptively benign opening track, 'Sunday Morning'. The musicians took real risks, and not just in the choice of lyrics that dealt with the purchase and taking of drugs or with sado-masochism as if they were among the unremarkable features of daily life.

The Velvets played rock 'n' roll that somehow wasn't. Or wasn't just yet, anyway. The stolid, remorseless two-chord guitar chug of 'I'm Waiting for the Man', prefigured in Cale's mono-chordal 'Summer Heat', had the form of a boogie, but sounded like something else altogether, flattened out by Tucker's dispassionate eighth-note pounding and undermined by the crashing piano dissonances (possibly Cale's tongue-in-cheek quote from 'X for Henry Flynt') that rose up behind the guitar riff in the closing half-minute. 'Heroin' and 'Venus in Furs' pinned back their listeners' ears not just through their subject matter but through the repeated accelerations of the tempo in the former, mimicking a junkie's rush, and the use of Cale's amplified viola in the latter, scraping out both the sort of double-stopped drone he had performed with Young's Theatre of Eternal Music and, in the verses, an upper-register squeal on the second and fourth beat of each bar – a novel way of articulating the backbeat, given that the band had seemingly abandoned the staple rhythmic device of rock 'n' roll. Only 'There She Goes Again', its riff stolen from Marvin Gaye's 'Hitch Hike', reverted to the backbeat formula; this sardonic take on Carnaby Street pop would surely have been the perfect song to perform during the 100 Club scene in *Blow Up*, had the group been able to accept Michelangelo Antonioni's invitation, made in early 1966. In 'The Black Angel's Death Song' Reed recites his cryptic cut-up poetry like a snarling anti-Dylan against a background of Morrison's hurried strumming and the hyper-intense scraping of Cale's viola.

Most extreme of all, the seven-minute 'European Son' includes the sound, placed just after a comparatively conventional first verse, of Cale hauling a metal chair across the studio floor and hurling it into a plate of glass, a symbolic Fluxus-style act forming the cue for Reed to take off on a solo designed to make Roger McGuinn's Coltrane-influenced guitar improvisation on the Byrds' 'Eight Miles High', released in 1966, seem like variations on a nursery rhyme. Behind him, the band pound on until disintegration sets in and anarchy takes over, Cale's bass guitar flailing furiously as pulse and tonality disappear into a vortex of noise.

Tom Wilson seems to have remained relatively unperturbed. 'Sunday Morning' aside, he made no attempt to tame the sounds the Velvets wanted to create or to frame them in structures more palatable to the mainstream rock market. And the unorthodoxy was maintained in the appearance of the album, its cover bearing just the image of a yellow banana, a Warhol silkscreen in the form of a removable sticker, with the instruction 'Peel slowly and see' and, as the only other wording on the otherwise plain white front of the gatefold sleeve, a stamp of the artist's name. No mention of the group's name, no other indication of what might lie inside: this was the most enigmatic artefact yet produced in the name of rock, a great deal more extreme even than those albums by English groups (the Rolling Stones, the Who) which had only a group photograph and no lettering on the front.

Tom Wilson was still in the producer's chair when the Velvet Underground assembled at Mayfair Sound Studios in New York in February 1968 to record their second album, *White Light/White Heat*. Nico, however, had gone off to pursue a solo career. Now a four-piece once again, the group produced a more focused and equally challenging second manifesto, full of formal experimentation making use of their varied interests and backgrounds.

The title track is two and three-quarter minutes of flat-out two-chord rock 'n' roll set in a buzzing, seething world of sound: high-revving guitars, hammered piano, howling bass, clattering drums and urgent backing vocals, drenched in distortion as a background to Reed's preening, jabbering lead vocal. 'The Gift', Reed's macabre short story, is read by Cale over a one-chord vamp, with Reed's screeching guitar providing an obligato that resembles someone trying to construct a raga out of feedback alone. 'Lady Godiva's Operation', another unsettling narrative intoned by Cale, is sung against a battering rhythm track, with the voices of Reed and Morrison making interjections as the story of a surgical intervention reaches its unhappy climax in the whirr of a saw cutting through bone and a sigh of expiration. The guitar arpeggios and relatively gentle viola of 'Here She Comes Now' echo the folk-rock approach of their earliest demos, but with a distinct strangeness in

Reed's stuttering delivery on the fadeout. 'I Heard Her Call My Name' returns to the high-octane mixture of a brusque Reed vocal emerging from a symphony of distortion and prefacing a guitar solo that seems determined to demolish the rhythm section and shatter the very air, leaving only splinters of noise.

Occupying most of the second side of the twelve-inch vinyl record is the seventeen-minute track that can probably claim, ahead even of 'All Tomorrow's Parties' and 'Heroin', to constitute the Velvet Underground's finest and most enduring achievement. 'Sister Ray' begins as a standard two-chord Reed song, albeit swathed in the now customary sounds of distressed amplification, but the freedom of movement and gesture with which the musicians exploit its open-ended structure shows what they have been up to during months on the road, enduring all sorts of derision as they turned snatches of songs into improvised symphonies of aggressive distortion. The anthology *Peel Slowly and See* contains a live improvisation titled 'Melody Laughter', recorded at the Valleydale Ballroom in Colombus, Ohio in November 1966, before Nico's departure: here is a ten-minute sequence (edited down from half an hour) of wonderfully reckless improvisation including feedback screeches, a drum hammering out slow time, viola scratches, and a wordless vocal from the *chanteuse*, before a backbeat-driven guitar riff is struck up with a couple of minutes to go, while Cale moves to the piano to pound broken chords. It's a harbinger of what was to come. The absence of bass guitar from 'Sister Ray' – Cale plays organ, Morrison guitar – means that Tucker's contribution comes into its sharpest focus, her indomitable slamming and rumbling forming a rubbly underpinning for the maelstrom that builds between each of the song's verses as Cale and Reed battle for supremacy. A sonic metaphor for the struggle going on between them off stage, the duel helps to provide the track with its sustained drama and constant changes of texture as one or the other switches roles or drops out.

Released in January 1968, 'Sister Ray' eventually did for rock what *Ascension* had done for jazz: it made everything and anything possible. And the cover of *White Light/White Heat,* with its stark white lettering against Billy Name's black-on-black photograph, created the aesthetic that, within a decade, would be espoused by another new wave. But 'Sister Ray' was also the sound of a band tearing itself apart. Cale followed Nico out of the band that September, at which point the Velvet Underground became a vehicle for Lou Reed's two-chord rock 'n' roll songs. Their work was done.

12 So Blue

What James Brown told Pee Wee Ellis

Although *Kind of Blue* had been an immediate success with his followers, Miles Davis did not attempt to repeat or recreate it. Instead he moved on, as he always had and would, while absorbing certain of its lessons into his operating method. For others, however, it would provide a very specific form of inspiration, with a particular emphasis on one of its individual pieces.

As Bill Evans, Cannonball Adderley and John Coltrane drifted away from his orbit, Davis retained only three of the modal compositions from 1958 and 1959 in his working repertoire. They were 'Milestones', its close relative 'All Blues', and 'So What', and it was the last of those that received the most frequent examination. Coltrane was less than a month away from his final departure from the band when the quintet was recorded by a French radio station at the Olympia music hall in Paris on 21 March 1960, performing a seven-tune set that included 'So What'. Just two weeks over a year since the first time it was played in Columbia's 30th Street studio, it had been stripped of its original impressionistic introduction and had already been speeded up to a sprightly fifty-eight bars per minute, not far from double its original languid pace.

More extraordinary than the increase in tempo is the execution of Davis's solo. Throughout his early career the trumpeter was criticised for not being Dizzy Gillespie; in other words, for refusing to emphasise the sort of technical prowess encouraged by bebop's demanding exercises. Those who defended his approach sometimes countered by claiming that Davis's fluffed notes were more interesting than the ones other trumpeters hit on the nose. In fact, as became obvious in the second half of the 1960s, when the demands of the music changed, his command of the instrument was more than adequate to make any ostensible faltering the product of choice, or at least of a decision-making process that embraced the right to fail. But in the course of the seven choruses of his solo on 'So What' at the Olympia, he steps away from the preconceptions to fashion an improvisation as absorbing, in its way, as anything he recorded.

Once a perfunctory theme statement is out of the way, Jimmy Cobb again launches Davis's opening solo by covering the switch from brushes to sticks with a wave-like cymbal crash. The trumpeter, however, enters in a much more tentative manner than before, as if testing the air into which he flights his terse opening phrases with an unusual reticence. By the middle of the second chorus he has taken wing and is spiralling into the upper register, moulding swift, liquid phrases before dropping back down for a sequence of sustained tones closer to the established Davis manner. But as his thinking unfurls, telling use is made of uncharacteristic intervallic leaps, while passages of phrases that sputter and crackle are alternated with other, more pensive interludes in which he seems to be intent on fashioning a separate pillow on which each individual note can rest. By the time he reaches the fifth and sixth choruses he is branching out into a kind of puckish freedom that admirers of Don Cherry would recognise, reaching for high notes he can't quite grasp but yet making something beguilingly lyrical of the resulting half-formed squiggles of sound before descending once more in the closing bars of the final chorus with serene phrases that form a perfect handover to the next runner. The trumpet even continues with a gently coaxing obligato under the opening bars of Coltrane's solo, the saxophonist picking up the baton with phrases that echo Davis's parting notes before turning up the pressure as he finds his own way towards his customary loquacious approach. Cobb's tendency to speed up in live performance is evident in this performance: by the time Coltrane has reach his full exhortatory mode, around the sixth or seventh chorus of his solo, the rhythm section has accelerated to a tempo of sixty-two bars per minute.

'So What' was also performed during Davis's famous Carnegie Hall concert of 19 May 1961, prefaced by Gil Evans's full-scale orchestration of the original piano and bass introduction. The recording of this event, as celebrated in the list of Davis's significant live performances as his Newport appearance six years earlier or his set at the Isle of Wight rock festival in 1970, finds him playing with unquenchable brio, silencing claims that he could not play fast or high. This 'So What' solo, stoked along at a flying sixty-four bars per minute and entirely different in mood from the one recorded in Paris fourteen months earlier, supports the claim, made by George T. Simon in his review for the *New York Herald Tribune*, that 'chances are nothing could match for sheer drama and excitement the sudden

transformation of Miles Davis from a cool, restrained jab-
ber into a hot, uninhibited swinger'. In *Down Beat,* Bill
Coss claimed: 'Davis has never played more brilliantly than
on this night . . . playing high-note passages with tremen-
dous fire, building magnificent solos that blazed with
drama.'

The piece remained a staple of his working groups until
midway through the life of the band that became known as
the Second Great Quintet, in which he was joined by the
saxophonist Wayne Shorter, the pianist Herbie Hancock,
the bassist Ron Carter and the drummer Tony Williams.
This group was very different from the *Kind of Blue* band:
its members' thinking on the question of independence and
interdependence was more closely aligned to that of the Bill
Evans–Scott LaFaro–Paul Motian trio, each musician operating as an individual voice in a collective whose interplay
operated at the highest possible level of sophistication. By
the time their work was completed, in 1967, they seemed to
be able to think of anything and make it work in the instant
of conception, individually and collectively: the drummer
could double and redouble the time while the bassist went
into a plunging rallentando; the horns could intone nothing
more than a spare, hauntingly baleful theme, leaving the
improvising to the rhythm section; or Davis and Shorter
could work off scales that only they could hear, but which
seldom sounded anything other than perfectly logical.

The way this group handled 'So What' is preserved most
effectively in the boxed set called *Live at the Plugged
Nickel,* documenting eight hours of music recorded over
three nights at a Chicago club in December 1965, by which

time the quintet had been together for more than a year and had fully developed its unique methodology. Surrounded by four young virtuosi sharing the highest ambitions, Davis gave them their head and did his best to match their desire to create form spontaneously. The technical demands were staggering: this group was accustomed to taking 'Milestones' at a supersonic eighty-five bars per minute, and the Plugged Nickel version of 'So What' moves at a whirlwind eighty, meaning that even when the rhythm section suddenly halves the tempo behind Davis's solo, the music is still travelling at more than the speed of the original recording. By this time, too, the horns' participation in the 'amen' chords of the theme has itself become another vehicle for interplay.

But 'So What', besides being the Davis tune most likely to be found in the repertoire of other musicians, and therefore the one through which musicians outside his circle (including the Don Rendell Quintet in London in 1961 and the Gerald Wilson big band in Los Angeles two years later) could most easily get to grips with the basic principles of modal improvising, also exerted an effect on the subcutaneous layers of music. The outcome could be transformative.

One night in the spring of 1967, after a show in New York, James Brown called his musical director, the saxophonist Alfred 'Pee Wee' Ellis, into his dressing room. He had a fragment of music in his head and he wanted Ellis to help him turn it into a song. 'He grunted a bass line of a rhythmic thing,' the saxophonist told a writer from *Down Beat* magazine after Brown's death in 2006. Thoroughly familiar with the singer's informal operating methods, Ellis jotted the idea down in rough, almost graphic form on a piece of paper and went away to see what he could do with it.

That night they were on the band bus from New York to Cincinnati, the home of King Records, to which Brown was contracted, when he assembled the raw outline of a piece that would prove to be a source of primal energy for a great deal of the music of the next forty years.

The next morning, according to Ellis, the bus pulled up outside the record company's offices. The musicians got out and went straight into the studio. 'We set up, and I went over the rhythm with the band. By the time we got the groove going, James showed up, added a few touches. He changed the guitar part, which made it real funky, and had the drummer do something different. He was a genius at it. Between the two of us, we put it together in one afternoon. He put the lyrics on it. The band set up in a semicircle in the studio with one microphone. It was recorded live in the studio. One take. It was like a performance. We didn't do overdubbing. It turned out to be "Cold Sweat".'

The performance was earthy, energetic, funky, and astonishing in the way the musicians interacted to create a lattice of sound. Two guitars (Jimmy Nolen and Alphonso 'Country' Kellum) scratched and flickered, Clyde Stubblefield's drums chattered, and the bass guitar of Bernard Odum scooped out a syncopated line that became recognised as the essence of funk. And yet the source of Ellis's inspiration was a familiar and surprising one.

'I was very much influenced by Miles Davis,' Ellis continued. 'I'd been listening to "So What" six or seven years ear-lier and that crept into the making of "Cold Sweat". You could call it subliminal, but the horn line is based on "So What".'

And so it is – not so much subliminal as seen through a vorticist's eyes, its forms stretched and distorted. The struc-ture of 'So What', in which the theme, played by the double bass, is answered by 'amen' chords from the three horns, is echoed in 'Cold Sweat' by the interplay in the opening four bars between Odum's bass guitar and the peremptory 'amens' of the horn section of Brown's band: two trumpets, trombone and four saxophones (alto, two tenors and bari-tone). Whereas 'So What' moves between two modes (D minor 7th and E flat minor) in a thirty-two-bar AABA structure, 'Cold Sweat' is structured, more unusually, in thirty-six-bar choruses consisting of an opening four-bar vamp on D major, sixteen bars of song over the same vamp, and a sixteen-bar second section moving down a major sec-ond to C before returning to the opening vamp (but try playing the E flat minor of 'So What's bridge over that C major on the second twelve-bar section of 'Cold Sweat', and it sounds fine – in effect Brown's musicians, too, are playing on scales rather than chords).

You didn't have to know jazz to play this music, but it certainly helped, particularly for the horn players. The musicians of Ray Charles's highly influential band – such as the trumpeters John Hunt and Phil Guilbeau, and the saxo-phonists Don Wilkerson, Hank Crawford and David 'Fathead' Newman – all had bebop backgrounds and were able to make names for themselves in the jazz world. Many years later the personnel of the Commodores and Earth, Wind and Fire were equally literate in the language of modern jazz: it rarely showed up in the external elements of the music that made them among the most popular bands of the disco era, but it gave them the chops they needed for music that may have been simpler in its concept but made other strenuous demands on technique, imagination and endurance. From the late 1940s to the late 1970s, bebop and its derivatives attracted the attention of ambitious young black musicians: from Maxwell Davis, the bandleader on countless Los Angeles R&B sessions, to Maurice White, the leader of Earth, Wind and Fire, it was the idiom that best represented their musical ideals: they studied everything by Art Blakey's Jazz Messengers, the quintets of Horace Silver and Cannonball Adderley, Thelonious Monk, Clifford Brown, Charles Mingus and, of course, Miles Davis. But while they worked hard to acquire bebop techniques, they also needed to earn a living in a world generally indifferent to jazz. Gigs with leading R&B and soul singers – who required flexible, competent horn players and rhythm sections – meant consistent work. And sometimes, too, it meant good music, even if – as with James Brown – the rules were strict and a fluffed note or a missed cue brought a $5 fine.

'Being able to improvise helped a lot,' Fred Wesley, Brown's long-serving trombonist, said, 'but you had to play James Brown parts as is. You had to improvise the part, but once you got the part, you had to stick with the part. There was no more improvising after you got it. That was important. After you got the part, you had to play it all the time just like that. The bass had to play his part, the horns had to play their parts, and you had to stay on your note. That's the way it worked. By rehearsing it over and over again it stuck to your mind and we took pride in making these difficult parts work.'

'Cold Sweat Pts 1 and 2' was released in June 1967, and caused a sensation. It was the fourth in a series of singles with which Brown revolutionised soul music, following on from 'Out of Sight' in 1964, 'Papa's Got a Brand New Bag Pts 1 and 2' in early 1965 and 'I Got You' in late 1965. Brown was a prolific artist, and several other singles were released during that time, but these four were the cornerstones of the mansion of funk, and 'Cold Sweat' was the one that completed its architecture.

'Out of Sight' had come as a pleasant surprise to dancers in the clubs of 1964. It had a smooth ride-cymbal beat with rimshots ticking on two and four, a laconic guitar double-chanking on the first backbeat of each bar, and widely voiced horns playing a baritone-anchored riff like the last piece of a jigsaw, all fitted to a twelve-bar blues pattern. It was utterly basic, and yet immediately identifiable as a thrust into the future.

The following year, 'Papa's Got a Brand New Bag' took the evolution of funk a stage further. Where 'Out of Sight' had been jumpy but fluid, almost every sound on the new record was staccato: the drums, guitar, the leaping bass, the horn flourishes. Even Brown's vocal was delivered in urgent spurts. The effect was heightened when Brown speeded up the tape of the original master take (recorded after a long bus journey, with a tired band) for its release as a single, making the track leap out of the grooves. It was the structure, however, that caught the ear. It was as if a cast-iron building had been stripped of its brick and plaster cladding to reveal the columns and cross-beams that held it together. Again the underlying structure was that of a twelve-bar blues, but the overall sound was wholly new.

This was a year in which one classic record after another reached the top of *Billboard*'s R&B chart: the Temptations' 'My Girl', Jr Walker and the All Stars' one-chord 'Shotgun' (the inspiration for Terry Riley's *Bird of Paradise*), the Four Tops' 'I Can't Help Myself', Wilson Pickett's 'In the Midnight Hour', Fontella Bass's 'Rescue Me', Marvin Gaye's 'Ain't That Peculiar'. Even in that distinguished company, Brown's record stood out. 'Shotgun' and 'In the Midnight Hour' shared its gritty directness, a characteristic of southern soul music, but neither of them felt like a great leap forward.

Brown finished the year with another hit that pointed to the new direction. 'I Got You (I Feel Good)' was at number one in *Billboard*'s R&B chart when Andy Warhol and Gerard Malanga took the members of the Velvet Underground, their newly signed group, uptown to see Brown's show at the Apollo in Harlem. It was a week after the Velvets had been sacked from the Café Bizarre for refusing to stop playing 'The Black Angel's Death Song'.

'I Got You' maintained the new staccato mode, but this time the twelve-bar blues structure of its verse led into a four-bar interlude for alto saxophone and drums and thence to an eight-bar bridge: it felt as if it were endlessly circulating, with no beginning or end. An early version, with a slinky, jazzier feel, had been recorded a year earlier and used in Brown's appearance in the film *Ski Party*, a Frankie Avalon vehicle. When Brown took a second pass at the song, at Miami's Criteria Studio in May 1965, he was looking for something different: 'I called my band director, Nat Jones,' Brown told a reporter. 'I said, "Nat, this song is too hip." He said, "What do you mean?" And I said, "It's too sharp. We're taking some of the funk out of it and making it too jazz. And the groove is really laid-back funk."'

Although Brown played keyboards by ear and was a proficient drummer, he could not read music and had no technical knowledge. But his instinct for feel and structure was both immaculate and far-sighted, and it made him a visionary artist. Somehow he knew what would be making people dance not just that weekend or the next month but a decade or two hence. He also produced his own records, which meant that no outside agency was second-guessing him in the studio.

'James Brown had no musical knowledge,' Fred Wesley said. 'He didn't know any music theory at all. So anything he put together came straight out of his mind, out of his heart, and that made it different right away. There was no basis in music theory for that. His energy is what made it work. He would give you rhythms that nobody else ever thought of. He would give you patterns that nobody else ever thought of and his energy made it work. That's what's important to know about him. Everything came out of his mind brand-new and we had to make it work.'

What Brown understood was the deep structure of popular music. He sensed that the time had come for the layers to be inverted, placing the emphasis on the bottom end, with the lead voices almost acting as decorative elements, and he knew the established time-frames needed to be dismantled, leaving modern musicians free to groove or loop to their hearts' content. Africa was reasserting itself, as it had in Miles Davis's mind when he came away from a performance by Les Ballets Africains with rhythms and sounds in his head.

If 'I Got You' had been a fine example of James Brown's ability to strip down, refit and supercharge a prototype, 'Cold Sweat' was an even better one. When he gave Pee Wee Ellis the germ of the idea, he had been thinking back to a slow blues called 'I Don't Care', recorded five years earlier on an album titled *James Brown and His Famous Flames Tour the USA*. His modifications to Ellis's newly sketched structure might have seemed minor, but they were crucial. It was Brown who asked Clyde Stubblefield to delay the backbeat on the fourth beat of each bar by an eighth note, so that instead of the regular *one-and-TWO-and-three-and-FOUR*, it becomes *one-and-TWO-and-three-and-four-AND*, providing an unexpected kick that moves the whole song along. He made a change to the guitar figures, too, and the way the upward guitar flick follows the ascending horn phrase on the second section creates the sort of internal rhythm-shift that few listeners would be aware of, but which formed part of the song's dance-floor irresistibility.

And it was certainly Brown who stretched the song to seven minutes that morning in the King studio by inviting Maceo Parker, one of the band's two tenor saxophonists, to take a solo that became the second side of the 45rpm release. He had done something similar, in a more discreet way, during Part 2 of 'Papa's Got a Brand New Bag', but this time the result was electrifying. 'Maceo,' Brown shouts, 'come on, now!' And Parker obliges with a trenchant, hard-edged solo that sticks to the D major tonality of the song's opening section, improvising on a one-chord vamp. A song that had begun with a hint of inspiration from 'So What' was now taking additional inspiration from the extended explorations of John Coltrane. (Brown's calls to Parker were probably the first occasion on which a tenor player had been summoned by name during a studio recording since Thelonious Monk's cry of 'Coltrane, Coltrane!', caught by the piano microphone, roused a nodding Coltrane during a septet version of 'Well, You Needn't' in 1957.) And Brown wasn't done. 'Give the drummer some!' he shouted, drawing attention to Stubblefield's jolting licks and emphasising the music's changed priorities.

Certain soul records from the golden age have a special kinetic energy: they seem to be composed of powerful forces held together only temporarily and with difficulty, straining against the limits of form and style. Marvin Gaye's 'Baby Don't Do It' is one; others are Derek Martin's 'Daddy Rolling Stone', Barbara Randolph's 'I Got a Feeling', Albert King's 'Crosscut Saw', Gloria Jones's 'Heartbeat Pts 1 and 2', the Soul Brothers Six's 'Some Kind of Wonderful' and Don Covay's 'It's Better to Have (and Don't Need)'. 'Cold Sweat Pts 1 and 2' belongs among that number, and is pre-eminent in the complexity of its internal design, in the perfect meshing of parts that fit together without any apparent connective tissue (no need here for the safety net provided by a walking bass or an eighth-note hi-hat pattern). Here is a miracle of collective syncopation.

'It was Brown's most significant record – innovative, influential, incendiary,' Adam White and Fred Bronson noted two and a half decades later in *The Billboard Book of Number One Rhythm and Blues Hits*. The passage of a further fifteen years only made the statement seem more secure in its judgement and even understated in its assessment of the effect 'Cold Sweat' had on the world. Funk and its tributaries, including the music of Sly and the Family Stone, the P-Funk style developed by George Clinton with his bands Parliament and Funkadelic, and Washington's Go-Go movement, would have been unthinkable without it. Even when the precise lineaments of 'Cold Sweat' were not being remanufactured, its underlying philosophy was feeding into the streams that became disco and electro. Its role in Brown's stage performances also signalled a change in the direction of popular music: away from Western song-forms, even those thoroughly reworked by African Americans of earlier generations, and towards the eternal, everlasting groove, exemplified by the new and seemingly heretical emphasis on the 'one' – the downbeat at the start of each bar – rather than the traditional backbeat, something on which Brown himself was insistent, creating a shift that emphasised the tension set up by the downbeat rather than the release provided by the backbeat. It was certainly where time stood still.

'The show was broken down into three sections,' Fred Wesley recalled. 'They had the opening section where the band would play a few tunes and then James would come out, he would sing a couple of pop tunes, he would do "If I Ruled The World" and then end up with "Kansas City". He would go off and change, come back and he would do a couple of slow songs. Then he would go off and change again, and when he returned he would do the real *get down, get down* part – "Cold Sweat" and all that stuff.'

Two years later Clyde Stubblefield's trademark licks were captured in the piece known as 'Funky Drummer', destined to become probably the most frequently exploited sample in the new world of music inspired by, or even pieced together from, appropriated snatches of other people's creativity. 'Funky Drummer' has since turned up in records by A Tribe Called Quest, the Beastie Boys, Coldcut, De La Soul, the Digable Planets, DJ Jazz Jeff and the Fresh Prince, Dr Dre, Enigma, Fine Young Cannibals, Gang Starr, George Michael, Ice T, LL Cool J, New Order, Nine Inch Nails, NWA, Prince, Public Enemy, Roxanne Shanté, Run-DMC, Salt-N-Pepa, Sinead O'Connor, Stone Roses, 808 State and numberless others. 'Cold Sweat' itself lives on in samples embedded in the recordings of 3Xdope, Chubb Rock, Cookie Crew, DJ Jazzy Jeff and the Fresh Prince, Ice Cube, King T, Public Enemy, Sweet T, Terminator X and UTFO.

James Brown and 'Cold Sweat' were certainly familiar to Ronny Jordan, a British guitarist who kicked off the acid-jazz movement in 1992 with his recording of 'So What'. Born Ronald Simpson in London in 1962, he secured a contract with Island Records – the label of Bob Marley, Roxy Music and U2 – and released an album, *The Antidote,* in which his evident fondness for such figures as Wes

Montgomery, Kenny Burrell, George Benson and Grant Green was applied to a kind of jazz aimed more at the feet than at the brain.

The new version of 'So What' was included in the album but also appeared as a single in various forms, including a 'jazz mix' and a 'dance mix'. The guitarist seemed to have been inspired by a track called 'Selim' ('Miles' backwards) recorded in 1967 by the vibraharpist Johnny Lytle, picked up and popularised twenty years later by a group of British disc jockeys who established a scene in which young audiences danced to records by Art Blakey's Jazz Messengers and the Horace Silver Quintet – music that had seldom been danced to when it was freshly minted, but now generated a new kind of dancefloor heat. The theme of 'Selim' was an unashamed crib of 'Milestones' and 'All Blues', although – like many musicians who took a brief ride on the modal bandwagon – Lytle and his sidemen (who included Wynton Kelly and Jimmy Cobb) reverted in the solo sections to a plain twelve-bar blues template that discouraged the higher forms of harmonic inquiry. At any rate, 'Selim' enjoyed its new life as a ballroom favourite, and a surprised Lytle was even invited to visit Britain to receive the homage of his new admirers.

Jordan had applied to 'So What' some of the techniques that the British disc jockeys who called themselves Us3 would bring to bear on Herbie Hancock's 'Canteloupe Island' a year or so later, principally by adding a halved-metre feel in the bass and drums as a lure for dancers. The tension between the guitar and the ride cymbal, which are playing at a bright fifty-two bars per minute, and the other musicians, who are effectively going at exactly half that pace, already gives the record a rhythmic hook. Jordan enunciates the familiar theme on the lower strings of his guitar, adding the amen chords with a mellow tone suggesting that, like Montgomery, he is using his thumb rather than a plectrum. As the ride cymbal falls away, the hi-hat and snare drum chop out a funkier beat alongside the bass guitar, which is playing heavily syncopated figures that might have come from Bernard Odum's practice book.

A new second section, invented by Jordan, adds a touch of breezy lyricism as the drums and bass shift up a gear, dropping the half-time rhythm: the bass player switches to a walking 4/4, Jordan performs an accomplished single-note solo incorporating a Bensonesque voice-and-guitar unison improvisation, a pianist produces a cheerful solo almost reminiscent of Wynton Kelly, and female voices punctuate the restatement of the theme with oo-wahs before the piece fades out.

This is light music of a very superior kind: crisp, charming, stylish, acceptable to a variety of radio formats. And with it Ronnie Jordan succeeded in attracting the sort of audience that Miles Davis had been courting for the last twenty years of his life, in albums such as *Bitches Brew* and *On the Corner*, in attempted partnerships with Prince and Scritti Politti, and notably in the collaboration with the rapper Easy Moe B in the months before his death in 1991. That final Davis studio project resulted in the album *Doo-Bop*, which, after its posthumous release, won the 1993 Grammy award for best R&B instrumental performance (the meaning of the term 'R&B' having gone through a considerable shift in the quarter of a century since 'Cold Sweat Pts 1 and 2').

Had Davis lived to hear Jordan's record, he might have found it a little too neat and freeze-dried for his taste. If, on the other hand, he recognised that it was getting him through to a new generation of young listeners who hadn't been attracted by his earlier adventures, he might well have concluded that it was the hippest thing on the block.

13 Blue Bells

Soft machines and curved air

In 1970 a rock group appeared for the first time in the BBC's Henry Wood Promenade Concerts, an eight-week season of classical music events founded in 1895 and held every summer, its headquarters being the Royal Albert Hall in London. The group was called the Soft Machine, and a couple of years earlier they would have been encountered about a mile away, on the other side of the West End, playing at a pioneering psychedelic club known as UFO, along with Pink Floyd, the Incredible String Band and the Crazy World of Arthur Brown. Somehow, though, they had acquired the quantum of intellectual credibility necessary to prompt the issuing of an historic invitation. The reason, mostly, was Terry Riley.

The man who introduced the members of the Soft Machine to Riley's music and his procedures, an Australian-born guitarist and psychedelic gypsy named Daevid Allen, was already long gone by the time they played the Proms. Allen had met Riley in Paris in 1963, when he was living in the Beat Hotel, taking acid and participating in William Burroughs's 'dream machine' experiments with consciousness. When he met Robert Wyatt and Hugh Hopper, two young Canterbury musicians, a couple of years later, Riley's tape-looping techniques were passed on.

Wyatt and Hopper, both jazz fans, started a band called

the Wilde Flowers with various other Canterbury-based musicians, playing jazz-influenced rock and R&B. Eventually the name changed, and with it the personnel: Allen came over to join Wyatt, and the line-up of the first of many versions of the Soft Machine was completed by the singer and bass-guitarist Kevin Ayers and the organist Mike Ratledge. Their influences included Stockhausen, Coltrane, Frank Zappa and Kurt Weill, but it was Allen's knowledge of Riley's methods that would have the most profound effect, even though the Australian left (after problems with an expired visa) before the group could make their first album. The Riley influence could be heard on Ratledge's complex layered keyboard figures on 'Out-Bloody-Rageous', Ayers' time-stretching vamp on 'We Did It Again' (lasting anything up to an hour), Wyatt's drones on 'Moon in June' and, once Hopper had returned in place of Ayers, the loops of the bass player's 'Facelift'.

Their first album was produced, in a mere four days while the group toured the United States with Jimi Hendrix in 1968, by Tom Wilson, who had supervised the Velvet Underground's debut two years earlier. During their stay in New York they were introduced to Riley and Gil Evans, but it would not be long before the collision of interests that made the band such an interesting proposition in the years between 1967 and 1970 turned into a deadening concentration on a vaguely quirky kind of jazz-rock. A succession of bona fide jazz musicians, drafted in to replace such idiosyncratic figures as Wyatt and Hopper, ensured that the last dregs of the original band's pungent, chaotic character were gradually drained away. The Proms performance, hindered by problems with Ratledge's organ, was perhaps the last significant occasion on which they played anything resembling full-strength Soft Machine music. 'Nobody in the band was trying to do the same thing at all,' Wyatt once said, 'which is why it was quite original and why, after a couple of years, it fell apart.'

In the late 60s Terry Riley began a deep study of Indian music. 'At first I thought that I was most interested in the rhythmic aspects of Indian classical music,' he said, 'so I started studying tabla. I'd heard Alha Rakha and some of the great Indian tabla players, and I thought, "Here's something in rhythm that I just haven't heard anywhere else." I wanted to know how it worked. Then in 1970 I met Pandit Pran Nath, the great vocalist, and my interest in the melodic aspects of Indian classical music started to really kick in.'

Pran Nath, a great teacher of the Hindustani tradition known as Kirana music, was born in Lahore (then in India) in 1918. He was taught by the Sufi master singer Ustad Abdul Wahid Khan, and from the age of nineteen he spent five years living in a cave and singing only for God. Instructed by his dying guru to give up the life of a recluse and take the music to the outside world, he became a staff artist with Delhi Radio and later spent ten years as a teacher at the University of Delhi. In 1968 his first recording, *Earth Groove: The Voice of Cosmic India*, was released in the United States, where it impressed La Monte Young and Marian Zazeela, who persuaded the singer to emigrate to the United States.

In New York he became an extremely popular teacher: his classes were attended by young classical composers such as Henry Flynt and Charlemagne Palestine, by inquisitive jazz musicians like Don Cherry and Lee Konitz (a member of Miles Davis's original *Birth of the Cool* nonet), and by musicians who would cross easily between genres, including the trumpeter Jon Hassell, the saxophonist Jon Gibson and the guitarist Rhys Chatham. Riley studied with him for twenty-six years, until his death in 1996. When Pran Nath performed a raga cycle over three days in Paris in 1972, he was accompanied by Young and Zazeela, both playing tamburas, and by Riley's tablas.

For Riley, this was another stage in the Western world's re-engagement with modal music. 'It really goes back to Claude Debussy, who made such an impact. To Erik Satie, too, to a great degree. And Ravel. I'd say that Satie was highly influential in his harmonic movement and also just general concepts about music, to free it from words that were kind of locking it in. And then you can go back to Gregorian chant, which was a modal music, and to all the world musics which have been around for thousands of years using modal processes in places like Java and Bali and India and Viet Nam. It goes on and on. It's a wonderful network and web of influences, all these geniuses feeding into it and creating one step at a time.'

During his time in New York Terry Riley had also met George Russell and Gil Evans. 'I've known George over the years and we've met several times and he's talked to me about it,' Riley said. 'I had his book at one point, and I looked it over. I think it has some good points. I can't say I understand all of what he's saying, although I was very interested in the Lydian scale because it's one of the great modes in Indian classical music – a raga is built on the Lydian scale, and I think George's connection of that to a way of playing on changes was very useful to a lot of musicians around him.

'One of the great thrills of my life was when I was living in New York, in about 1967, and George brought Gil Evans over to my loft and I was able to play him "Poppy Nogood and the Phantom Band", which I'd just done. Gil was really interested in this piece and in the process of the long looping delays. He sat there and asked me to play it for him twice and he sat there with his eyes closed. I was so thrilled that he liked it because I, of course, was a big fan of his and was so influenced in many ways by his harmonic ideas and his arrangements.'

'Poppy Nogood and the Phantom Band' was the title given to a series of all-night concerts in the late 60s in which Riley used his soprano saxophone and an electric organ to set up complex repetitive and overlapping patterns. Growing out of 1966's 'Dorian Reeds', the piece appeared in 1968 as the second side of Riley's second Columbia album, titled after the piece on the first side: *A Rainbow in Curved Air*.

Was the eighteen-minute 'Rainbow' a more influential work than *In C*? In terms of its profound impact, certainly not. But this pioneering work for keyboard synthesiser, the unfamiliarity of its unashamedly inorganic timbres softened by shimmering fragments of bright melody over a strong tonal foundation, exerted a strong appeal to a generation of young rock musicians just beginning to explore a new generation of electronic music-making devices. Its cascades of notes, falling in waves over a constant pulse, offered an instant and unthreatening welcome to a new world of sound. By happy coincidence, the piece was scheduled to be recorded on the day the first eight-track recorder arrived at Columbia's 30th Street studio; the layers of hyperactive keyboards and the chattering tablas which pace the second half still seem to sparkle with the composer's delight at being able to extend his range.

This time there were no earnest sleeve notes or quotes from admiring reviews. Instead Riley contributed a poem: *'And then all wars ended / Arms of every kind were outlawed and the masses gladly contributed them to giant foundries in which they were melted down and the metal poured back into the earth / The Pentagon was turned on its side and painted purple, yellow & green / All boundaries were dissolved / The slaughter of animals was forbidden / The whole of lower Manhattan became a meadow in which unfortunates from the Bowery were allowed to live out their fantasies in the sunshine and were cured / People swam in the sparkling rivers under blue skies streaked only with incense pouring from the new factories / The energy from dismantled nuclear weapons provided free heat and light . . .'* And so on, in a charming summary of the hippie creed to which Riley, unlike many others, would remain faithful throughout his life.

On the other side of the Atlantic, rock musicians were certainly tuning in; Pete Townshend's synthesiser playing on 'Won't Get Fooled Again' and 'Baba O'Riley', from *Who's Next*, released in 1971, was clearly indebted to 'A Rainbow in Curved Air'. The title of 'Baba O'Riley' formed a joint tribute to Townshend's guru, Meher Baba, and to Terry Riley. A popular band, featuring a classically trained violinist, called itself Curved Air. Emphasising its futuristic but genial other-worldliness, the piece was also used as background music for the original BBC radio dramatisation of Douglas Adams's *A Hitch Hiker's Guide to the Galaxy* in 1978. More recently, and less predictably, it has turned up in the soundtrack to the computer game *Grand Theft Auto IV*, employed as chill-out music.

And just eight and a half minutes into 'A Rainbow in Curved Air', when the piece has paused to catch its breath after the sheer exhilaration of the opening sequences, a new sonority enters the mixture: an electronic rendering of the sound of the kalimba, the African thumb piano, the humblest of tuned percussion instruments, the one Miles Davis had in his head when he approached the recording of *Kind of Blue*.

Very different moods were being explored a couple of years later when Riley collaborated with John Cale, his old colleague in the Theatre of Eternal Music, on a Columbia album titled *The Church of Anthrax*. John McClure, the director of the Masterworks series, had suggested the idea, which teamed the two men with a pair of session drummers. One, Bobby Colomby, was a member of Blood, Sweat and Tears; the other, Bobby Gregg, had played the famous snare and bass drum lick that prefaced Bob Dylan's 'Like a Rolling Stone' in 1965 and had become a temporary member of the Hawks, replacing Levon Helm, when the band joined Dylan on tour later that year.

Recorded over three days at the 30th Street studio, the album is notable principally for its title track, a nine-minute vamp on a punishing bass-guitar riff, with what sounds like the drone of a fleet of bombers in the background and a succession of improvised solos on top, first from Riley's organ and then his soprano saxophone. Cale takes over at the keyboard as Colomby and Gregg thrash away underneath until, in the closing minutes, the piece gradually falls apart in a welter of clanging noise. Something about the track's ominous intensity, and the relentless, emotionless drumming in particular, suggests the work of German rock bands yet to come: Can, Neu!, and the rest.

Cale takes his seat at the studio's Steinway – the very same instrument on which Bill Evans played the introductions to 'So What' and 'Blue in Green' – on an eight-minute piece called 'The Hall of Mirrors in the Palace of Versailles', holding down the piano's sustain pedal so that his ringing chords collect a cluster of overtones which surround Riley's multi-tracked soprano, the prevailing tonality shifting slowly as the piece resists the incursion of unplaceable incidental noise. The piano receives harsher treatment on 'Ides of March', Cale and Riley hammering away at the uncomplaining instrument in what at times becomes a battle with the two drummers over a kind of stiff-legged boogie-woogie rhythm, and on 'The Protégé', which is introduced by a double-stopped bass-guitar riff that Cale could have brought directly from the repertoire of the Velvet Underground.

But Riley's studies with Pran Nath were taking him away from well-tempered keyboards such as Columbia's venerable Steinway and towards the non-tempered scales of Indian music. It was a journey that La Monte Young – obsessed with the mathematical relationships between pitches – had begun in 1964, with his large-scale piece for solo performer titled *The Well-Tuned Piano*, performed on a specially pre-pared Bösendorfer piano retuned to just intonation with single rather than double strings and an extra octave at the bass end (the Dia Foundation, which presented the American première in 1975, had an instrument remodelled for the occasion). In just intonation, intervals are calculated and tuned according to precise mathematical divisions rather than the adjusted and compromised tunings of the well-tempered scale; hence the harmonics literally ring truer. The intention of Young's massive piece, an episodic composition lasting up to six and a half hours and incorpo-rating slow and fast sections divided by silences, was to use simple harmonic relationships to create 'clouds' of harmon-ics over an underlying drone.

Among those exploring similar territory was a pianist, singer and composer known as Charlemagne Palestine. Born Charles Martin in New York in the mid-1940s, Palestine had been a teenage bell-ringer in a Manhattan church and the experience seems to have profoundly affect-ed his approach to music. His many piano pieces, including 'Strumming Music', first performed in 1974, are often based on two notes played in alternation at very fast tempo, perhaps starting an octave or a fifth apart, and then appear-ing to move gradually away from or towards each other. The tempo of the 'strumming' can vary, but the music's rich-ness is derived from the tintinnabulating build-up of the harmonics, which makes the piano sound like a carillon. In 2007 Palestine recorded a series of pieces on an instrument built by Luigi and Paolo Borgato in Padua, Italy, with two separate grand piano bodies: a normal keyboard-operated body with eighty-eight keys, and a lower body with only the bottom four and a half octaves, operated by pedals. The music emerging from the Doppio Borgato (Double Borgato) is even richer in overtones as the performer drives his minimalist resources through highly active passages towards others in which the instrument seems to be idling. In between are moments irresistibly recalling the keyboard ostinato underpinning 'All Tomorrow's Parties'.

Another musician working on similar lines was Jon Hassell, the trumpeter who played on the first recording of *In C*. Hassell's studies with Pran Nath led him towards a completely different approach to the trumpet, in which he renounced the attack normally associated with the instrument in favour of a completely legato approach, notes issuing from his instrument in a seamless skein of controlled exhalation, with barely more weight than that of breath alone. Electronic devices enabled him to produce two notes simultaneously, providing a parallel harmony that added another element of character to an already unique sound. The rhythms of his music borrowed from the flowing long-metre patterns of tabla drumming, while synthesisers provided the equivalent of a tambura's drone.

In his first album, *Vernal Equinox*, issued in 1977, it could be seen that the singing of Pran Nath – a master of slow tempos, and of the out-of-tempo prelude to a raga called the alap – had profoundly influenced Hassell's timbre, his phrasing and his use of microtonal intervals. In this he had jumped ahead of Miles Davis, who used Khalil Balakrishna and Badal Roy on sitar and tabla in various mid-70s concerts and studio dates but never quite managed to make the Indian instruments into anything more than an additional tone colour within the soundbed.

While these musicians were looking to India for inspiration, Steve Reich searched other terrain. In 1965, the year after the first performance of *In C*, he created a piece of music out of a taped snatch of a Pentecostal preacher's sermon. 'It's gonna rain,' the preacher said: a sentence as loaded with dread as a verse from the Book of Revelation. Reich had two tape machines replaying the phrase simultaneously; they were running at slightly different speeds, and as they ran out of phase he noticed the effect that was created, both on the voices and on the listener. 'It's Gonna Rain' became a piece that would have a profound impact on others wanting to enter the same world. The longer 'Come Out' (1966), in which he used testimony from a race riot, extended the approach.

For Reich, the next step was to apply the phase-shift technique to his notated music. In *Piano Phase* and *Violin Phase* (1967), two players perform the same twelve-note phrase initially in unison, with one later speeding up fractionally to create the phase-shift effect. The ambitious hour-long *Drumming* (1971) and the more modestly proportioned *Clapping Music* (1972) explored similar preoccupations in an almost entirely percussive mode. *Drumming*, written after a visit to Ghana, also featured voices, piccolo, whistling and the tuned percussion – glockenspiels, marimbas, vibraphones – that would become virtually a trademark of the compositions that brought Reich to prominence.

With *Music for Mallet Instruments, Voices and Organ* (1973) and *Music for 18 Musicians* (1976), he created extended pieces that combined the ability to ravish the ear with a modernist asceticism reassuring to those listeners wary of falling for anything that might be considered too easy on the senses. The precision of the performance combined with the dry sound of the mallet instruments – and in particular the wood-keyed marimba, a close relative of the African balafon – to give the music an aura of integrity. This was a tonal music whose complexities were laid out for the listener to examine: there would be none of the headaches caused by searching for the retrograde or the inversion in a dodecaphonic composition.

These two pieces – the earlier of them sixteen minutes long, the later clocking in at just over an hour – resembled *A Rainbow in Curved Air* in as much as they created an unbroken sound world in which a listener could bathe, knowing that the feeling of constant evolution would not be disrupted by a sudden outburst of chromaticism, an ill-matched instrumental colour or a guitar solo. But they were more controlled, more rigorous, more self-contained and less spiritually importunate than Riley's composition, and suggestive in a different way: they seemed to hold within them the blueprint for an entire physical environment. This was music for modernist architects and interior designers, as well as for modern musicians.

At this stage it was hard to locate the emotional content

in the music of a composer who had been so transfixed by his early exposure to Miles Davis and by Coltrane's nightly sermonising at the Jazz Workshop. Music does not have to scream or cry to display its emotions, of course, but some listeners found the moiré patterns of Reich's 70s music cold and forbidding, however absorbing in mathematical terms. Later, with the lyrical *Electric Counterpoint* (1987), written for the guitarist Pat Metheny, and the multi-layered narratives of the Holocaust meditation *Different Trains* (1988), for string quartet and taped voices, Reich was able to dispel all doubts about his ability to transmit emotions through music.

Philip Glass, Reich's friend and contemporary (they were born four months apart), and John Adams, who is ten years younger, are the two composers associated (not always helpfully) with the minimalist movement whose own music shows the fewest external traces of the changes that came via Miles Davis, John Coltrane and Bill Evans. But it is there, somewhere. Glass would have found it hard to create his monumental *Music in 12 Parts* (1974) or his score for the opera *Einstein on the Beach* (1976) without the dual influence of the modal harmonic slowdown and the distension of time in vernacular music. A meeting with Ravi Shankar in Paris in 1965 proved of great significance to him; before that, however, his student days in New York were 'the days of Kenneth Brown's *The Brig* and Jack Gelber's *The Connection* . . . they were part of the general avant-garde mix of the time, a mix that included the Beats (Jack Kerouac, Gregory Corso and Allen Ginsberg), the hard bop of John Coltrane, and Claes Oldenburg's *Store Days*.' And no doubt Adams's love of *Kind of Blue* propelled him towards the modal investigations of *Phrygian Gates* (1978) and helped him achieve the integration of classical and vernacular idioms that we hear in *Grand Pianola Music* (1982) and *Naive and Sentimental Music* (1998). There is also the use of just intonation in *The Dharma at Big Sur* (2003) – 'In almost all cultures except the European classical one,' Adams has said, 'the real meaning of the music is between the notes.'

Terry Riley spent the 1970s allowing the influence of Pandit Pran Nath to permeate his music. Using the techniques of layering and delay already built into his general method, he gave concerts of extended real-time improvisation in which his Yamaha organ was tuned to just intonation. One night in November 1975, in the apartment of the producer of the Metamusik Festival in the old West Berlin, John Cale, Brian Eno and I listened to the recording of a concert Riley had given a few nights earlier, as part of the festival, in the black glass box of Mies van der Rohe's Neue Nationalgalerie. Cale and Eno were just back from their own festival appearance at the gallery, with Nico, in a concert that was part Velvet Underground, part Fluxus (Nico sang 'Deutschland über Alles', to the fury of an audience consisting largely of students, accompanied by Cale thumping out thunderous arpeggios on a grand piano while Eno smashed a table full of wine glasses).

Riley had shared his concert with a group of Tibetan monks, to whose extraordinary drone-based vocal music we also listened. His own performance, later released as *Descending Moonshine Dervishes*, consisted of almost an hour of unbroken improvisation on a keyboard whose output had been split into two channels, one sounding fractionally later than the other. Using a fixed mode and a predetermined rhythmic cycle, and absorbing the different tone colours of the non-tempered tuning into his conception, he sent skeins of melody spinning and spiralling off against drones that resembled the sound of the portable harmonium used in Pakistani qawwali music. He seemed, in fact, to have cracked the problem of creating a seamless East–West unity.

All these musicians loosely and often misleadingly grouped together under the heading of minimalism – Young, Riley, Hassell, Reich, Glass – had made their mark by reacting against the prevailing orthodoxy of classical music education at college level in the post-war years. They had learnt all about Schönberg, Webern and Berg, and they could make a tone-row dance on the head of a pin. But what was the point? To them, the music of the serialists suffered from emotional sterility. By rejecting it, they were repeating the struggle of Miles Davis and his colleagues to emerge from the restrictions of bebop. And it was Davis who would help them find a way out of the academic cul-de-sac.

But all things happen for a purpose, including bebop and the Second Viennese School. 'These forces are all in play all the time,' Terry Riley said, 'and sometimes it's necessary for chromaticism, say, to come into music, as it did with serialism and bebop, to thicken the plot. Sometimes modal music can become too precious – it just doesn't have enough grit. So a lot of times musicians will draw on this music just to give it more grit, to express other emotions. It's the job of the musician to be a kind of antenna, to feel what's needed at the time in the energy of music.'

14 Code Blue

The art-school hop: Brian Eno and the bush of ghosts

When I visited Brian Eno in his Notting Hill studio in the autumn of 2008, he was keen to show me his latest project: a piece of software capable of turning your iPhone or your iPod Touch into a musical instrument. Its name is Bloom, and it was derived from his experiments with ambient music – designed for specific environments – and generative music, which is set up to evolve by itself once the relevant trigger mechanisms have been activated. Created in collaboration with Peter Chilvers, it was already a success; a blogger had called it 'a teasing, addictive ambient masterpiece'.

Eno showed me how you could touch any one of a dozen or so buttons to start the process of creating music automatically. Each button corresponded to a set of notes: a scale, a mode. Each mode was named after a perfume appropriate, in Eno's judgement, to the sound it produced (he is very interested in aromas and their effects): Vetiver, Labdanum, Ylang, Neroli, Ambrette, et cetera. 'This one,' he said, 'is called Bergamot. It's actually a Dorian mode.' He pressed it lightly, and gentle sounds began to unfurl over a drone, like raindrops on glass. Each note also produced a little splash of colour on the screen of his iPod Touch, a meeting of ambient music and synaesthesia – the phenomenon that creates associations between sounds and hues.

It reminded me that the terms 'mode' and 'modal' have

236

their source in the Latin *modus*, from which the English word 'mood' is also derived. Modes, as Miles Davis and his collaborators realised, can set up moods: a discovery first made more than two thousand years earlier by those who began the codification of the range that came to include the eight-note scales – used in, among other things, Gregorian chant – known as Dorian, Lydian, Myxolydian, Aeolian, Ionian, Phrygian and Locrian.

In the world of modern music, Eno has become a kind of filter. Everything seems to pass through him, as it were, before re-emerging in an altered form: sometimes embellished, sometimes simplified. Initially scorned after entering public consciousness as a self-proclaimed 'non-musician' in eyeliner and a feather boa, later he attracted criticism from those who accused him of lacking genuine originality. Even the Bloom software was immediately compared unfavourably (and inaccurately) with Erik Satie's 'Vexations', a short written piece intended to be repeated eight hundred and forty times, and composed a hundred and fifteen years earlier. Yet that is to misunderstand Eno's role. He does not necessarily do things first. What he does is bring new or relatively new things to wider attention without compromising their original intellectual integrity, often by blending or juxtaposing them in creative combinations.

In this way, after graduating from Winchester College of Art in the summer of 1969 with a diploma in fine art, he animated the work first of Roxy Music and then, as contributing musician, songwriter or producer, of Harold Budd, Robert Fripp, Devo, Cluster, John Cale, David Bowie, Jon Hassell, Laurie Anderson, Robert Wyatt, Talking

Heads, U2, Coldplay and Paul Simon, among many others. His range is one of his characteristics: he helped found the Long Now Foundation, whose purpose is to get people thinking seriously about the very distant future, and he composed the start-up music for Windows 95, which lasts six seconds.

Eno did not hear, or was not aware of, *Kind of Blue* until he had absorbed its teachings from other sources, and passed them on. He became aware of Miles Davis towards the end of his time at art school, and at first more as a personality – a *cool cat* – than through his music. His first serious exposure came through the *Lift to the Scaffold* soundtrack, which he heard via the painter Peter Schmidt, later to become a frequent collaborator. Like a lot of painters, Eno said, Schmidt (who died in 1980) listened to music all the time while he was working.

Eno was attracted by the epigrammatic quality of the music. The fact that he had not seen Malle's film merely increased the appeal of 'those very short, mysterious pieces that didn't have a context. As always when listening to film music without the film, you're immediately stimulated to imagine what this was music for.'

For a while, Eno ran the student entertainments at Winchester. He organised events and hired a number of young artists and musicians, including the lighting designer Mark Boyle, who performed with Schmidt. Boyle was becoming well known for the light shows he created for Soft Machine, but at Winchester he gave what Eno described as a 'Fluxus-type' performance. Thanks in part to Schmidt, Eno also

developed an interest in the new American minimalist composers, including La Monte Young, Philip Glass and Steve
Reich. 'La Monte was a mysterious guru figure,' Eno said. 'I
had no idea who he was. I thought he had such an interesting name.'

Like John Cale, Eno was drawn to Young's 'X for Henry
Flynt', which became the first piece of music he ever performed in public on his own. For 'X', the number of repetitions required of the performer, he somewhat rashly chose
3,600, the number of seconds in sixty minutes, calculating
that it would take him an hour to smash as many notes as
possible on the piano keyboard just over three and a half
thousand times. In the event it took him two and a half
hours. There were, he said, two ways of approaching the
composer's instruction. 'One is that you do the first one and
then try to repeat it exactly throughout the piece. The other
is that you try to repeat the last one you played. So if a drift
starts to happen, you follow it. I had the sustain pedal down
– I put a brick on it – and the piano was just ringing with
this amazing sonic world.' He paused, and laughed with
pleasure at the memory. 'This was like the ultimate in modal
music because it was every mode playing at the same time.
Every chord was possible. There wasn't much audience left
at the end but for me it was an amazing musical experience.'

The recording of Terry Riley's *In C* impressed him
straight away, its simplicity of means appealing to his love
of economy. He also liked the sense of immersion in a piece
that was not concerned with giving the impression of going
anywhere in particular. He had already started experimenting with a very simple synthesiser and a tape recorder that

he could use for overdubbing. Here, as we talked, he picked up a pencil and started to draw a diagram. 'On track one I'd have a note fading up and fading out, and on track two I'd have its octave doing the same thing but with a different cadence, and a fifth, maybe, and I'd build it up so that there's basically a mode being explored, just like this Bloom thing.' He gestured towards his iPod Touch, which was still emitting a constantly changing ribbon of notes. The idea, he said, came from the tambura: the same few strings being played but with harmonics coming in and out and a continually shifting ripple of sound. In fact he thought he would be happier listening to the tambura by itself, without a solo instrument on top, so he tried to develop the idea of music that could sound like one big tambura.

'You could get variety by lack of synchronisation, for example,' he said. 'The idea was that sounds would have their own life and they wouldn't all be bolted together. When you think about it, nearly all music until then was about tying everything together with bar lines and so on to make sure everything was synchronised. And suddenly to find that I could make this sound I liked by *not* synchronising – that was amazing. You could have a whole other way of doing things. But of course when I heard *In C* I thought, 'Oh, right, yes, you could indeed – *now* I see.'

Another powerful influence at that time was Cornelius Cardew's choral work, *The Great Learning*. 'That was a very interesting balance for me,' he said, 'because each singer in that piece behaves as an individual in the sense that nobody's synchronising them or telling them all to do things together, so each person has their own programme that they work through, just like the players on *In C*. But there are certain very simple rules that make you occasionally pay attention to what other people are doing, and that changes what choices you have available. I thought that was really brilliant as well, something that had the combination of free individuals and occasional moments where things connected and information fed across from one to the other. The Cardew piece offered the possibility of both.'

Eno was starting to get interested in how systems work, and in the balance between control and freedom. A totally free system, he found, was inherently random and not very interesting. A totally controlled one meant an orchestra, and classical music. He was trying to find the places in between.

Having absorbed Young's interest in long durations and Riley's use of tape delay into his own thinking, Eno was also affected while at college by encounters with the music of Reich and Glass. He came across Glass first, at a concert at the Royal College of Art in London in 1970. 'It was one of the most impressive things I'd ever seen. He had an all-electric band – seven players, I think. Four of them were playing electric organs, Farfisas, and the other three were electric viola, clarinet and something else – I don't remember what. But the sound was so strong and heavy. It was not a very big room, and there weren't very many people there, and it was so powerful.

'It was a time when those kinds of composers weren't really getting hired at all in the classical world. It wasn't until they cleaned up their act and started writing for classical musicians that they started getting grants and so on. So they played in art schools, which were the only places that were interested in that kind of thing. Music schools weren't at all interested. In fact the college that I was at had a huge music school in the same building – you only had to go along a corridor and you were in the music school. And I had these amazing people coming down, like Christian Wolff and Cornelius Cardew and Morton Feldman, and none of the music students ever came. It would be like if you had a painting college and you knew Picasso was in the next building and you thought, "I won't bother." So that was really a divide. Actually, art colleges were the places where people were thinking hardest about music at that time. So strange, isn't it? And of course the diaspora from that became the rock music of the 1970s and later.'

It was Schmidt who alerted him to Reich's experiments with rhythm and his studies of African drumming, with its use of polyrhythms. The phase-shift effects of the overlapping of two simultaneous metres particularly intrigued Eno, in the way they continued independently before coming back into temporary synchronisation: a dramatic effect that he also noted in Gnawa music in Morocco. 'They do this trance thing where they play very strongly on one beat for a while and they gradually start fading in the cross-beat. You suddenly reach the point at which the music flips – after maybe an hour of listening – and you're hearing a completely different tempo. It's astonishing when that happens because it's entirely to do with perception. There's really nothing much changing in the music. What's changed is that you've suddenly seen it differently.

'That's a big element of this area of music – the perception is part of the music. The classical idea is that it's all there and you receive it. What happened with a lot of this repetitive stuff is the idea that the brain doesn't just receive things neutrally: it's constantly working on what it receives. These composers were working with the fact that your brain is constantly active, and faced with repetitive material it keeps looking at it in different ways. Your perception is that the material is changing, but what's happening is that your perception is changing. The material becomes a way of monitoring the way in which you're changing. So it's a way of looking at your brain at work, actually.'

Eno heard that effect, implying the audience's move from a passive role to an active one, in the early Steve Reich tape pieces, such as 'It's Gonna Rain'. 'You know what the music is, you know how simple it is, you know all the ingredients, and yet you hear so much going on. Once you realise that that's part of the compositional process, it liberates so much. It means that as a composer you don't have to do nearly as much as you thought. What you have to do is make interesting provocations.'

The key to Eno's own switch from passive to active was the Velvet Underground. Although he loved Young, Riley, Reich and Glass because he thought they were opening up new ways of thinking about making music, the Velvets answered his personal preference for what happens when the new ways get into the hands of people who just assume their existence as a set of tools and simply go to work. 'I knew that they were connected. I could hear it, especially in what John [Cale] was doing – when he's playing those long drones, like on "Venus in Furs" and "All Tomorrow's Parties". I could see that, as is so often the case, pop music covers more bases. So in terms of music, they had a much bigger effect on me.'

Despite his fine-art background, he was unimpressed by the group's Warhol connection. 'I didn't really see anything of Andy Warhol in what they did, although I was very grateful to him for sponsoring them.' The connection that became vital to him was much more personal and direct, because it enabled him to link the two impulses – art and pop – hitherto working separately inside him. He had grown up thinking he could only follow one path or the other, and had been trying to make the choice between the two. When he discovered the Velvet Underground, he recognised that they had gone a stage further than his previous favourite rock band, the Who, who stopped at the edge of pop music and didn't cross the border. With the Velvets, followed by the Fugs, Captain Beefheart's Magic Band and a handful of others, Eno could see a new music appearing, in which there might be a place for him. 'I didn't want music to be a place where I had fun and art was where I got serious,' he said. 'I wanted music to be a place where I could do everything I wanted to.'

The minimalist composers, Eno believed, still felt the urge to remain part of the academy and to be taken seriously, so there were certain vulgarities they could not contemplate. He remembered getting into trouble at a new-music seminar in New York in the early 1970s, at which he remarked that Steve Reich's music would have been improved by choosing better instruments to play it on.

'I thought a lot of that percussion stuff he'd been doing, which was very interesting intellectually, sounded so boring because the instruments were so boring – they were just not sounds that would engage you. They were like drawing the system with an engineering pencil so you could really see what was going on. So, okay, I understand the value of that: if part of your message is to say that this is another way of making music, you want to show people how it's done. But I wanted a sensory experience, and I felt that he couldn't go there because it would muddy the message up. People would think, "Oh, he's just trying to make music." And Steve at that point – and lucky he did, perhaps – would want to insist, "No, actually, what I'm doing is making systems, okay? Get it? That's what you're listening to: a system. Not music."

'He might disagree with that interpretation. But, anyway, I got shouted at. Pauline Oliveros' – a former colleague of Reich, Young and Riley in California – 'came up to me afterwards and said, "Who do you think you are to talk about our music like that?" She was really upset about it, like I was an upstart. I suppose I was, really.'

When I first came across Brian Eno, at the 100 Club in London in December 1971, his contribution to Roxy Music was expressed from a desk next to the club's back wall, on which sat his VCS3 synthesiser. Using this primitive device, controlled by a joystick, he added squeaks and squiggles and swooshes to the sound, while modifying the signals emanating from the five musicians on the stage: the first such intervention in popular music.

By the time the group became famous he would be up on stage himself, flamboyantly arrayed and not just adding a vaguely Rileyesque synthesiser solo to 'Virginia Plain', their first hit single, but providing such a powerful alternative focus that the band's ostensible front man, Bryan Ferry, would eventually find it necessary to ease him out, just as Lou Reed contrived the departure of John Cale (in both instances, curiously enough, before the recording of their respective bands' third albums). But the idea of intervention had taken hold, along with the possibility of incorporating elements of the music of the California and New York minimalists.

'What fed into Roxy was the sonic material that tended to be generated by that kind of thing,' Eno said. 'There are always two outputs: the body of ideas and impressions and feelings about personalities, and the sounds themselves. When people buy a record, they think they're buying the sounds. But of course they're buying all the other stuff as well. Miles Davis hasn't remained popular for so many years only because he made great records; it's because he has a cultural position, and you get all that with it.

'So what Roxy took from that, finally, was more the types of sound that were being made, the repetitive things, and the kind of darkness of the sound compared to how a lot of pop had been. It became a whole set of colours that we could use, if you were talking in painting terms – a whole palette that didn't exist in most pop music until then.'

His ejection from Roxy Music turned Eno into one of the great collaborators, who brought his knowledge and instincts to bear on the work of a remarkable diversity of musicians. (Curiously, his collaborations with fellow *provocateur* John Cale, first on the ex-Velvet Underground musician's mid-70s solo albums – *Fear, Slow Dazzle* and *Helen of Troy* – and in a jointly authored song cycle called *Wrong Way Up* in 1990, failed to strike sparks.) The first of his important partnerships, with Robert Fripp, the leader and guitarist of King Crimson, had begun even before his departure from Roxy in the summer of 1973. Once Eno was free of other obligations, his work with Fripp gathered momentum and towards the end of the year an album titled *(No Pussyfooting)* was released, containing the first examples of their collaboration. 'The Heavenly Music Corporation', the first of two extended pieces, had been recorded in Eno's apartment, employing just Fripp's guitar and two Revox tape recorders linked up in the manner of Terry Riley's 'time-lag accumulator'.

Using the characteristic long sustain of his Gibson Les Paul guitar, Fripp improvised lines which Eno then looped and layered, creating sound beds over which fresh improvisations would be laid. This was music in slow motion: sounds would emerge and decay, blending with their own shadows and traces. *(No Pussyfooting)* and its successor, the even gentler *Evening Star*, provided Fripp with a new means of self-expression – his personal adaptation of the tape-delay technique became known as 'Frippertronics' – and took his partner a step closer to what would become, half a dozen years later, the most radical move of his career.

It was the sound of *(No Pussyfooting)* that attracted David Bowie to invite Eno to participate in a series of three albums recorded in Berlin and Montreux between 1977 and 1979. In *Low, 'Heroes'* and *Lodger*, Eno was able to give Bowie a sharp new identity by deploying the tactics learnt from the minimalists. 'I got the songs going in some strange new directions,' he said. 'Things like "Warsaw" and "Subterraneans" started very mathematically, which is to say I just thought, okay, I'm going to put a grid down – I'd divide a piece of blank recording tape up like a tape measure and say, okay, something's going to happen on event number three, lasting to event number seven, something else there and a change there. That way of composing, where you're starting off from the mind rather than the senses, is completely from that (minimalist) school – in all of their experiments, these people were saying, "Let's try to make music *this* way." It wasn't "Oh, I've got this feeling – I've got this sound in my head."'

The agenda of American experimental music in the 60s, he said, and that of a lot of English as well, was to think about what music consisted of and what behaviour constituted composition. 'What did it mean to compose? Was it different from playing? Was it different from being a painter? Was it like writing books? What was special about composing? I had belonged to the Scratch Orchestra, whose lasting gift to the world is a publication called *Scratch Compositions*, which has loads of ideas for compositions, and some of them are completely incomprehensible – you know, it would be something like "Take a stone" – and that's it. That's the composition. Hmm, okay. And some of them are very rigorous in the sense that they tell you precisely something to do, but it isn't usually something musical – it's something to do, and when you're doing it, listen.

'So what happened with these is that I laid out structures and, using my synthesiser, I'd lay out notes. Now with the choice of notes, of course, is when the thing of "I prefer some notes to others" starts to come in. This was really the separation from Steve Reich and La Monte Young. They had an attitude that taste shouldn't be a part of it, that it was giving in to leftover tendencies of some sort. Terry Riley was never quite as doctrinaire. But the experiment for these guys was, "Let's get taste out of the picture. Let's see what happens if that isn't part of the story" – which was a very great experiment to make and many wonderful things came out of it, but I wanted to make records that I wanted to listen to, and I wanted to be moved. For me, all these techniques were ways of finding a different territory to get into, but once in the territory I wanted to enjoy being there. So as soon as the structure started to pay off in terms of me getting some feelings from it, after that I would just run with the feelings.'

All of that, he said, was a way of finding new starting points to which he would not have been led by taste-based decisions. Nor, in his case, was musical skill a navigating tool. 'I had to find other ways of pushing myself, and the nice thing about being in strange territory is that you're very alert, just as you are in a strange town – you're looking out everywhere for signs, and the brain starts working when you're alert like that. So there was a lot of that on the first two of those three Bowie albums, a lot of us finding strange structures, just for the sake of it.'

*

Not much of that thinking, he said, went into his work with Talking Heads between 1978 and 1980 on *More Songs About Buildings and Food*, *Fear of Music* and *Remain in Light*, the albums with which art paid a return visit to the discothèque. While the band worked on one song in rehearsals, Eno would be working on another. The resulting ideas would sometimes be blended in a cut-and-paste way, but always with an ear open to emotional consequences that could overtake the emphasis on process.

One of the reasons people want to work with him, he suggested, is that he believes music is a place where you can put your most serious thoughts. 'I have a different attitude from most producers, who are interested in hits. I'm not at all interested in that. Luckily, the bands I work with are. It's good that someone is, but that isn't me. I always want to get more of something in the music. I want it to be able to hold more content and to be richer, and I don't want it to have a date-stamp on it. I don't want you to listen to it and think, "Oh yes, that sounds like September 1994", which a lot of things do have – although sometimes things are charming because they sound like September 1994, but I'm not so keen on it. And so with U2, I think they responded to the fact that I was interested that they wanted to do something in particular with music.

'Funnily enough, they don't just want to have hits, although they could easily do if they wanted to because they write very good songs, but they want music to be almost a religious experience. So they have the attitude that they're making music for a reason other than that it's quite a well-paid job – in their case, a very well-paid job, but it isn't their motive and I don't think it ever has been. They came out of punk and they still have a lot of that sensibility in terms of why they think they're doing music.'

At a time when music was becoming obsessed with sequencers and robotic rhythms, with Kraftwerk exerting a heavy influence on disco and early hip-hop, Eno had veered off in pursuit of greater emotional content. Having moved to New York as the 1970s drew to a close, he sought out the trumpeter Jon Hassell, in whose album *Vernal Equinox* he had become interested.

'Jon's experiment was to imagine a "coffee-coloured" world – a globalised world constantly integrating and hybridising, where differences were celebrated and dignified – and to try and realise it in music,' Eno wrote many years later. 'His unusual articulacy – and the unexpected scope of his references – inspired me. In general, artists don't talk much about how or why they make their work, especially "why". Jon does. He is a theorist and a practitioner, and his theories are as elegant and attractive as his music; because in fact his music is the embodiment of those theories. We spent a lot of time together, time that changed my mind in many ways. We talked about music as embodied philosophy, for every music implies a philosophical position even when its creators aren't conscious of it. And we talked about sex and sensuality, about trying to make a music that embraced the whole being and not just the bit above the neck (or the bit below it).'

They worked together on an album titled *Fourth World Vol 1: Possible Musics*, the first instalment of a series exploring the trumpeter's desire to create a pan-ethnic approach to music. Hassell played his trumpet through a variety of devices that enabled him to make it sound more like a Japanese flute than a Western brass instrument: almost all breath, very little metal. Its distant pre-echoes could be heard in Miles Davis's mid-50s tone, just as the music's procedures gathered inspiration from some of Davis's 70s bands, the ones that had impressed Eno on albums such as *Get Up With It* and *On the Corner*.

Together they devised settings suffused by the textures and timelessness of Indian and Malaysian music: weightless drones and gentle plip-plopping percussion surrounded Hassell's playing, whose dominant quality recalled Davis's comment many years earlier, when talking about Spanish *cante hondo*: 'The softer you play it, the stronger it gets.'

It was in the conversations between Eno and Hassell that the idea was nurtured which came into being a year or so later as *My Life in the Bush of Ghosts*, an album by Eno and David Byrne in which some of the intellectual procedures of systems and structures were applied to the 'found sounds' of singers and preachers whose voices supplied unmediated passion. 'I suppose I'm still searching for that sense of mystery,' Eno told me at the time, describing the origins of a recording that ended up featuring the voices of faith healers, Islamic singers, radio evangelists and a gospel choir from the Georgia Sea Islands.

Hassell was supposed to have been a third partner in the project, but removed himself after an argument (not settled until some time later) that blew up when the trumpeter felt his ideas were being exploited. Additionally inspired by

Holger Czukay's *Movies*, a 1979 album in which the co-founder of Can created sound collages from pre-existing voices and music, much of it taken from short-wave radio broadcasts, Eno and Byrne similarly pieced their work together with pre-digital technology, painstakingly blending the voices into freshly made rhythm beds. The combination worked well on practically every level and became widely influential, most obviously on the work of Moby, whose simplified version of the Eno/Byrne formula ended up providing the incidental music for countless television programmes and advertisements.

'It was a really brilliant trick, in a way, because the music sounded not dissimilar to things you might have heard before, but suddenly to drop in these very charged voices, with all the stuff that they bring, was an amazing piece of chemistry,' Eno said. 'And it was very easy to do, which made it surprising that no one had done it before. You just say, "Okay, I'm not going to write the song." That was my main reason for doing it in the first place, actually, because I just didn't want to write songs – I thought, "A lot of people can do that part better than me." So it started with something I heard on the radio, this argument between a politician and a call-in listener, and the dynamic between the two voices. I thought, "That's so musical – I wonder what'll happen if I put it in music." It was such a pay-off because of course one is used to singers – that's what it relies on, you rely on the fact that people are used to listening to songs with singers who are trying to say something, so they automatically connect the what's-being-said to the what's-being-played, although there was no connection here. The voices weren't done in response to the music – but it sounds like they are, because we make that assumption. So there was a huge assumption of value in there.'

Eno and Byrne had been reading John Miller Chernoff's *African Rhythm and African Sensibility*, excited by the author's description of the push-pull effect of overlapping counter-rhythms. 'We were really high on that idea. We didn't know how to explore it other than either to hire in people who could do it, which we did occasionally, but not very often. We mostly tried to do it ourselves – and we had to do it purely mathematically, because neither of us could play it. But we sort of knew how it worked. So we'd get metronomes – the way it started was so clumsy and non-organic. But to get us to the point where we could understand it, we had to do it mathematically. We'd put these time signatures together and then sit and listen to them and try to understand what they were. Could we play with it? Early on it was completely feel-less. We didn't know how to feel it. We just knew that you could. But as soon as it began to pay off, then you kind of knew what to do.'

The homespun techniques used to create *(No Pussyfooting)* and *Evening Star* became the foundation of the music that Eno released in 1978 on an album titled *Ambient 1: Music for Airports*, which proposed nothing less than a reinvention of background music. He saw no reason why public spaces should be condemned to exist on a diet of Muzak, music that was neither stimulating nor anonymous, and in his further explorations of wordless music, with the German group Cluster and on certain tracks from his own albums, he had developed an appropriate sonic vocabulary. At the Notting Hill studio of Island Records he worked with Robert Wyatt, Fred Frith and his engineer, Rhett Davies, to create something that might fill life's physical environment more interestingly, complementing the spaces and lifting the senses of the passer-by without insisting on its own presence.

Wyatt played piano, Frith played electric guitar and bass guitar, Davies played electric piano and Eno played an ARP synthesiser. They were recorded separately and then Eno started to combine the results. Finding a section of tape in which the pianos, although played in isolation from each other, created a pleasing combination, he looped them on to a twenty-four-track machine and slowed the result down to half-speed, creating a gently floating effect. The first piece of ambient music, it lasted seventeen minutes. When Eno again used loops, pitch adjustment and editing on a recording of his synthesiser to produce further pieces in a similar vein, he had his album.

There would be others, and in 1996 he took it a stage further by using a piece of computer software called Koan to create generative music: a form of music which, once triggered into life, evolves by itself. 'The basic idea, adapted from systems and minimalist music, is setting in motion a number of procedures and letting them work themselves out,' he told me then. 'The appeal to a man not overconcerned with the proprietary pride of authorship is that it presents me with more than I put in.'

The ultimate goal, however, was to break the stranglehold of the recorded form. 'The finite nature of the result was frustrating. I was always rather unhappy with the idea that I took a bit of this process, made it into a record, and sold that to people. What they got was an experience that repeated itself, like recordings always do.' In the technology used to create humble screensavers, and in the discovery of Koan, he found his solution.

First he could choose a note, then change the attack, the decay, the timbre. He chose notes from a scale, and assigned probabilities. He might tell it not to choose the flattened fifth, but to use a lot of the major third. He might tell it to leave lots of gaps in the music, or to use a lot of dotted notes. Then came the really interesting part: the relationship between two voices. 'Although you can tell them how to respond to each other,' he said, 'you don't know how they're going to inter-react. So you put the seeds into the system and then it starts growing music for you. And it might make something quite beyond what you had imagined, something you didn't expect and couldn't predict, in fact something you could never be around long enough to listen to in its entirety. I think it's quite possible that our grandchildren will look at us in wonder and say, "You mean you used to listen to exactly the same thing over and over again?" And some of the works I've made with Koan sound to me as good as anything I've done.'

They also sounded quite similar to many of the sounds he had produced before discovering this 'probabilistic' system of self-generating music: drifting lines of consonant melody, a soft clanging like church bells under water, gentle patterns coagulating and recombining with a moiré effect, the coming twenty-first century's equivalent of Debussy's *La*

Cathédrale engloutie or the Bill Evans Trio's 'Jade Visions'.

'The sensory side of ambient music came from the idea that I wanted to make music that was like environment,' he said. 'I didn't want to make music that was stories. I liked the idea of creating music-producing systems where you set the machine going and it just keeps doing it, just keeps permutating the ingredients. It connected with the idea of music as a place rather than an event.'

Thanks to Eno, the terms 'ambient music' and 'generative music' entered the general lexicon. Unfortunately the music it was invented to displace still survives, some of it – although not nearly enough – displaying the benign influence of *Music for Airports* and its successors, all the way to the push-button modalities of Bloom, where the ripples spreading from *Kind of Blue* can be heard at their faintest.

15 Blue on Blue

Northern latitudes and the most beautiful sound
next to silence

The five seconds of silence that precede the music on any
ECM album may be the most important statement a record
company could make. That pause is a recognition that
music exists within silence; only by acknowledging it can a
listener become wholly involved.

Manfred Eicher is the author of that silence, and of the
silence that appears to surround all the recordings produced
on his remarkable label. The quality of that silence is
intended to lead us towards a heightened awareness, a contemplative state where we are encouraged to listen harder
and more acutely to the music, and to the spaces between it.

When he was asked, almost forty years after founding
ECM, if he had any patterns or models in mind when he
started the label, Eicher's answer was straightforward and
immediate: 'A very good model, all the time, was for me the
sound of Miles's *Kind of Blue* and Bill Evans, how he
sounded there.'

The first ECM album dropped on to my desk at the *Melody
Maker* one day in 1970. It was a trio recording by the
American pianist Mal Waldron, previously known for his
work as Billie Holiday's accompanist and for his recordings
with the saxophonist Eric Dolphy. Called *Free at Last*, it
came in a black-and-white sleeve with an abstract drawing

258

on the front and there was nothing very remarkable about it, beyond two considerations: first, as the title suggested, Waldron had chosen to break the shackles of the conventional song form, and second, someone in Germany had decided it was the right time to start a new record company devoted to jazz.

That man was Eicher, and over the next four decades he would have as much effect on the evolution of modern music as any industry executive you could imagine. Despite his decision to found his little company at a time when the music business as a whole was doing its best to limit its engagement with jazz to a largely forced marriage with rock, Eicher's sensibility, combined with an ability to supervise the business side of running an independent record label, ultimately gave a voice and a home to music that might otherwise have remained unaware of its own existence.

ECM, which stands for Editions of Contemporary Music, is the place where Keith Jarrett, Jan Garbarek, Terje Rypdal, Pat Metheny, Bill Frisell, Steve Reich and Arvo Pärt found a platform. Its other featured artists have included the Argentinian bandoneon player Dino Saluzzi, the Italian clarinettist Gianluigi Trovesi, the Tunisian oud player Anouar Brahem, the Greek composer Eleni Karaindrou, the Polish trumpeter Tomasz Stanko, the American viola player Kim Kashkashian, the Latvian violinist Gidon Kremer, the Franco-Ivorian drummer Manu Katché, the Indian tabla player Zakir Hussain and the Norwegian saxophonist Trygve Seim.

Like Alfred Lion and Francis Wolff at Blue Note in the 1950s and 60s, Eicher has always encouraged the permutation of his favourite musicians: someone who bought a Jarrett record because he liked Jarrett's playing might find out that he liked Garbarek, too; and then, buying a Garbarek record, might find out that he also liked Stanko; and so on. Sometimes the juxtapositions would be obvious, at other times unexpected, yet there was never a sense that they had been foisted on the musicians. This was a form of creative marketing matched by every other aspect of the label's presentation, from the care with which the sleeves (first LPs, then CDs) were designed to the configuration of the point-of-sale units that gave ECM a distinctive identity in a crowded record store. Eicher's instincts and judgements were attuned to those of his musicians, and to those of the audience he hoped to attract to their music.

All that, however, was a few hundred albums in the future when Mal Waldron's *Free at Last* emerged from its packaging. And the point of ECM, the unique proposition, did not make itself apparent until a few months later, when Eicher started releasing albums of solo piano music by Paul Bley, Chick Corea and Keith Jarrett.

At the time, these were three of the most interesting pianists in jazz. Bley had been around for fifteen years, recording with Charles Mingus and participating in the 1968 October Revolution in Jazz, a short-lived New York movement whose initial protagonists also included Archie Shepp and Cecil Taylor. While Bley was associated with the new avant garde, his playing set him at a distance: it was spare, flinty, avoiding all forms of rhetoric in favour of a bare-bones examination of his materials.

What Jarrett and Corea had in common, apart from a

greater propensity to lyricism than Bley, was that both had recently been members of Miles Davis's band. This was the time when Davis was being invited to perform at Bill Graham's Fillmore auditoriums in San Francisco and New York, and at the 1970 Isle of Wight pop festival, where on a beautiful summer evening he played a demanding half-hour set to a crowd of 600,000, who gave every indication of enjoying the experience. Prominent alumni such as Corea and Jarrett could have been forgiven for thinking that rock-style stardom was theirs for the taking, but here they were releasing records of solo acoustic piano music on a label hardly anyone had heard of. And, as it turned out, without any form of contract. (Even when Jarrett's popularity reached extraordinary heights, he and Eicher operated on the basis of a handshake.)

Whereas the appeal of Bley's music, heard in the seven pieces making up the solo recital titled *Open, To Love*, lay not just in his sharp-angled melodic inventiveness but in a complete absence of ingratiating gestures, Jarrett's *Facing You* and Corea's *Piano Improvisations Vols 1 & 2* were far more approachable, without sacrificing much in the way of intellectual rigour. Jarrett's improvisations, in particular, contained the seeds of what would later be seen as his gift for inventing folk-like melodies that sounded as if they had been lying around for a couple of centuries. Corea's albums were distinguished by his marvellous touch and deftness. And if you had to make a guess about the preferences of the man who produced these albums, you might come to the conclusion that it was probably someone who held Claude Debussy and Bill Evans in equally high regard.

*

Born in Lindau on Lake Constance in 1943, Manfred Eicher was as deeply affected by his childhood environment as La Monte Young had been by a very different setting. 'I remember that the light and the winds would become sometimes very intense and wild,' he once said.

Given a violin by a music-loving mother, he listened to a great deal of classical music, and to the work of twentieth-century composers in particular. At the age of fourteen, having discovered Miles Davis, he switched to the double bass, but maintained his interest in classical techniques through studies at Augsburg conservatory, followed by enrolment at the Berlin Musikhochschule. After graduating, he played in orchestras and with jazz groups while working part-time for a small publisher of jazz compositions and as a production assistant for Deutsche Grammophon, the prominent classical label.

At eighteen he visited New York, where he heard the Bill Evans Trio at the Village Vanguard during their historic season in the summer of 1961. Later came a chance to hear the John Coltrane Quartet at the Deutsche Museum in Berlin. These experiences, like the discovery of *Kind of Blue*, would create a deep impression and remain with Eicher for the rest of his life, shaping the music that he, in turn, helped bring into the world.

In 1969, aged twenty-six, he began the adventure. Paul Bley remembered Eicher paying him a visit in New York and remarking on the shelves of unreleased tapes in the pianist's apartment. 'When he decided to begin a record company, he offered to buy some of my previously recorded music,' Bley wrote in his memoir. Among the first releases was a trio album titled *Ballads*, with the bassist Gary Peacock and the drummer Barry Altschul. 'With that album it was my desire to do a project in which each ballad would be twenty-plus minutes long and be unlike the other ballads on the LP. At that time I was working at being the slowest pianist in the world. Manfred was always very helpful. We were on the same wavelength. He knew all there was to know about the intentions of the musicians he recorded.'

If there was something slightly indiscriminate about certain releases in the first year or so of the label's life (there would be no follow-ups to albums by Just Music, the German multi-instrumentalist Alfred Harth, and by the American saxophonists Marion Brown and Robin Kenyatta), the founder's vision soon came into focus. The profusion of solo piano records helped to make it clear that the label's recordings would be characterised, first of all, by a concern for sound quality. 'The most beautiful sound next to silence' is a phrase the company borrowed from a review of one of its early releases in *Coda*, the Canadian jazz magazine, and it worked as a slogan because Eicher believed in breaking a silence only if he could replace it with something equally worthwhile.

As Eicher's repertory company of musicians also began to take shape, it became obvious that he enjoyed recruiting from northern Europe. Two young Norwegians, Jan Garbarek and the guitarist Terje Rypdal, both of whom had studied and played with George Russell, were the first to make an impact, not least because both men seemed to have achieved something hitherto deemed almost impossible: as European jazz musicians, they infused their improvisations

with qualities that seemed to spring from their own indige-
nous music. Garbarek's tenor and soprano saxophones
internalised the obvious (and virtually inescapable) debt to
Coltrane while singing with a lyricism that seemed to echo
from the mountains and fjords of his native land. Rypdal
made electronic effects an integral part of his playing, doing
to jazz what Jimi Hendrix had done to the blues: he seemed
to think in soundscapes rather than bars or choruses. I
remember reviewing the first of Rypdal's many ECM
albums in 1972, having heard him playing with Robert
Wyatt and the violinist Don 'Sugarcane' Harris during the
Berlin jazz festival a few months earlier, and suggesting that
Miles Davis might be better off were he to abandon his
attempts to copy Sly Stone and build a new band around
Rypdal. It still sounds like a promising idea.

ECM's visual signature was also becoming increasingly
obvious in sleeve designs that used a strong but understated
approach, with photographs – almost invariably black and
white – or abstract paintings and drawings that formed a
kind of poetic allusion to the atmosphere of the music, with
the bare details – artist, title, sidemen, label and catalogue
number – given in a sans serif type so plain as to be virtually anonymous. Very seldom was the artist's photograph in
evidence (an obvious exception being the label's biggest sell-
er, Jarrett's *The Köln Concert*). Explanatory or biographical
sleeve notes were rare.

The impression, as with the music, was of something
carefully distilled, the product of a refined sensibility. The
sound of the records, too, reinforced the impression of emotional containment. Eicher had taken his cue from the

ambiance of Columbia's old wooden-walled church on 30th Street, with its gorgeous echo, both natural and enhanced. He worked almost always with the same engineers and studios: Jan Erik Kongshaug in Oslo, at the Arne Bendiksen Studio, the Talent Studio, or the Rainbow Studios, and James Farber in New York, at the Power Station or Avatar. The invention in 1971 of a digital reverb machine by the Lexicon company of Utah gave him the tool he needed. Like pipe-smoking Fred Plaut in the 1950s, Eicher and his engineers used echo and microphone placement to establish two vital parameters: the spaces between the instruments, and the closeness of the musicians. The former allows the timbre of the individual instruments to bloom, while the latter directs the listener's attention to the quality of the interaction between the performers.

After the label had established itself Eicher endured a great deal of criticism, both for his concentration on manipulating sound and for the apparent aesthetic sameness of many of his releases. The use of reverb, it was claimed by some musicians outside ECM's magic circle, was nothing but a cosmetic addition, a commercial gimmick aimed at pleasing listeners who looked to music for nothing more than social reassurance. It was the aural equivalent of the magnolia wash that an aspiring young couple might give to the walls of the old house.

To his detractors, Eicher was creating a hand-made version of the mass-produced music represented by the guitarist Mike Oldfield's *Tubular Bells*, the virtually single-handed instrumental album that appeared from nowhere in 1973, in which Oldfield had applied some of Terry Riley's long-form techniques (as a teenager, he had played in a band with the former Soft Machine members Kevin Ayers and Robert Wyatt) to gentle chord sequences suggestive of folk music, with a garnish of soft-rock textures. By selling around 15 million copies around the world, *Tubular Bells* not only established Oldfield's career but played a significant part in the rise of Richard Branson, the founder of Virgin Records, to the status of an international business tycoon. When Jarrett's wholly improvised *Köln Concert* unexpectedly started selling in vast numbers a couple of years later, unfriendly observers called it Eicher's very own *Tubular Bells*.

No doubt Jarrett's success did provide a carefully run label with a bedrock of financial stability, but Eicher refused to indulge in tycoonish gestures. The company resisted buyout offers from major labels, its handful of employees staying put in their unprepossessing offices over an electrical supplier in an anonymous Munich suburb. And a curious thing happened: as a relentless recording schedule threw up more and more releases, often with the same musicians reshuffled, the artistic quality seemed to rise.

The accusation that Eicher favoured a bloodless Europeanisation of jazz had long been undermined by the presence in the catalogue of Don Cherry, the Art Ensemble of Chicago, Leo Smith, Charles Lloyd and others. As for Jarrett, his albums of solo improvisations and classical pieces began to be outnumbered by those devoted to the occasional trio in which he was joined by the bassist Gary Peacock and the drummer Paul Motian, exploring the territory delineated by Motian with Scott LaFaro and Bill Evans.

Following a long and debilitating period of illness, Jarrett returned in 1999 with a solo piano album, *The Melody at Night, With You*, in which he recorded himself at home, interpreting a group of standard tunes in the concise and unpretentious manner that was all his reduced physical capacity permitted. Mysteriously investing the songs with a new lustre, he seduced even many of those listeners long since alienated by his haughty manner on the concert platform and by his implied suggestion that his long stream-of-consciousness improvisations were being channelled from some higher authority.

As time went on, too, Eicher's interest in the northern latitudes led to music of increasing scope and depth. The childhood on Lake Constance appeared to have made him unusually sympathetic to the culture of the Baltic and the Scandinavian countries; gradually it became obvious that in this context, and in the recordings of the music of such leaders as Edward Vesala, Jon Balke, Trygve Seim and Christian Wallumrod, 'cool' was not a synonym for 'cold'.

As the label travelled through its fourth decade, the list of ECM classics grew rapidly. Tomasz Stanko's *Litania* revisited the neglected music of a great Polish composer, the late Kryszstof Komeda. Marilyn Crispell's *Nothing Ever Was, Anyway*, a recital of compositions by Annette Peacock, reflected Eicher's admiration of Bill Evans in extending the label's catalogue of exemplary piano trio recordings (as did releases by Bobo Stenson, Tord Gustavson and Marcin Wasilewski). Seim's *Different Rivers* offered a set of orchestral colours as fresh as those devised by Gil Evans had seemed in the 1950s. The two quintets heard in Manu

Katché's *Neighbourhood* and *Playground* updated the appealing formula of Herbie Hancock's 'Maiden Voyage', offering serenity with substance. The Norwegian accordionist Frode Haltli (*Passing Images*) and the Finnish pianist Iro Haarla (*Northbound*) made interesting, unsentimental use of folk materials. The trumpeters Arve Henriksen and Mathias Eick made promising appearances first as sidemen, then as leaders.

But when the adventurous trumpeter Nils Petter Molvaer, following the success of his albums *Khmer*, *Ligotage* and *Solid Ether*, wanted to release an album of disc-jockey remixes in 1999, Eicher said no. Molvaer's music, heavily influenced by that of Jon Hassell, already made use of samples, turntables and laptops, but the producer refused, in effect, to concede final authorship to outside agencies. His continued willingness to venture beyond the established frontiers, however, can be seen in two albums released by the self-described 'zen-funk' group Ronin, a quintet led by the Swiss pianist Nik Bärtsch. In their two ECM albums, *Stoa* (2006) and *Holon* (2008), Bärtsch creates small rhythmic and melodic cells which are allowed to develop over time. Bass clarinet and percussion, added to the basic piano trio, operate between the functional and the decorative. The result is like a cross between Terry Riley, James Brown's rhythm section and *Bitches Brew*, recorded in an imaginary studio somewhere between Kyoto and Oslo: yet another intriguing recombination of durable components.

A lot of people tried to be the new Manfred Eicher, but no one came closer than Rune Kristofferson, a Norwegian

Blue on Blue

musician who spent several years working for ECM in Oslo before setting up his own label. Rune Grammofon, as it was called, was intended to be a vehicle for Norwegian music that moved away from ECM's supposed concentration on wintry tone poems and meditative moods towards a more aggressive blend of free improvisation with the techniques of electronic and post-rock music.

'The most characteristic thing about these Norwegian musicians,' Kristofferson told me in 2005, 'is their complete disrespect for genre. It's about people from jazz and more hardcore improvisational music, and from electronic music and rock, playing with musicians from other fields and trying to create something that's not very identifiable. The music academies in Trondheim and Oslo have been very important in that respect, encouraging musicians to step outside their own fields and experiment in ways that might help them find their own voices.'

As with ECM, a strong visual identity helped the new company to establish itself in the minds of critics and other listeners. 'I've always been fond of labels that had a more artistic attitude to their sleeves, like ECM, 4AD and Factory,' Kristofferson said. Rune Grammofon's art director, Kim Hiorthoy, developed a style based on a coolly underplayed typography and his own pale abstract paintings on white backgrounds.

No sleeves were more understated than those of Supersilent, Rune Grammofon's first and best known group, in whose work, whatever claims are made for genre-bending, the legacies of *Kind of Blue* and the minimalists remain clear. For the four members of Supersilent, free

269

improvisation is based on a common language derived from the givens, even when the vocabulary of sounds is unfamiliar. Although Stale Storlokken (keyboards), Helge Sten (guitar, electronics), Jarle Vespestad (drums) and Arve Henriksen (trumpet) make few compromises with melody, harmony or rhythm, they achieve moments of powerful beauty amid the outbreaks of noise terrorism. Henriksen, moving on from the influence of Hassell and Molvaer, exploits a narrow spectrum of timbres ranging from a bugle-like tone reminiscent of early Miles Davis to a synthe-sised sound mimicking the finely nuanced breathiness of the shakuhachi.

Three of Henriksen's solo albums appeared on Rune Grammofon. *Sakuteiki* (2001), *Chiaroscuro* (2004) and *Strjon* (2007) are full of graceful impressionistic miniatures, tiny essays in timbre and space that go beyond category and place. I don't think I've ever heard music that so precisely responds to the analogy made by Bill Evans in the original sleeve note to *Kind of Blue*: 'There is a Japanese visual art in which the artist is forced to be spontaneous. He must paint on a thin stretched parchment with a special brush and black water paint in such a way that an unnatural or interrupted stroke will destroy the line or break through the parchment. Erasures or changes are impossible . . . The resulting pictures lack the complex composition and tex-tures of ordinary painting, but it is said that those who see will find something captured that escapes explanation.'

In December 2004 I saw Henriksen give a concert, with Stale Storlokken, at the church of St Martin-in-the-Fields in Trafalgar Square. It was arranged, as is the custom, by the

Norwegian embassy to celebrate the country's gift to London of a giant Christmas tree, an annual expression of thanks for the assistance given by Britain to Norway during the second world war. Storlokken, performing on the church's large pipe organ, was perched high up in the loft by the west door. Henriksen, located in front of the congregation, began by using an echo device on his trumpet to set up multiplying waves of sound, creating the illusion of a whole section of soft-focus shakuhachi-trumpets, over which he laid a heart-piercing lead line. Storlokken made his presence felt on a subsequent piece in which he exploited the organ's capabilities to produce a dramatic fusillade of lower-register stabs and groans. Henriksen set aside his trumpet to sing a lyric in his native tongue, first in a soprano voice of shocking purity and then in a keening tenor.

The duo finished their set with Joe Zawinul's 'In a Silent Way', the title track of the 1969 album which was the closest Miles Davis ever came to replicating the effect of *Kind of Blue*. Storlokken provided an ostinato powerfully reminiscent of Terry Riley's raga-influenced organ pieces while Henriksen, a diminutive cherub who, but for his facial stubble, could have fallen off a carving on the church roof, enunciated the graceful tune as if it were a prayer.

The world is full of interesting music now, much fuller than it was in 1959. And I think the new music I would find it hardest to do without, fifty years after *Kind of Blue*, is that produced by the Necks, an Australian trio who have been working together since the late 1980s. They are Chris Abrahams (piano and other keyboards), Lloyd Swanton (bass) and Tony Buck (drums): a piano trio, in other words, but not like any other piano trio you ever heard, even though one of their albums (fourteen of them, up to 2008) is called *Piano Bass Drums*.

Almost everything they play lasts around an hour. One member begins with a repeated melodic or rhythmic cell, the others join in, and the material is subjected to a process of gradual change. The harmonies are either static or modulate only very slowly, the grooves are often locked in, and there is little melodic development in the conventional sense. Yes, at their most austere they tend to make Keith Jarrett's solo improvisations sound like a résumé of the week's Top 20. The listener has to adjust. But these musicians have the gift of choosing motifs that make you want to listen to them, and developing them in ways that create a slow-burning tension which, since the music generally lacks rhetorical flourishes, ultimately also serves as its own release.

The term 'trance' is sometimes used to describe their music, but that seems to me to be as much of a mistake as it would be to apply it to one of Ravi Shankar's raga recitals. The listener who goes into a trance while listening to Shankar or the Necks is missing almost everything that makes such music worthwhile, not least the creative imagination at work on detailed motivic development, and would be oblivious to its often half-hidden moments of emotional intensity. There is a great deal of joy in the Necks' music, and it is the more rewarding for being hard-won.

The musicians were all born at the beginning of the 1960s. Each of them spends most of his time away from the group, working in other contexts, from orchestral music through free improvisation and straight jazz to singer-song-writer music. They pursue their own projects: Abrahams makes dreamy solo albums, Swanton leads a well-regarded band with horns and a guitar called The catholics (yes, lower-case c), and Buck has a hardcore outfit called PERIL (yes, all upper case). They meet a few times a year for concerts in Australia, for the occasional foreign tour, and for sessions to produce their studio albums. Many awards have come the way of a group that can claim a devoted following around the world.

If variety is not the dominant characteristic of their individual performances, there is a considerable difference between the pieces themselves. At one end of the scale stands 1994's studio-recorded *Aquatic*, a groove-based piece lasting fifty-three minutes which takes a leisurely journey across several electronically enhanced exotic landscapes before culminating, with nine minutes to go, in an explosion of euphoric riffing which gains its emotional charge from all that has come before it: as the electronics fade to make way for the driving acoustic piano, the slow accretion of harmonic information and rhythmic intensity gets its pay-off. At the other end is the live recording called *Townsville* (2007), half a minute longer than *Aquatic* but entirely different in process. Swanton's sombre introductory bass figures are joined by Buck's slow-motion cymbal washes and reverberant arpeggios from Abrahams's piano, the latter coalescing over the course of the piece into a kind of ecstatic strumming not a million miles from the basic method of Charlemagne Palestine (and everything else of

273

which that is a reminder). Although nowhere in the entire length of *Townsville* is an explicit regular tempo stated, the three musicians nevertheless generate a kind of unmetred collective propulsion that conducts the listener through the work's gradual unfurling. This is not the 'free time' of the avant-garde jazz of the 1960s, in which momentum came principally from nervous energy: it springs from a deeper level of communication, and at times like this the Necks sound like nothing more than a deconstruction of the great Bill Evans Trio, transported to and reassembled in a world with a different scale of chronological time.

Actually, what I hear in their music is a direct lineage from *Kind of Blue*. Abrahams's keyboard strumming is the tremolo laid by Evans under the theme of 'All Blues'. Swanton's slowly changing bass figures are Paul Chambers's underpinning riff, half a century on. And everything Buck plays is a descendant of the cymbal crash with which Jimmy Cobb gave Miles Davis a prod in the back at the start of his solo on 'So What', the happiest of accidents. More than that, however, *Kind of Blue*'s legacy is apparent in the ease with which the Necks exploit the spaces that were opened up for them all those years ago: spaces in harmony, rhythm and melody, but also spaces in the mind.

16 Coda: Permanent Blue

Inside the Dream House

Through the unobtrusive doorway of 275 Church Street, set in a typical row of downtown buildings that once housed small factories and sweatshops on what used to be New York's Lower West Side, between a pair of little restaurants and just across the street from the understated chic of the TriBeCa Grand hotel, a long straight flight of stairs leads up to the third floor. This is the Dream House. A young man opens the door, invites the visitor to remove his shoes and drop an optional $5 in a perspex donation box, and offers a sheaf of explanatory documents. Then he gestures down a white corridor to the place from which the sound is emanating.

The room, which measures about forty feet by thirty feet, has white walls and ceiling and a dozen white cushions scattered around a white wall-to-wall carpet, but the whole space is washed and suffused with magenta light. Against one wall, a small table covered with a cloth sits below portraits of Pandit Pran Nath, the great Indian singer and guru; the young man renews the lightly perfumed incense stick burning in a holder beneath the pictures. Three windows in the west-facing wall, looking out on to the street, are covered in sheets of transparent magenta plastic which have the unintended effect of making the brake lights of the cars going north up 6th Avenue glow with an unusual intensity.

Ceiling-mounted spotlights pick out four mobiles, each one a slender curl of thin sheet metal, two of them suspended in front of each of the longer walls, defined in yellow, red, blue and white, their bright chromatics repeated in their shadows on the wall. This is the work of Marian Zazeela, the wife of La Monte Young, whose own contribution to the environment is issuing from the room's only other significant physical feature: a set of loudspeakers in each corner of the room, huge sub-woofers hidden within white-painted wooden plinths about seven feet high, on top of which are mounted conventional black-boxed, open-faced speakers dealing with the higher frequencies.

There are thirty-two of those frequencies in all, issuing in *en bloc* from each speaker, their exact registers and relationships calibrated with infinite care in relation to the harmonic series and to each other. Their source is a custom-built Rayna Syn-1 sine-wave synthesiser residing one floor down and filling the air in the colour-washed room with such density that the effect is at first disconcerting. As the listener settles down on a cushion, frivolously wondering whether it is compulsory to cross his legs in imitation of the lotus position, the sound envelopes him in layers that begin with the ground-shaking bass and go all the way up to the highest audible partials.

The title of this audio installation is 'The Base 9:7:4 Symmetry in Prime Time When Centered Above and Below the Lowest Term Primes in the Range 288 to 224 with the Addition of 279 and 261 in Which the Half of the Symmetric Division Mapped Above and Including 288 Consists of the Powers of 2 Multiplied by the Primes Within the

Ranges of 144 to 128, 72 to 64 and 36 to 32 Which Are Symmetrical to Those Primes in Lowest Terms in the Half of the Symmetric Division Mapped Below and Including 224 with the Ranges 126 to 112, 63 to 56 and 31.5 to 28 with the Addition of 119'. The frequencies are selected by Young in reference to prime numbers, with which he is apparently obsessed.

At first the listener holds himself still, imagining that the purpose of the environment is to replicate the experience of meditation and that movement would break whatever spell the sound and light are intended to cast (there is indeed a notice in the corridor asking visitors to the installation area to remain silent). But when a small involuntary physical movement inevitably occurs, it has a surprising effect: the sound changes.

Intrigued, the listener is soon moving his head carefully from side to side, flexing his neck, bowing slightly or straightening his back, or shifting from one sit-bone to the other. And each time he moves, in ways that mimic the exercises of physical therapy (the Alexander technique, perhaps, or Pilates), the same result occurs: the sound changes. Or rather the relationships within it change.

The powerful thrum of the deepest layer of bass seems to remain unaltered, but the drones in the middle and upper ranges respond: a slow but distinct pulse in the alto register disappears with a small inclination of the head, reappearing as the movement is reversed. Slight shifts seem to bend notes through microtonal gradations, the drone pitches themselves being already calibrated in microtones, since they are fixed to the intervals of just intonation. Groups of pitches can seemingly be opened up or closed down. Tilt the chin downwards towards the right shoulder blade and the ominous flutter of a helicopter rotor blade appears, accompanied by a sharp increase in the volume of the highest tones. New tones are introduced to the mix imperceptibly but unmistakeably, sometimes with an effect that is almost spectacular: here, coming into view like a vehicle in a desert heat-haze, one of Terry Riley's 'Poppy Nogood' organ improvisations seems to be making a spectral guest appearance.

Yet each one of these shifts and oscillations and additions is an illusion. Or, rather, they are caused not by the massed drones, which had already been formulated, generated and held in a steady state for fifteen years by the time I entered the Dream House, but by their effect on the listener's neural pathways, from the spinal column to the cerebral cortex. You are playing the music, and the music is playing you.

References

1 Introduction

Bill Evans: sleeve note for *Kind of Blue* (Columbia, 1959)

Dom Joly: 'Jazz: Love the lifestyle, can't stand the music' (*Independent*, 29 September 2008)

Kristin Scott-Thomas: interview on *Soul Music* (BBC Radio 4, 30 September 2008)

Robert Wyatt: interview with David Toop (*Wire*, October 2007)

Benny Green: *Drums in My Ears* (Davis Poynter, 1973)

Kingsley Amis: *Memoirs* (Hutchinson, 1991)

Richard Cook: *It's About That Time* (Atlantic Books, 2005)

Andy Summers: *One Train Later* (Pavilion, 2006)

Chris Rea: conversations with the author

John Adams: *Hallelujah Junction* (Farrar Straus Giroux, 2008)

Manfred Eicher: speech to a symposium in Bath, England (1999)

3 The Sound of Blue

Wallace Stevens: *Selected Poems* (Faber and Faber, 1953)

Glen MacLeod: *Wallace Stevens and Modern Art* (Yale University Press, 1993)

John Richardson: *A Life of Picasso*, Vol. 1: *1881–1906* (Jonathan Cape, 1991)

Michel Pastoureau, trans. Markus I. Cruse: *Blue: The History of a Colour* (Princeton University Press, 2001)

Johan Wolfgang von Goethe: *Theory of Colours* (John Murray, 1840; MIT Press, 1970)

John Gage: *Colour and Culture* (Thames and Hudson, 1993)

John Gage: 'Into the Blue' from *Blue: Borrowed and New* (New Art Gallery, Walsall, 2000)

Henri Matisse: *Le bleu de l'été* (Réunion des musées nationaux, 2000)

F. Scott Fitzgerald: *The Great Gatsby* (Scribners, 1925)

Kieslowski on Kieslowski, ed. Danusia Stock (Faber and Faber, 1993)

Annette Insdorf: *Double Lives, Second Chances: The Cinema of Krzysztof Kieslowski* (Miramax Books, 1999)

Nat Hentoff: sleeve note to *Sketches of Spain* (Columbia, 1960)

4 Blue Moods

André Hodeir: *Jazz: Its Evolution and Essence* (Grove Press, 1956)

Nat Hentoff: interview with Gil Evans (*Down Beat*, 7 and 16 May 1957)

Gil Evans: conversations with the author (1978)

Raymond Horricks: *Gil Evans* (Spellmount, 1984)

Laurent Cugny: *Las Vegas Tango* (POL, 1989)

Gerry Mulligan: sleeve note to reissue of *The Birth of the Cool* (Capitol, 1978)

Gerry Mulligan: interview with the author (*The Times*, 27 June 1988)

Gerry Mulligan: interview on promotional disc for *Miles Davis and Gil Evans: The Complete Columbia Studio Recordings* (Columbia, 1996)

Ingrid Monson: 'Russell, Coltrane and Modal Jazz' from *In the Course of Performance*, ed. Bruno Nettl with Belinda Russell (University of Chicago Press, 1998)

Michael Zwerin: sleeve note to *The Complete Birth of the Cool* (Capitol, 1998)

Miles Davis with Quincy Troupe: *Miles: The Autobiography* (Macmillan, 1989)

The New Grove Encyclopaedia of Jazz, ed. Barry Kernfeld (Macmillan, 1988)

Philippe Carles: interview with Juliette Gréco (*Jazz* magazine, May 2006)

Gene Santoro: *Myself When I Am Real: The Life and Music of Charles Mingus* (Oxford University Press, 2000)

Robert Levin: interview with Booker Little (*Metronome*, October 1961)

Kenneth Tynan: *Tynan Right and Left* (Longmans, 1967)

Ken Vail: *Miles' Diary: The Life of Miles Davis 1947–1961* (Sanctuary, 1996)

Bill Coss: sleevenote to *Blue Moods* (Prestige, 1955)

5 Blue Dawn

Miles Davis with Quincy Troupe: *Miles: The Autobiography* (Macmillan, 1989)

Ian Carr: *Miles Davis: The Definitive Biography* (Harper Collins, 1998)

Michael Cuscuna: 'The Jazz Message' in *The Blue Note Years: The Jazz Photography of Francis Wolff* (Rizzoli, 1995)

Ken Vail: *Miles' Diary: The Life of Miles Davis 1947–1961* (Sanctuary, 1996)

Francois Postif: interview with John Coltrane (*Jazz Hot*, January 1962)

John Coltrane: sleeve note to *A Love Supreme* (Impulse, 1964)

Neil Tesser: sleeve note to *Ahmad Jamal: Ahmad's Blues* (Original Chess Masters, 1994)

Keith Jarrett: interview from promotion disc for *Miles Davis and Gil Evans: The Complete Columbia Studio Recordings* (Columbia, 1996)

Mike Hennessey: *Klook: The Story of Kenny Clarke* (Quartet, 1990)

Barney Wilen and René Urtreger: interviews in *Echoes of a Genius* (Arte TV, dir. Ulli Pfau, 1992)

Pierre Michelot: sleeve note to *Miles Davis, Ascenseur pour l'echafaud: The Complete Recordings* (Fontana, 1988)

George Russell: quoted in *Dizzy: To Be or Not to Bop* by Dizzy

Gillespie with Al Fraser (W. H. Allen, 1980)

Paul Bley with David Lee: *Stopping Time* (Véhicule Press, 1999)

6 Six Colours (Blue)

Gunther Schuller: 'Sonny Rollins and the Challenge of Thematic Improvisation' (*Jazz Review*, November 1958)

André Hodeir: *Towards Jazz* (Grove Press, 1962)

Peter Pettinger: *Bill Evans: How My Heart Sings* (Yale University Press, 1998)

Miles Davis with Quincy Troupe: *Miles: The Autobiography* (Simon and Schuster, 1989)

Ken Vail: *Miles' Diary: The Life of Miles Davis 1947–1961* (Sanctuary, 1996)

John Szwed: *So What: The Life of Miles Davis* (William Heinemann, 2002)

Ian Carr: *Miles Davis: The Definitive Biography* (Harper Collins, 1998)

7 Interlude: Outside in Blue

Albert Camus: 'Sketches for a Self-Portrait' from *Selected Essays and Notebooks* (Penguin, 1979)

Albert Camus: *L'Etranger* (*The Outsider*) (Gallimard, 1942; Hamish Hamilton, 1946)

Jean-Paul Sartre: *La Nausée* (*Nausea*) (Gallimard, 1938; Penguin, 1963)

Colin Wilson: *The Outsider* (Victor Gollancz, 1956)

Alberto Moravia: *La Noia* (*Boredom*) (Bompiani, 1960; NYRB, 1999)

John Tynan: 'Caught in the Act: Miles Davis Sextet' (*Down Beat*, 6 August 1959)

John Clellon Holmes: 'The Philosophy of the Beat Generation' (*Esquire*, 1958)

William Morris: 'cantiba high', published in *The Jazz Word*, ed. Dom Cerulli, Burt Korall and Mort Nasatir (Dobson, 1960)

Jack Kerouac: *On the Road* (Viking, 1957)

Peter Bondanella: *Italian Cinema: From Neorealism to the Present* (Continuum, 1996)

Dizzy Gillespie with Al Fraser: *Dizzy: To Be or Not to Bop* (W. H. Allen, 1980)

Frederic Raphael: screenplay for *Darling* (1965)

8 The Blue Moment

Conrad Silvert: sleeve note to *Bill Evans: Spring Leaves* (Milestone, 1976)

Bill Evans: manuscript sleeve note included in *Kind of Blue*, 50th anniversary edition (Columbia, 1959)

David Simons: *Studio Stories* (Backbeat Books, 2004)

9 Blue Waves

John Tynan: 'Caught in the Act: Miles Davis Sextet' (*Down Beat*, 6 August 1959)

Ben Ratliff: *Coltrane: The Story of a Sound* (Faber and Faber, 2007)

Don DeMichael: 'John Coltrane and Eric Dolphy Answer the Jazz Critics' (*Down Beat*, 12 April 1962)

Nat Hentoff: sleeve note to John Coltrane's *Meditations* (Impulse, 1966)

Peter Pettinger: *Bill Evans: How My Heart Sings* (Yale University Press, 1998)

Orrin Keepnews: *The View from Within* (Oxford University Press, 1988)

Brian Hennessey: 'Re: A Person I Knew' (*Jazz Journal*, March 1985)

Conrad Silvert: sleeve note to *Bill Evans: Spring Leaves* (Milestone, 1976)

10 Blue Horizon

Robert Dean: interview with Terry Riley, 1995 (sleeve note to *Music from The Gift / Bird of Paradise / Mescalin Mix*, Organ of Corti, 1998)

Alex Ross: *The Rest is Noise: Listening to the Twentieth Century* (Fourth Estate, 2008)

James Gavin: *Deep in a Dream: The Long Night of Chet Baker* (Knopf, 2002)

Morton Subotnick: sleeve note to *In C: 25th Anniversary Concert* (New Albion, 1992)

David Behrman: sleeve note to *In C* (Columbia Masterworks, 1968)

Walter Boudreau: sleeve note to *In C* (*Mantra*) (Organ of Corti, 1999)

David W. Bernstein (ed.): *The San Francisco Tape Music Centre: 1960s Counterculture and the Avant-Garde* (University of California Press, 2008)

Terry Riley: conversations with the author (2001, 2002, 2008)

Tim Mitchell: *Sedition and Anarchy: A Biography of John Cale* (Peter Owen, 2003)

Edward Strickland: *Minimalism: Origins* (Indiana University Press, 1993)

11 Dark Blue

David Fricke: notes to John Cale: *Sun Blindness Music, Dream Interpretation* and *Stainless Gamelan* (Table of the Elements, 2001)

Tim Mitchell: *Sedition and Alchemy: A Biography of John Cale* (Peter Owen, 2003)

David Fricke: notes to the Velvet Underground: *Peel Slowly and See* (Polydor, 1995)

Richard Witts: *The Velvet Underground* (Indiana University Press, 2006)

'Rock 'n' Roll: Everybody's Turned On' (*Time*, 21 May 1965)

12 So Blue

Richard Cook: *It's About That Time* (Atlantic Books, 2005)

George T. Simon: review of Miles Davis at Carnegie Hall (*New York Herald Tribune*, 20 May 1961)

Bill Coss: review of Miles Davis at Carnegie Hall (*Down Beat*, 6 July 1961)

Aaron Cohen: 'James Brown's Musicians Reflect on His Legacy' (*Down Beat*, 2007)

James Brown (with Bruce Tucker): *The Godfather of Soul* (Macmillan/Sidgwick and Jackson, 1987)

Geoff Brown: *James Brown: A Biography* (Omnibus, 1996)

James Brown (with Marc Eliot): *I Feel Good* (New American Library, 2005)

Adam White and Fred Bronson: *The Billboard Book of Number One Rhythm and Blues Hits* (Billboard Books, 1993)

13 Blue Bells

Ian MacDonald: 'Soft Machine Pts 1 and 2' (*NME*, January–February 1975)

Rob Chapman: 'Soft Machine' (*Mojo*, June 1997)

Tim Mitchell: *Sedition and Alchemy: A Biography of John Cale* (Peter Owen, 2003)

Edward Strickland: *Minimalism: Origins* (Indiana University Press, 1993)

Philip Glass: *Opera on the Beach* (Faber and Faber, 1988)

Terry Riley: conversation with the author (2008)

14 Code Blue

Edward Strickland: *Minimalism: Origins* (Indiana University Press, 1993)

David Sheppard: *On Some Faraway Beach: The Life and Times of Brian Eno* (Orion, 2008)

David Toop: *Haunted Weather: Music, Silence and Memory* (Serpent's Tail, 2004)

Brian Eno: conversations with the author (1972, 1973, 1980, 1996, 2006, 2008)

Brian Eno: 'The studio as compositional tool', lecture at the New Music, New York seminar (The Kitchen, New York City, 1979)

Brian Eno: 'The debt I owe to Jon Hassell' (*Guardian*, 9 November 2007)

15 Blue on Blue

Paul Bley with David Lee: *Stopping Time* (Véhicule Press, 1999)

Manfred Eicher, Lars Müller, Dieter Rehm and Barbara Wojirsch (eds): *Sleeves of Desire: A Cover Story* (Lars Müller Publishers, 1996)

Steve Lake and Paul Griffiths (eds): *Horizons Touched: The Music of ECM* (Granta, 2007)

Stuart Nicholson: interview with Manfred Eicher (jazz.com, 2007)

Rune Kristofferson: conversation with the author (2005)

Bill Evans: sleeve note to *Kind of Blue* (Columbia, 1959)

16 Coda: Permanent Blue

La Monte Young: *Some Historical and Theoretical Background on My Work* (1987, 1999)

Ed Howard: 'The Dream House' (*Stylus*, 17 November 2003)

Sandy McCroskey: 'Dream Analysis' (*Journal of the Just Intonation Network*, Vol. 8, No. 3, May 1994)

Acknowledgements

The idea of writing a book about *Kind of Blue* occurred to me several years ago and began to take shape during conversations with Graham Coster. I started work, but put the project aside when two other books on the subject were announced for publication in 2002. On reading (and admiring) them, I realised that I had been about to attempt a quite different task, which was to place Miles Davis's album in a wider context, and to reflect on some of its more far-reaching implications. And when, after a decent interval, I returned to it, there was encouragement in the realisation that intervening events had only confirmed the soundness of the underlying thesis. For their enthusiasm and assistance I must thank my agent, Clare Alexander; my editor at Faber and Faber, Neil Belton, and his assistant, Kate Murray-Browne; my copy editor, Charles Boyle; and my friend Steve Beresford, who took time out from his busy teaching and playing schedule to read the manuscript and make several helpful observations. The responsibility for any residual errors and provocations is, of course, entirely my own.

R.W.

Index